ALSO BY EMMANUEL CARRÈRE

The Adversary
Class Trip
The Mustache
Gothic Romance

I AM ALIVE AND YOU ARE DEAD

I AM ALIVE AND YOU ARE DEAD

A JOURNEY INTO THE MIND OF
PHILIP K. DICK

EMMANUEL CARRÈRE

TRANSLATED BY TIMOTHY BENT

METROPOLITAN BOOKS
HENRY HOLT AND COMPANY | NEW YORK

Metropolitan Books
Henry Holt and Company, LLC
Publishers since 1866
115 West 18th Street
New York, New York 10011

Metropolitan Books ™ is a registered
trademark of Henry Holt and Company, LLC.

Originally published in France in 1993
under the title *Je suis vivant et vous êtes morts*
by Éditions du Seuil, Paris, France.

Library of Congress Cataloging-in-Publication data
Carrère, Emmanuel, 1957–
    [Je suis vivant et vous êtes morts. English]
    I am alive and you are dead : a journey into the mind of Philip K. Dick /
Emmanuel Carrere ; translated by Timothy Bent.
        p.   cm.
    ISBN 0-8050-5464-2
    1. Dick, Philip K.—Criticism and interpretation. 2. Science fiction,
American—History and criticism. I. Bent, Timothy. II. Title.
PS3554.I3Z63 2004
813'.54—dc22   2003067710

Henry Holt books are available for special promotions and
premiums. For details contact: Director, Special Markets.

First American Edition 2004

Designed by Kelly S. Too

Printed in the United States of America
1   3   5   7   9   10   8   6   4   2

For Anne

I am sure, as you hear me say this, you do not really believe me, or even believe that I believe it myself. But nevertheless it is true. . . . You are free to believe me or free to disbelieve, but please take my word on it that I am not joking; this is very serious, a matter of importance. I am sure that at the very least you will agree that for me even to claim this is in itself amazing. Often people claim to remember past lives; I claim to remember a different, very different, *present* life. I know of no one who has ever made that claim before, but I rather suspect that my experience is not unique; what perhaps is unique is the fact that I am willing to talk about it.

—FROM A SPEECH GIVEN BY PHILP K. DICK
IN FRANCE, SEPTEMBER 24, 1977

CONTENTS

PREFACE

The book you hold in your hands is a very peculiar book. In it I have tried to depict the life of Philip K. Dick from the inside, in other words, with the same freedom and empathy—indeed with the same truth—with which he depicted his own characters. It's a trip into the brain of a man who regarded even his craziest books not as works of imagination but as factual reports. This is a book about the mind, its alterations, its remotest and most dangerous territories. It's about drugs and mystics, about the Zeitgeist of the sixties and the seventies and its legacy to our New Age. As I say, it's a very peculiar book—how could it be otherwise? Dick's life was as much marked by the fictions he created as those fictions bear the mark of his lived experiences.

But no account of a life, however tenuous its relationship to "reality," can emerge ex nihilo, or solely from the mind of the biographer. And this account is no exception. Especially in my imaginative recreations of scenes in Dick's life and of his state of mind, I have drawn from a wealth of sources. After Dick's death, his survivors temporarily entrusted the role of literary executor to Paul Williams, the journalist who had aided and abetted him in the creation of his legend. A small van filled with papers, including his unpublished Exegesis and carbon copies of letters, was unloaded into Williams's garage in Glen Ellen, California, which would become a mythic place for "Dickheads" the world over. It was from this garage that the *Philip K. Dick Society Newsletter* issued forth from 1982 to 1993. For more than a decade, the newsletter recorded the progress of a cult that to this day endeavors—and actually manages—to keep him alive.

The attentive ministrations of his fans, friends, and family, however, are only partially responsible for Dick's long and fruitful afterlife. Ridley Scott's film *Blade Runner* did much to enshrine him in the popular imagination in the United States and Europe, as did the film *Total Recall*, starring Arnold Schwarzenegger, which was based on Dick's short story "We Can Remember It for You Wholesale," and, more recently, the screen adaptations of Dick's stories "Minority Report" and "Paycheck." There has also been an opera based on *Valis*, numerous other film projects, dozens of books on Dick, books with references to Dick, and novels in which Dick is the protagonist. Given the uniform Vintage editions of his complete works and the many articles about Dick that have appeared in both academic and popular journals, his fans must feel a little like the early Christians did when their faith was officially adopted by the Roman Empire: triumphant, of course, but also slightly nostalgic for the days when they lived in the catacombs. The Happy Few cease to be happy when they are no longer few. Dick has become part of the mainstream. The present book is yet another indication.

My book has benefited from those that have preceded it. Lawrence Sutin's *Divine Invasions: The Life of Philip K. Dick* served as an indispensable reference, as did *In Search of Philip K. Dick* by Anne R. Dick, which the author was kind enough to let me see even prior to its publication. I have read too many other books to note here and therefore cannot recognize all my debts, but there are two I must acknowledge: my understanding of the history of LSD in America was guided by Jay Stevens's inquiry in *Storming Heaven: LSD and the American Dream;* the game of "Rat" was described—I believe invented—by Thomas M. Disch. While I've consulted and talked with Dick's contemporaries, my primary text throughout has been Dick's own work, which I've approached as an admiring literary critic. In straddling the line between autobiography and fiction, Dick's novels and stories provide the best window onto a man who, in a far more radical way than any of his contemporaries, effectively abolished the difference between life and literature.

I would like to thank the Philip K. Dick Trust for graciously allowing use of extensive quotes from the works of Philip K. Dick. It should be noted that such permission is granted in the spirit of promoting discussion and debate about Dick's life and works, and in no way signifies the Trust's endorsement of or agreement with my portrayal of characters or events.

My thanks as well to Anne Dick, Ray Nelson, Joan Simpson, Tim Powers, Jim Blaylock, Doris Sauter, and Paul Williams, all of whom spoke to me about Philip K. Dick; Stéphane Martin, who got me to read *Ubik* many years ago; Gilles Tournier and Nicole Clerc, for their hospitality; Hélène Collon and Robert Louit, for having generously opened their archives and their wisdom to me; François-Marie Samuelson and Elizabeth Gille, my agent and my editor, respectively, for having put their faith in such a hazardous project; everyone at Metropolitan Books for the same; and finally, those who kindly read the manuscript and helped me to improve it: Hélène and Louis Carrère d'Encausse, my parents; Jacqueline-Frédéric Frié; Françoise and Patrice Boyer; and Hervé Clerc. My special thanks to Arthur Denner, without whose discernment and creativity this English version might not have seen the light of day.

I AM ALIVE AND YOU ARE DEAD

CHAPTER 1

BERKELEY

On December 16, 1928, in Chicago, Dorothy Kindred Dick gave birth to twins, a boy and a girl. The babies were six weeks premature and very underweight. Unaware that she was not producing enough milk for both infants, and because no one—neither a family member nor a doctor—suggested to her that she supplement their diet with formula, Dorothy undernourished the twins during the first weeks of their lives. On January 26, 1929, the baby girl, whom her parents had named Jane, died. She was buried in the cemetery in her father's hometown of Fort Morgan, Colorado. The little boy survived. His parents had his name, Philip, engraved alongside Jane's on the headstone; under his name, next to the dash that followed the date of birth he shared with his sister, a blank space was left. Not long afterward, the Dicks moved to California.

A rare family photo shows a hatchet-faced Edgar Dick in a rumpled suit and wearing a fedora, the kind later made famous by Treasury agents in films like *The Untouchables*. And in fact Edgar was a federal employee, though with the Department of Agriculture rather than the Treasury. His job involved rooting out fraud in a federal price-

support program that paid farmers to reduce their herds: he had to
verify that farmers had actually slaughtered the numbers of cows they
claimed; if not, he had to kill the animals himself. Hunched over the
wheel of his Buick, he crisscrossed a California countryside hit hard by
the Depression, encountering grim, suspicious locals along the way
who might well show their hospitality to a government agent by shoving under his nose the rat they were roasting on a makeshift spit. The
one bright spot in these trips was occasionally coming across a fellow
World War I veteran with whom he could swap stories. Edgar, who
had volunteered for active duty, had come back from Europe with stories of bravery, sergeant's stripes, and a gas mask. Once, he took the mask
out of its box and pulled it over his head to amuse his son, who was
three at the time. At the sight of the round opaque eyes and the sinister-
looking rubber trunk, the boy screamed in terror, convinced that a
hideous monster, a giant insect, had eaten his father and taken his place.
For weeks afterward Phil kept scanning his father's face for other signs
of the substitution. Edgar's attempts to tease his son out of his anxieties
only heightened the boy's fears. From then on, Dorothy couldn't bring
herself to look at her husband without rolling her eyes and huffing self-
righteously. She had her own ideas about how to raise children.

Dorothy had been a beautiful woman when Edgar married her,
shortly after the war; people said she looked liked Greta Garbo. Age
and illness took their toll, however, and left her looking rather like a
scarecrow, bereft of the sex appeal she had once possessed although
not without a certain seductive severity. A voracious reader, Dorothy
divided humanity into two camps: those who devoted their lives to
creative pursuits and those who did not. Unable to conceive of anyone
of any worth who did not fall squarely within the first camp, she spent
her life in a state of intellectual bovarysme, trying but never managing
to break into that elite circle, the ranks of published authors. She
despised her husband, who, apart from things military, was interested
only in football. He tried to pass on his passion to his son, sneaking
him out of the house and taking him to games. Phil, however, was his
mother's child, even when he disobeyed her; he couldn't understand
how grown-ups could get so worked up about a stupid game.

Phil was one of those pudgy, brooding little boys who grow up to become chess champions or musical prodigies; in fact, his childhood had much in common with that of Nabokov's Luzhin or Glenn Gould (his contemporary and in some respects his spiritual cousin). People praised him for his maturity and his precocious appreciation of music. More than anything else in the world, though, Phil loved spending hours on end hiding in old boxes, silent and safe from the world.

He was five when his parents separated and divorced. Dorothy had taken the initiative, having been assured by a psychiatrist that her child would not suffer from the separation (he complained about it his entire life). Edgar had not wanted to sever all ties to his son and ex-wife, but his first visits following the divorce were so coldly received that he soon gave up and moved to Nevada. Hoping to find work that was both more interesting and better paid than the secretarial position in which she felt she had been stagnating, Dorothy took Phil and moved to Washington, D.C.

The next three years were horrendous. Having left Chicago as a baby, Phil knew only the West Coast and its mild winters; in Washington he discovered the dull misery of rain and cold, poverty and loneliness. Dorothy spent her days working at the Federal Children's Bureau, editing and correcting the proofs of educational pamphlets. Every day Phil would come home from Countryside School in Silver Spring, Maryland, the Quaker academy where the children gathered silently in circles awaiting the direct experience of God, and spend hours alone in the dark, sad apartment waiting for his mother to return. Since she came home late, too tired to tell him stories, he had to tell himself stories he already knew. His favorite was the one about the fairy who grants three wishes to a farmer and his wife. The wife asks for a nice fat sausage, and instantly one appears before her, fat and juicy. Her husband is furious. "Idiot! How can you waste one of your wishes that way?" he asks her. "May this sausage always hang from your nose!" And no sooner does he utter these words than the sausage attaches itself to the woman's nose; to get rid of it, they have to use the third wish. Phil invented endless variations on the theme. When he learned to read, he discovered *Winnie-the-Pooh* and not long afterward, an abridged version of *Quo Vadis*. This story, which seemed to bring to life everything he had been hearing at his Quaker school, troubled him deeply. Unbeknownst to his mother, Phil spent his afternoons for an entire winter playing at being one of the first Christians hiding in the catacombs.

Phil and Dorothy's lonely exile in Washington ended in 1938, when Dorothy took a job in the U.S. Forestry Department office located on the Berkeley campus of the University of California. Mother and son could breathe again. Anyone who lived there for more than a week knew that Berkeley was the center of the world. A feminist and pacifist, a tireless proponent of progressive ideas, Dorothy blossomed in this academic enclave in which one could be both an office worker and a women's rights activist. As for Phil, he loved to watch the water in San Francisco Bay sparkling in the sun; he also loved the green lawns of the Berkeley campus and the small creek running through it in which local children were allowed to play and the bells of Sather Tower, whose joyous, peaceful tones echoed over the rooftops. School was a different matter. Phil had asthma and episodes of tachycardia, and he took full advantage of his conditions to miss school at every opportunity. Even when she could tell he was faking symptoms, Dorothy played along and let him stay home. Deep down, she was delighted that he took so little after his father, that he hated sports, horseplay, and all those other mindless tribal activities that absorbed the interest of the average red-blooded American male. He was more like her—an artistic soul, an albatross whose enormous wingspan prevented him from walking on the earth.

By the age of twelve, Phil was already immersed in the things that would become his lifelong passions: listening to music, reading, and typing. He had his mother buy him classical records, 78s at first, and he soon developed a talent—of which both mother and son were not a little proud—for identifying any symphony, opera, or concerto after hearing only a few measures played or, for that matter, hummed. He collected illustrated magazines with titles like *Astounding!* and *Amazing!* and *Unknown!*, and these periodicals, in the guise of serious scientific discussion, introduced him to lost continents, haunted pyramids, ships that vanished mysteriously in the Sargasso Sea. But he also read stories by Edgar Allan Poe and H. P. Lovecraft, the recluse from Providence, Rhode Island, whose protagonists face abominations too monstrous for them to name or even describe.

Early on, Phil stopped merely reading these writers and began to imitate them. In Washington he had written a few lugubrious poems—one about a kitty eating a birdie, another about an ant that drags the carcass of a bumblebee into the forest and leaves it there, a third about a tearful family burying its blind dog. Typing freed Phil's creative energies. As soon as he had a typewriter of his own, he became a wizard at the keyboard. No one could type faster than Philip Dick or for as long; it took him only ten days to finish his first novel, a sequel to *Gulliver's Travels* called *Return to Lilliput* (the manuscript has been lost). His first published works were macabre tales inspired by Poe; they appeared in the "Young Author's Club" column in the *Berkeley Gazette*. The magazine's literary editor, who signed her name "Aunt Flo," favored realism of the Chekhov or Nathanael West school. Even as she continued to publish his work, she exhorted him to write about what he knew—everyday life with its actual little details—and to keep his imagination in check. At thirteen, feeling unappreciated and misunderstood, Phil founded a magazine of his own. Foreshadowings of the future Philip K. Dick are everywhere apparent in this endeavor: in its title, *The Truth*, in the editorial statement that opened the magazine's first and only issue ("This paper is sworn to print only that which is beyond doubt the TRUTH"), and in the fact that this uncompromising truth took the form of intergalactic adventures, the fruit of the feverish daydreams of the prolix adolescent who was the magazine's sole contributor.

Around this time Phil began having a recurring dream in which he found himself in a bookstore trying to locate an issue of *Astounding!* that would complete his collection. The rare, indeed priceless, issue contained a story entitled "The Empire Never Ended" that, if only he could get his hands on it, would reveal the secrets of the universe to him. The first time he had the dream he awoke just as he had worked his way down to the bottom of a pile of old magazines he was sure contained the prized issue. He waited anxiously for the dream to recur, and whenever it did he found the pile of magazines exactly as he had left it. Again he started rummaging through. With each recurrence of the dream, the pile became smaller and smaller, but he always awoke before he could get to the bottom of it. He spent days reciting the story's title to himself, until he could no longer distinguish it from the sound of the blood beating in his ears when he had a fever. He could see the letters that formed the words of the title; he could picture the cover illustration. The illustration worried him, even though—or because—he couldn't quite bring it into focus. Over the course of weeks, Phil's desire to find the magazine turned into anxiety that he actually might do so. He knew that if he read "The Empire Never Ended" the world's secrets would be revealed, but he also understood the danger of such knowledge. He had read it in Lovecraft: if we knew everything, we would go mad with terror. Eventually, Phil began to see his dream as a diabolical trap. The buried issue was lying in wait, ready to devour him whole. Instead of tearing through the pile of magazines as he had at first, Phil tried to slow his fingers as they pulled one magazine after another from the pile, bringing him closer and closer to the final horror. He became afraid to fall asleep.

Then, for no apparent reason, he stopped having the dream. He awaited its return, first nervously, then impatiently; at the end of two weeks, he would have given anything for the dream to come back. He remembered the story of the three wishes, how the last one had to be squandered to remedy the catastrophe of the previous two. He had wished that he could read "The Empire Never Ended"; then, sensing danger, he wished that he wouldn't have to; now, once again, he wished he could. Then again, it was probably better for him not to get his third wish, because he wouldn't get a fourth wish to undo it. Still, he was disappointed that the dream didn't recur. He longed for it. Then he forgot about it.

Phil lived alone with his mother. Dorothy and he called each other by their first names, treating each other with a curious combination of formality and intimacy. At night they left their bedroom doors open and held conversations from their beds. Their favorite topics were books, diseases, and medications. A lifelong hypochondriac, Dorothy maintained a supply of pharmaceuticals nearly as extensive as her son's record collection. When tranquilizers started hitting the market, right after the war, she was among the first to set off for the new chemical El Dorado. She tried Thorazine, Valium, Tofranil, and Librium the instant they became available; she ranked them according to the quality of the stupor they induced and enthusiastically recommended her favorite brands to her friends.

From time to time Phil saw his father, who had remarried and settled in Pasadena, where he worked for the Department of Commerce and became a regular on a local radio program called *This Is Your Government*. His broadcasts impressed the shy teenager, who dreamed of exercising power over others. Like everyone else during the war years, Phil was patriotic but he was also fascinated by Nazi propaganda, priding himself on being able to admire a plan for the way it was being executed even though he found its goals abhorrent. Within him, he felt, there was a leader among men, but, as he had no followers, he stuck close to his own little world.

He contented himself with ruling over that little world, filling it with possessions. His mother constantly begged him to straighten up his room, but he was one of those compulsive personalities who, like Sherlock Holmes, can date a file by the thickness of the dust covering it and relish being the only one who can make sense of the reigning chaos. In Phil's case, the chaos was an imperceptibly organized jumble of model airplanes and army tanks, chess sets, records, science fiction magazines—and, somewhat better hidden than those other things, pictures of naked women.

Of course, Phil was starting to become aware of girls, and even though, thanks to his lack of self-confidence, his interest remained fairly theoretical, it was enough to threaten the osmotic unity of mother and son. This interest, coupled with Phil's bad grades, introversion, and anxiety attacks, persuaded Dorothy that her son should see a psychiatrist. He was fourteen when she took him to his first session, the first in a series that would continue nearly uninterrupted until his death.

It took only a few sessions—along with hours in between spent leafing through books that his mother had feverishly annotated—for young

Phil to begin speaking knowledgeably about "neuroses," "complexes," and "phobias." He subjected his classmates to various personality tests of his own devising from which, without revealing the sources of his wisdom, he drew conclusions that were to varying degrees flattering and welcome.

Toward the end of the 1930s, psychological tests had begun influencing middle-class Americans' notions of what was going on in their heads—as well as in the heads of their neighbors. Administered to over fourteen million recruits subsequent to America's declaration of war, these tests revealed that more than two million of them had one neuropsychiatric disorder or another that was serious enough to disqualify them from military service. Before the establishment of these new, reputedly scientific parameters of mental illness, no one had suspected the number of misfits would be so astronomically high. The result was panic—as well as a vast infusion of public money into the mental health sector and growing, popular interest in psychoanalysis, which, it was hoped, would turn these problem cases into responsible, mentally balanced citizens.

Freud, who on his first visit to New York in 1909 had seen himself as bringing the plague to the New World, would have smiled at this naive confidence in the powers of psychoanalysis. American psychiatrists and psychoanalysts lagged behind their European counterparts; they were less up-to-date on the latest squabbles and newest theories. They had also tailored Freudianism to fit their pragmatic outlook; they were not so such interested in their patients' gradual journey toward self-knowledge and self-acceptance as in helping them adapt to social norms. The tests they were administering—at every opportunity—evaluated the progress their patients were making toward normal behavior, or at least toward the appearance of normal behavior.

Phil himself became adept at taking these tests, learning to recognize the trick questions and figuring out the expected answers. Like a student who has managed to get his hands on the teacher's manual, he knew exactly which answer bubbles in the Wordsworth Personal Data Sheet or the Minnesota Multiphasic Personality Inventory he should blacken if he wanted to please the doctor, which figures he should see in the Rorschach splotches if he wanted to confound him. At will he could appear normal, normally abnormal, or (his forte) abnormally normal, and, by varying his symptoms, he ran circles around his hapless first psychiatrist.

Phil's second therapist, a San Francisco psychoanalyst, was more intelligent. He was, after all, a Jungian, and anyone in Berkeley who knew anything about psychoanalysis knew that Jungians were the crème de la crème, that they specialized in the creative personality. Twice a week, Phil took the ferry across the bay to San Francisco. He told a friend who wondered where he was going all the time that he was taking a course for people with exceptionally high IQs and—naturally—that he had gotten in by cheating on the exam. Anyone who succeeds in convincing someone else that he's a genius, Phil added slyly, when his friend snickered conspiratorially, proves that he's superior even to an authentic genius. The friend began avoiding him after that.

With his new psychiatrist Phil discovered the extraordinary effect he could achieve by talking about his dead sister. He understood that a trauma like Jane's death made him interesting, and he spent long sessions speculating as to who had revealed to him the dramatic circumstances of his birth and on what occasion. Obviously it was his mother, and she must have told him fairly early on. But it seemed to him that he had always known. In his earliest recollections, he had an imaginary friend named Jane with black hair and dark eyes who had a flair for wriggling out of danger—so unlike Phil, the awkward, overweight little boy who hid in old cardboard boxes. He also claimed to remember his mother's once screaming in a moment of anger that she wished he had died instead of Jane.

His psychiatrist's revelation that Phil had a castrating mother felt to the boy like some sort of betrayal: why was Dorothy paying this man to say bad things about her? But the information didn't fall on deaf ears. Indeed it soon became the source of new anxieties. The signs were all there: castrating mother, absent father, interest in art and culture. Phil was sure he was going to become a homosexual.

Fear of homosexuality was one obsession of Phil's teenage years but not the only one. He suffered from dizziness and agoraphobia. He was afraid of public transportation and was incapable of eating even a sandwich in public. At fifteen, during a concert, he was suddenly overcome by a panic attack. He felt as though he were sinking away and looking at the world through a submarine's periscope.

Another time he fell ill watching a newsreel that showed American troops on a Pacific island using flamethrowers to kill Japanese soldiers. What was worse than seeing images of men being turned into human torches was the delight of the audience. Phil ran out of the theater, followed by a horrified Dorothy; it was years before he set foot in a movie theater again.

He also stopped going to school, preferring instead to stay at home reading his schoolbooks while listening to records. He enjoyed studying German most of all, as it seemed to go so well with the music in the background. Choosing German had been a fairly brave thing to do; these were, after all, the war years. He reveled in the poetry, which seemed written to be sung. The melodies of Schubert, Schumann, and Brahms pervaded his existence. He could think of nothing better to do with his life than listen to music, and so, at the age of sixteen, he decided to make a profession out of it.

Phil took a part-time job at University Radio, a store that sold records, radios, record players, and the first television sets. The store also did repairs, and the repairmen constituted a kind of aristocracy among the store's personnel. Philip envied them. These were men who could fix things—and fixing things was the essence of human genius. The heroes of his novels would often be tinkerers, handymen, jacks of all trades. Though this might seem a little strange, given that he had grown up in a college town and read voraciously, Phil made his choice very early on—well before anyone could accuse him of sour grapes. The university, the local hangouts where students talked endlessly about how to remake the world—these were not for him. He would always prefer the mom-and-pop store, the small establishments whose owners swept the sidewalk every morning before raising the metal shutters and greeting their first customers.

Phil's job at University Radio was to shelve the classical records as they arrived from distributors, as well as to sweep the floors and change the toilet paper rolls in the bathrooms located behind listening booth number 3. It also meant buying records for his private collection at a discount and getting into debates with fellow employees and customers alike over the best recording of the *Magic Flute*. The store became his world, a stable and familiar environment where nothing disruptive would happen, a place that seemed to shield him from panic attacks and agoraphobia. His self-confidence grew. If he found a female customer attractive, he would take her into one of the booths and play the brilliant young baritone Dietrich Fischer-Dieskau, who sang Schubert lieder as no one had sung them before. While the record was playing, Phil would watch the girl with his intense blue eyes, humming along, a little off-pitch, in the deep, resonant register that had now replaced the piping voice of his adolescence.

Phil dreamed of hosting his own radio show. What better way to pick up women? He worked at a station in Berkeley, but unfortunately not as a disk jockey. His job was to choose the music, while a guy with slicked-back hair, saddle shoes, and an argyle sweater whom he heartily despised wielded control over the microphone. In one of Phil's favorite daydreams, he is an astronaut circling high above an earth devastated by atomic catastrophe. From the spaceship he is condemned to call home for the rest of his life, he sometimes receives radio messages from survivors on the planet's surface. And he starts to broadcast back. After a while his listeners wait as anxiously and eagerly for his broadcasts as Resistance fighters did for the BBC during the war. He plays records for them, reads books, and relays news. Thanks to his tireless efforts, a bond forms between isolated groups of survivors, inspired by the warmth of his voice not to lose heart. People huddle around crude homemade radio sets, their most precious possession. Without them, and without that lonely but valiant disk jockey somewhere up there in the sky looking down at them, they would revert to a state of barbarism. If civilization were ever to take root again, it would be because he had somehow managed to protect its fragile seeds. For Phil, the most exquisite moment of this daydream was when he resisted the temptation of allowing himself to be treated like a god by the people below. He always managed to triumph over this temptation, but just barely.

Mother and son remembered differently the circumstances surrounding his moving out of their apartment. According to Phil, his mother took it hard and threatened to call the police to prevent him from leaving home and ending up the homosexual he would surely become without her to watch over him. Dorothy, on the other hand, maintained that she practically had to push her son out the door; he was too old to be living with her. Whichever the case, Phil moved his collection of books, records, and magazines and his beloved Magnavox record player into an apartment shared by a group of bohemian Berkeley students. Here only "great literature" had a place: academic interest in popular culture was still some ways off. Phil stopped reading science fiction, put away the pulp magazines that had fascinated him in his adolescence, and began to read Joyce, Kafka, Pound, Wittgenstein, and Camus. An ideal evening for him meant listening to Buxteude or Monteverdi while budding avant-garde poets recited long passages from *Finnegans Wake* by heart, stopping only to point out traces of Dante's influence. Everyone was trying to write, engaging in frenetic name-dropping, exchanging manuscripts, and offering advice. Phil wrote a number of short stories which he tried unsuccessfully to place in magazines, and two novels, about which we know only what he later said about them. The first was a long interior monologue involving Jungian archetypes and a hopeless romantic quest; the second, set in Maoist China, was about the relationship of two men and a woman trapped in a complex web of secerts and lies.

Around this time Phil lost his virginity and, with it, his fear that he was a homosexual. The girl was a customer at the store whom a more experienced fellow employee had steered him toward. Refusing to sell her the saccharine Christmas carols she had come in to buy, he took her into a listening booth and played his favorite records. Then he took her down to the basement; its usual occupants, the repairmen, had gone to lunch. One week later he proposed, thus beginning his long career of compulsive monogamy. Phil and Jeanette rented a dark little studio apartment. There Phil discovered the rigors of being an impoverished newlywed; he also learned how little he had in common with his wife.

She fell asleep as he read her William James's *Varieties of Religious Experience* or his own short stories; she found *Finnegans Wake* incomprehensible. Worse, she got sick of listening to his records and after a few weeks started threatening to smash them: Phil knew then that it was over. The judge found the threat of smashed records less than compelling as grounds for divorce; Phil, on the other hand, never quite recovered from it. The idea that someone might destroy his precious record collection haunted him for years. Dick wrote novel after novel in which a cruel wife sets upon her husband's cherished albums, and in his second-to-last novel, it is to the threat of this very action that Yahweh himself must resort to rouse the reluctant hero; nothing else has worked.

With Phil's second marriage, the danger receded. Once again, he met his wife-to-be in the record store. She was perusing the Italian opera section as he hovered nervously nearby, unwilling to make a move until he made certain she had tastes similar to his. Kleo Apostolides was a dark, pretty nineteen-year-old from a Greek family; an avid reader, she was remarkably even-tempered compared with Phil's future companions. Phil and Kleo married in June 1950. Borrowing money, they bought a ramshackle house in a working-class neighborhood down by the Berkeley waterfront. The roof leaked and the paint was peeling off the walls. Whenever it rained, they had to put pans everywhere. Neither Kleo nor Phil had realized how much work was involved in owning a house. The difficulties didn't seem to faze them, though—Phil spent most of his money buying records and his free time listening to them, and Kleo was determined to resist anything resembling a bourgeois lifestyle. A stalwart foot soldier of local radicalism, Kleo wore jeans and horn-rimmed glasses and sang the songs of the Spanish Civil War that the members of the Abraham Lincoln Brigade had sung as they marched on Madrid. She discussed everything with equal vehemence, whether out of enthusiasm or indignation. She especially loved feeling indignant.

A political science major at Berkeley, Kleo did odd jobs to pay her tuition. Phil spent his days at University Radio. Unlike practically every other young person in Berkeley, he was not a student. Several days after he had signed up for courses on *Sturm und Drang* and the philosophy of David Hume, a severe panic attack had put an end to his academic career. Not particularly ambitious in conventional terms, to say the least, he quickly got over whatever disappointment he may have felt. On the other hand, now that he had become a full-time record salesman with no prospects other than maybe—someday— managing the store, he began to worry that he might turn into another Berkeley eccentric, one of those old guys beloved of generations of students. Remember him? The guy at the record store who would rap for hours if you got him going on German idealism or the '53 recording of *Tristan* where Schwarzkopf sings the top notes for Kirsten Flagstad?

Phil's meeting a writer named Anthony Boucher at University Radio thus proved a turning point. Boucher was a sort of impresario of popular literature, writing, editing, and reviewing detective novels and science fiction under a variety of pseudonyms. Here, to Phil's astonishment and, ultimately, to his relief, was a grown man, a person of obvious distinction and discriminating taste in music, who did not look down on a genre that Phil had felt obliged to abandon rather than risk the scorn of his former housemates. Shyness kept Phil from attending the weekly creative writing course Boucher gave at his home. But Kleo went, taking with her several of her husband's pieces, including one science fiction story. Phil's second great surprise came when Boucher told him that he found his work promising. Heartened, Phil gave up writing self-conscious and overwrought character analyses and interior monologues and let his imagination run free. Thus it was that in the October 1951 issue of the *Magazine of Fantasy and Science Fiction*, of which Boucher was editor-in-chief, Philip K. Dick's first published short story appeared. In "Roog," a barking dog chases after the garbage men, sensing that they are predatory carnivores from another planet who make off with the earthlings' garbage in order to analyze it, in preparation, one suspects, for their abduction of the earthlings themselves.

Phil was not paid much for the piece, but he was paid, and thereupon concluded that he could actually make a living from writing. He quit his job at University Radio and began writing full-time. He got an agent. In 1952, he sold four short stories; in 1953, thirty; in 1954, twenty-eight; and in 1955 he published his first story collection, as well as his first novel.

CHAPTER 2

LITTLE GREEN MEN

When he set himself up at the age of twenty-four to write science fiction, Philip Dick did not imagine it was something he would do his whole life. SF was a temporary solution to a temporary predicament. Yet once it was clear that a career in academia was out of the question, there were few professions that his various phobias and anxieties would allow him to pursue. All those psychological tests he had undergone over the years had established that, if nothing else. Sure, he could play the game during a job interview and appear as serious and earnest as the next guy, but he also knew he could never pull off the charade day after day, week after week, stuck behind a desk. He liked power, but not the kind you get from being a middle manager or even a senior executive. As for the white-collar existence that the American advertising industry was touting to a country swept up in the postwar boom, no self-respecting Berkeleyite could look at suburban America and see anything other than a grotesque nightmare: grinning robots in suits and ties filling their commuter trains every morning with the reek of aftershave and, in the evening, after a day of meaningless activity, returning to their ranch houses and smiling blond wives, who hand them a martini and ask them the same question in the same tone of voice—day after day, week after week, year after year: "So, honey, how was your day?" Better to cultivate one's own peculiarity—in Dick's case, an adolescent affinity for science fiction. To a young writer whose "literary" works no one would touch, the genre at least offered a chance to earn a living from writing—a meager living, but enough to cover expenses while he wrote other things. Of course, writing science fiction also meant playing the game—working fast and cheap and putting up with editorial interference, inane titles, and garish illustrations of little green men with bulbous eyes. Terry Carr, the Ace paperback editor, used to joke that if the Bible had been published as science fiction, it would have had to be cut down to two volumes of twenty thousand words each; the Old Testament would have been retitled "Master of Chaos," and the New Testament "The Thing with Three Souls." Phil hoped that things would change, that it wouldn't be long before people would be reading his stories in the *New Yorker*; that his real books would be published by real publishers and receive real reviews; that someday he would be mentioned in the same breath as Norman Mailer and Nelson Algren; indeed, that the whole period of his science fiction writing would merely add an appealingly common touch to the biography of one of America's greatest living novelists.

The strangest thing about Dick's literary dreams may be that they never materialized. His "serious"—or, as publishers like to say, "mainstream"—works may not have been all that good, but far worse ones were getting published all the time. In a world in which remainder shelves overflow with yesterday's brilliant discoveries, Dick ought to have had a shot at making it among mainstream readers. But something held him back, something that seemed to him at first an inexplicable piece of bad luck, then (though much later) a sign that a far higher calling awaited him.

In the 1950s, in addition to the eighty or so short stories and seven science fiction novels he turned out, Dick managed to write no fewer than eight non–genre novels; each was rejected. Kleo, who subscribed wholeheartedly to the myth of the misunderstood artist, took the

rejections in stride: the true artist had to be rejected by the bour-
geoisie, at least in the beginning. She saved his rejection letters (one
day he received seventeen) and pinned them to the wall—silent testimony both to the obtuseness of the zombies in suits who ran the publishing houses and to her husband's originality, which the world would
soon be forced to recognize. Newspapers were starting to talk about
the Beat Generation, and its laid-back rebels offered a plausible model
for someone like Phil, at least sartorially: he had been wearing jeans,
checked shirts, and old army boots for years. Kleo's dream was for her
husband to become as famous as Kerouac, and on their rare excursions
across the bay and into San Francisco she tried to drag him into the
smoky little cafes of North Beach where the Beat poets listened to jazz
and read their works until all hours of the morning.

Unfortunately, Phil didn't like crossing the bay, and he didn't like
smoky cafes, jazz, or writers' gatherings either. He was petrified of the
moment when some obscure but published poet would ask him what
he wrote and then look on with a superior smile as Phil mumbled,
"Science fiction." Less confident than Kleo and lacking her sense of
righteous indignation, Phil wasn't so sure that failure was the mark of
genius, and without daring to ask her to take down the rejection letters she so prized—"What!" Kleo would have screamed. "Don't tell me
you're ashamed of them!"—he merely scowled and turned away from
the accusing wall. He preferred, when he was alone, to take out his
wallet and contemplate a file card autographed by a novelist named
Herb Gold, whom he barely knew, on which the anodyne inscription
read: "To a colleague, Philip K. Dick."

If Phil found it mortifying to find himself in the company of those
he would have loved to regard as his peers, he soon came to feel that
way around so-called normal people, people who weren't writers, who
had careers, lived in nice houses, and took home a weekly paycheck.
Of course, he could always follow Kleo's example and despise these
people for their success, except that he knew that the sword cut both
ways and that they looked down on him for his failures. The pride and
pleasure he took in not having to answer to a boss meant little next to
the nagging daily realities of being poor. Not far from where they lived

was a pet-supply store, the Lucky Dog Pet Store, where Phil some-times went to buy horse meat, supposedly for his dog. One day as he was making his purchase, the salesclerk looked at him and said, "You're not going to eat this stuff yourself, are you?" When he recounted the incident to Kleo, she laughed and tried to console him by reminding him that his first name meant "lover of horses" in Greek. He replied by asking whether his being a horse lover meant that he should eat their flesh or be repulsed by the very idea of it. Hindus didn't eat cows, which they considered sacred; Jews didn't touch the flesh of the pig, an animal they regarded as unclean. Kleo and Phil couldn't decide what to make of this paradox, except to conclude the two strictures were probably equally valid. Whatever the case, they ate horse meat, and in California in the mid-1950s this was the food of pariahs.

Phil wrote at night, keeping to the habit he had got into while work-ing at the record store. In the morning he would stroll around his neighborhood, in ever-smaller circles, coming home to scan his collec-tion of secondhand records or sit out in his overgrown backyard and read. What he didn't do was attend to home repair, to the sorts of little jobs his next-door neighbor would surely have done if he could have spent his days at home as Phil did. Leaving for work every morning, the neighbor would eye Phil suspiciously, and once he was gone, Phil would turn a sly, longing gaze over the fence and stare at the man's wife, who invariably would be starting her housecleaning just as he was thinking of going to bed. They must have flirted with each other, but nothing came of his flirtations with his female neighbors until later.

Phil read widely—Dostoevsky, Lucretius, the transcripts of the Nuremberg trials, German poetry and philosophy, and science fiction; he also read psychoanalysis, mostly Jung, buying each new volume of the Bollingen Press edition as it came out. This was how he discovered *Seven Sermons to the Dead*, which Jung had published in 1916 under the pseudonym Basilides—after a twelfth-century Gnostic from Alex-andria. In pseudoarchaic prose, Jung recounted a mystical experience filled with weird sounds and lights and with revelations from such figures as the prophet Elijah, Simon Magus, and Philemon, whom Jung recognized as an embodiment of his own spirit, only wiser and more knowledgeable. Phil became obsessed with this strange work and toyed with the idea of using it as the basis for a novel about a struggling writer, along the lines of Thomas Mann's newly published *Doctor Faustus*, which he had read with enormous admiration. Then he dropped the idea.

Generally speaking, the mainstream novels Dick was writing during this period reveal few traces of what he was reading. Their protagonists are aging television repairmen, disgruntled record salesmen who dream of becoming disk jockeys, and unhappily married couples. Instead of unfolding in any dramatic way, the lives of these lost souls seem predetermined, as they trudge with weary resignation along a path toward even greater despair. Sloppily written, turgid, full of inanely portentous dialogue, these works reflect the deep melancholy of their author, who would have given anything to be called another Thomas Mann. Stories about little green men and flying saucers, on the other hand, were what he was paid to write, and the most they offered in terms of literary recognition was comparison to someone like A. E. Van Vogt, a writer with whom Phil had once been photographed at a science fiction convention. The photo appeared in a fanzine above the caption "The Old and the New." Three years of hard work had raised him to the level of "promising young writer" in the science fiction community.

Van Vogt's specialty—like that of certain other writers, such as Lafayette Ron Hubbard, the future founder of the Church of Scientology—was galactic foundation myths known as "space operas." Featuring valiant earthlings doing battle against invading mutant hordes, they served up a standard fare of initiation rites, awesome displays of supernatural powers, the clash of titans. But alongside this naive if demanding genre, which some critics saw as merely offering compensatory fantasies to an unsophisticated readership, there existed a slightly more adult school of science fiction that emphasized the "science" rather than the "fiction," attempting to extrapolate the shape of things to come from existing or plausible technologies. Readers of the future, an author could only hope, would marvel at his prescient depiction of their world.

Phil had little affinity for either of these schools of science fiction, but he catered to the market and churned out Van Vogtian space operas while keeping up his subscriptions to various popular science magazines to stay abreast of developments in science and technology. Reading an article about a recent Soviet discovery that supposedly disproved Einstein's special theory of relativity, he immediately dashed a letter off to one of the researchers, a Professor Alexander Topchev of the Soviet Academy of Sciences. Phil hoped he might get some firsthand physics information, a scoop that would provide material for a new story, but no one ever wrote back. In any case, SF publishers were beginning to realize that good science made for dull reading, and the writers soon got the message and started to let their imaginations run wild again with stories of time travel, journeys to the fourth dimension, and space taxis that took pleasure seekers out to the rings of Saturn for an evening of adventure.

In the mid-1950s, however, another style was starting to take shape, one in which Dick felt much more at home. Writers like Robert Scheckley, Fredric Brown, and Richard Matheson were publishing dark, terse narratives in which the ordinary somehow turns into the nightmarish. Often involving a loss of innocence, their stories were crafted with an eye toward a denouement that reversed the normal order of things and left the reader with a feeling of disorientation. Lying somewhere between traditional fantasy literature and conventional science fiction, this school is peculiarly American, as I discovered when I published a novel called *The Mustache*. Although it was deeply influenced by Matheson, not a single review in my native France mentioned him, whereas Kafka's name came up repeatedly. The style was popularized by television and the movies, its spirit infusing such TV shows as *The Twilight Zone* and *The Invaders*, for which Scheckley, Brown, and Matheson all wrote teleplays, and Don Siegel's remarkable film *Invasion of the Body Snatchers*.

―――――――

Phil didn't see the film when it came out in 1956. Ever since the panic attack he had had as a child while watching a wartime newsreel, movie theaters made him uncomfortable and he rarely saw movies until they were shown on TV. Friends who had seen the film, however, told him about it, and as he listened to them recount the story of the residents of a small town being taken over, body and soul, by extraterrestrial pods, he was convinced that someone had stolen the idea from him. It seems that two years earlier he had published a short story on the same theme, told from the point of view of a young boy who believes that a monster has taken possession of his father's body. The more the person standing before him actually looks like the father he has always known, the more the boy is convinced the man is not his father at all but an alien imposter. And while the boy is in the garage looking in the incinerator for his father's remains, the monster sits in the living room complaining to the boy's mother about their son's wild imagination and how someday it will get him into trouble.

Invasion of the Body Snatchers, however, was based on a short story by Jack Finney that had come out several months before his own. Phil eventually decided that the general idea must have been in the air at the time.

CHAPTER 3

GEORGE SMITH AND GEORGE SCRUGGS

During these years of the Cold War and the Communist witch-hunts, everyone was suspicious of everyone else. The FBI, galvanized by urgent warnings from Senator Joe McCarthy, regarded every American citizen as a possible crypto-Communist—this despite the fact that, as J. Edgar Hoover himself acknowledged, the Communist Party of the United States had fewer than twenty-five thousand members, of whom one out of six was actually an FBI agent or government informant. Meanwhile, American citizens who, though not necessarily Communists, felt vulnerable to accusations that they were, considered every neighbor a possible police agent or at least an informant ready to report their names to the authorities. The evil creatures who had insinuated themselves among us in *Invasion of the Body Snatchers* and in scores of comparable stories could be read as Soviet agents or, just as easily, as FBI agents trying to track the Soviet agents down: the authors' intentions counted less than the public's response to these fantasies. Consciously or not, nearly everyone saw an enemy lurking behind the terrifyingly familiar face of his neighbor: for the Midwest farmer, the enemy was the dirty Commie; for a Berkeley bohemian, it was the stinking cop. Berkeley had been a center of radicalism since the 1930s, not simply because of the small kernel of actual card-carrying party members who lived there, but because Berkleyites tended to think of themselves as fellow travelers for whom *capitalist* and *fascist* were interchangeable terms that applied to anyone who was connected in any way with authority—or, for that matter, who simply wore a tie.

Phil had grown up in this world. His babysitter, a young woman whom he would later refer to as Olive Holt, never tired of telling him how much better the lives of workers in the Soviet Union were than those of the American proletariat, who sweated and toiled only to fatten the bloodsuckers on Wall Street. His mother, who never went so far as to join the party, had approved of these little speeches. His wife, Kleo, talked a similar line, adopting the slogans she heard at the meetings she sometimes went to after class. As for Phil himself, he was hardly sympathetic to Communism, and the friends Kleo brought back to the house considered him a complete reactionary. From his reading of Orwell and Hannah Arendt, he had developed a political philosophy that equated Communism with fascism and, refusing to give the former any credit for having better intentions, looked only at their similar outcomes, the totalitarian regimes that both systems had produced. A discussion he had one day with an actual Communist left him feeling exasperated; he found the man dogmatic and small-minded. None of this diminished his admiration for Communism's great revolutionary figures, however, or prevented him from following his natural inclination to side with the underdog and despise the middle class. In this regard, then, Phil was not out of step with the people around him; like them, he was a "radical"—or, as the FBI might have put it, he was "favorably disposed toward groups and persons themselves favorably disposed toward Communism."

Phil could of course not have missed the remarkable debut of a young congressman from California named Richard Nixon, who had surfaced in the late 1940s in Orange County, the stronghold of political reactionism a few hundred miles south of Berkeley. To Berkeleyites, who would never dream of setting foot in Orange County, Nixon—the shifty politician with a perpetual five o'clock shadow and greasy hair who liked to have himself photographed standing in front of his gun collection—was its signature product. Although no one had yet asked in so many words whether anyone would buy a used car from the man, Richard Nixon had already earned the nickname "Tricky Dick." The Berkeley *Gazette* had printed articles describing how Nixon won his Senate seat by red-baiting his Democratic opponent, Helen Gahagan Douglas, whom he had insinuated was a lesbian and famously characterized as being "pink right down to her underwear." Earlier, as a member of the House Un-American Activities Committee, he had carried out its anti-Communist mission with exceptional zeal. Next to Nixon, Joe McCarthy was a schoolyard bully, a paper tiger whom Congress knew how to muzzle once it no longer needed him. Nixon was a different kind of creature— soft-spoken, more the back-stabbing type. In 1952, when Phil Dick published his first short story, Tricky Dick had just been elected vice president as Eisenhower's running mate. The days when baby-sitters could openly avow their membership in the Communist Party were well over.

One winter day in 1955, Phil was alone in his house listening to a Beethoven symphony when two men came to the door. At first, he mistook them for salesmen. One was tall and fat, the other short and thin, but they were dressed identically in gray three-piece suits, Stetson hats, and black shoes polished to a high shine. They looked as though they might have just walked off the set of the new TV show *The Untouchables*, which is to say, they looked like Phil's father, who had become so rigid, narrow-minded, and conservative that Phil had not seen him for years—in fact not since the end of World War II, when they had fought over the morality of the atomic bombing of Hiroshima. (According to Edgar, the slant-eyeds had it coming to them.)

At any rate, the two men weren't selling anything; they were from the FBI, and had the badges to prove it. Wanting to affect an air of sang-froid, he tried to tell a joke, something he'd read in the *New*

Yorker: some FBI agents checking on a suspect question his neighbor, who tells them that the suspect listens to symphonies. Suspicious, one of the agents wants to know what language they're in.

Simple as the joke was, Phil garbled it in the telling. As always happened when he was upset, his voice jumped an octave or so. The two agents stood at the door listening to him in silence, unsmiling.

He couldn't have been from their office, one of the men finally replied. They asked if they could come inside, and, as soon as Phil let them in, they began to look around, making note of Phil's typewriter and his record player, which he immediately switched off. Phil sensed their disapproval—here he was in his shirtsleeves, unshaven, hanging around the house at eleven in the morning when everyone else either had gone off to work or was out shopping. The fat man asked what it was exactly that he wrote, and Phil's reply, that he wrote stories about Martians, little green men, stuff for kids, produced the expected reaction—the disdainful little smile—that in this instance particularly offended him, given his interlocutor. He wondered for a moment if they were interested in him because he was a science fiction writer. That made sense to him. Had he been an FBI agent, he, too, would have been suspicious of science fiction writers. After all, they wrote for a wide audience of unsophisticated—and therefore impressionable—people who generally read nothing else. Someone like him was in a perfect position to poison the minds of the masses, the same way a hydraulic engineer could poison the water supply for a large city. Not to mention the fact that the SF writer, believing he was merely following his imagination, might discover and expose classified technological information relating to national defense. No question about it: had he been one of the witch-hunters, Phil wouldn't have bothered with fashionable East Coast intellectuals or Hollywood scriptwriters who wore their Communist sympathies on their sleeve; they were red herrings. He would have kept his eye on the true manipulators of public opinion, the guys working down where it counted, turning out fodder for the masses, working-class literature that intellectuals affected to disdain.

The fat man began to question Phil about his political activities.

Phil told him he had none. He had never been a political activist, he said, had never even voted, for that matter, and the most subversive thing in his life was his passion for Dostoevsky and for *Boris Godunov*— of which he owned two recordings.

But what about Kleo? Everyone knew she had some connection to the student wing of the Socialist Workers Party. Didn't she talk to him about what happened at the meetings?

No, Phil said, she didn't. He wasn't interested in what went on there and she knew it.

The agent told Phil that it might be a good idea to start showing some interest in those meetings and to listen carefully to what his wife had to say about them.

Phil could hardly believe what he was hearing. Were they really asking him to spy on his wife? The request seemed so preposterous that it occurred to him that he was dealing with a pair of imposters. Why were they questioning him when everyone, Kleo included, knew that the SWP, like every other left-wing organization in the United States, was riddled with government informants? Even if for some reason they really did need him to infiltrate these organizations, weren't they supposed to take their time, make subtle approaches, lay some sort of intricate trap? Surely they wouldn't show their hand before they had made it impossible for him to refuse them. Could it be, he wondered, that they not only had already laid the trap but had sprung it, too?

Unable to figure out just what sort of game his two visitors were playing, Phil thought the safest thing to do was to play dumb, and he said simply that he wasn't interested in any of what they were talking about. Neither, it seemed, was the fat man's partner, the thin, silent agent who had been standing over Phil's desk and, without making any attempt to hide what he was doing, was reading the sheet of paper that was still in the typewriter. That was when the fat agent asked Phil if he had Communist leanings.

Phil, of course, was no Communist sympathizer, at least not in any intellectual sense, but once again he couldn't figure out what lay behind the question. What sort of answer did they expect him to give? He suddenly remembered how a famous English spy used to answer this kind of question. He had always admired the simple elegance of the formulation and had been waiting for a chance to try it out for himself.

"No," Phil told the agent, "I can assure you I'm not a Communist sympathizer. But then you and I both know that if I were one my answer would be the same."

Apt as it was, the reply seemed to irritate the two men. They exchanged glances, then turned to leave, telling Phil as they were going out the door that they would be back. Alone again, Phil wondered whether he had cleverly deceived two imbeciles or, on the contrary, had walked into a trap. He remembered something he'd read in a work by Bertolt Brecht, a committed Communist and Kleo's favorite author: "He laughed because they couldn't hit him; he didn't know they were trying to miss."

Initially, Kleo took the whole business very seriously, telling anyone who would listen that America had become a fascist country. Then things quieted down. For a while, George Smith and George Scruggs— those were the agents' names—came to visit once a week. Smith, the fat one, asked the questions and talked about this and that. Scruggs, the thin one, kept silent, as if, having nothing better to do, he had decided to join his friend on house calls that were actually none of his business. Kleo decided Scruggs was the more dangerous of the two, though she had nothing to back up her hunch. On one of their visits they dropped off questionnaires—surveys, they said, that they would stop by to pick up later. Rather than surveys, the forms seemed to be tests intended to gauge how right-thinking the subject was. What was most disturbing about these two tests—like the general behavior of the two Georges—was that it was hard to know how seriously to take them. The questions were like the ones immigration officials used to ask: "Do you have any addictions? Are you a terrorist? Do you intend to attempt to assassinate the president of the United States?" The stupider the question appeared, and the more obvious the desired answer, the greater the chances, Phil reasoned, that they were traps—like the famous "K Scale" of the Minnesota Multiphasic, which supposedly measured a test taker's "degree of defensiveness." One question, for example, was a multiple-choice completion with three answers to choose from:

Russia is
(a) growing weaker
(b) growing stronger
(c) maintaining about the same level of strength as the Free World

Of course, the best answer was (b) if one wanted to demonstrate that one shared the fears of the nation's leaders that Russia was growing more powerful and hence their belief in the need for ever-larger military budgets. But the second question complicated matters. It went as follows:

Russian technology is
(a) very good
(b) average
(c) useless

By choosing (a), one would appear to be paying the Commies a compliment. The best choice seemed to be (b), and was probably the closest to the truth. On the other hand, what right-thinking citizen could fail to choose (c), for how could technology produced by victims of totalitarianism be anything other than useless? But in that case, how was it that a hopelessly backward country could be growing in strength? Luckily, the answer was suggested by the next question:

The greatest threat to the Free World is
(a) Russia
(b) our high standard of living
(c) subversive elements hiding within our midst

Kleo said they should choose (c)—even though it referred to them. They laughed and pretended to be scared. They knew they were small fry.

———————

Eventually, George Scruggs started dropping by on his own or with Merton, his German short-haired pointer. The Dicks wondered whether these solo visits signaled a new tactic or an easing up of surveillance. It turned out that Scruggs lived fairly close by and simply liked stopping by to chat with Phil on his way to the office. His visits seemed innocent enough. Unlike his sneering, boorish partner, he was impressed that Phil was a writer. He asked him where he got his ideas and even read one of his books. Phil was flattered. Though he suspected that Scruggs was trying to gain his confidence in order to make it easier to trap him, he started forming a sort of friendship with the man. When Scruggs learned that Phil didn't know how to drive, he offered to give him lessons in his sports car. Every Sunday morning, Phil went into contortions to fit his long legs into the car, and, jammed between the driver's seat and the steering wheel, he spent an hour or two talking with Scruggs. He began to enjoy trying to psych him out. Beneath the humorless platitudes—which his job required of him—there was in Scruggs an underlying honesty and generosity of spirit that made him the ideal victim of a sophist like Phil. More than he should have been, given his line of work, he was open to arguments of reason, and Phil took advantage of this to get him to swallow the most subversive notions.

One day, for example, as they were driving slowly around the block, Phil asked Scruggs about the files the FBI had on him and Kleo. The question embarrassed Scruggs. He muttered something noncommittal, but Phil wouldn't let go and pressed him to admit that he still thought Kleo was a Communist. Scruggs was apologetic. There was no way of getting around it, he said: Kleo attended meetings of the Socialist Workers Party, and the Socialist Workers Party was a front for the Communist Party. And she had signed the Stockholm statement, which pretty much settled the matter.

Phil smiled indulgently and pointed out that Kleo's going to meetings, spouting leftist slogans, and signing petitions proved only one thing, namely, that she couldn't be a Communist. Scruggs knew as well as he did, Phil said, that if Kleo were a Communist, she would have to be more careful.

Scruggs conceded the point, a sure sign that Phil had succeeded in flustering him—George Smith would never have made such a concession—but he wasn't going to give up so easily. If Communists didn't go to meetings or spout slogans or sign petitions, then how was one supposed to spot them? Well, Phil said, the Communists obviously were the ones who didn't do any of those things. The FBI pretended to monitor harmless fellow travelers like Kleo when in fact the people they were really after were those who didn't make waves—or those who were railing loudest against the Communists.

Scruggs scratched his head. Phil had noted that it was easy to throw the man off balance by ascribing Machiavellian motives to him, for then he wondered whether he ought not to have them. The FBI had no choice but to go on the evidence, Scruggs insisted, and to judge people on the basis of what they did. How else could it learn what was going on in their heads?

Phil told Scruggs not to take him for a fool, which only made Scruggs more nervous. Somehow he seemed to have switched places with the man he was supposed to be interrogating. He wouldn't have been surprised if Phil had revealed himself not only as an FBI agent himself but as someone higher up in the hierarchy than he was, if this whole time Phil had simply been pretending to be a struggling writer. Scruggs tried one last time to counter Phil's arguments. If one followed Phil's line of reasoning, he told him, everyone in the whole country would have to be considered dangerous. Even Nixon would be a Commie! Phil flashed a sardonic grin. It was Scruggs, not he, who had said it, he pointed out to the agent.

The conversation provided food for thought, particularly Scruggs's admission that it was difficult to know what was going on inside people's heads. Phil wondered what it would be like to be inside the head of someone as different from him as George Scruggs or, worse, George Smith, or his father, or Richard Nixon.

He played for a moment with the notion of trading brains with Richard Nixon—just for the time it would take to write a book—but then dropped the idea. Phil Dick's waking up one morning to find himself in the skin of the politician from California, and Dick Nixon's waking up to find he had become an SF hack in Berkeley—it would probably make a wonderful story, one with all sorts of interesting dimensions, but that wasn't what was on his mind. He had recently come on a distinction in a philosophy textbook between the *idios kosmos*, the individualized vision of the universe each of us carries around inside our head, and the *koinos kosmos*, what people tend to think of as the objective universe. The notion of "reality" is merely a convenient way of referring to the *koinos kosmos*, but the *koinos kosmos*, strictly speaking, doesn't exist; our perception of an objective reality is a matter of convention, an agreement among people trying to create some stable basis for their interrelations. The *koinos kosmos* is a sort of diplomatic fiction, the lowest common denominator of my *idios kosmos* and those of my neighbors—assuming that my neighbors truly exist and that I am not alone in the world.

Phil wasn't interested in what it would be like to exchange his *idios kosmos* for someone else's—not that he would necessarily have been aware of the exchange, since once it had been made he would have been the other person and not himself anymore. What intrigued him was the possibility of visiting someone else's *idios kosmos* without losing his own. It would be like traveling to a foreign country. All he needed was the device that would allow him to take the trip. If nothing else, the literary genre in which he had been toiling for the past few years provided just what he was looking for—in spades. That same evening, he typed the following sentences, managing to assemble in just a few lines all the elements of science fiction that put so many people off:

> The Proton Beam Deflector of the Belmont Bevatron betrayed its inventors at four o'clock in the afternoon of October 2, 1959. [Phil was writing in 1956 about the near future.] What happened next happened instantly. No longer adequately deflected—and therefore no longer under control—the six billion volt beam radiated upward toward the roof of the chamber, incinerating, along its way, an observation platform overlooking the doughnut-shaped magnet.
>
> There were eight people standing on the platform at the time. . . .

They fell to the floor of the Bevatron chamber and lay in a state of injury and shock until the magnetic field had been drained and the hard radiation partially neutralized.

He tells us in the next paragraph that the eight accident victims regain consciousness and are taken to the hospital. Those with the least serious injuries are sent home. Everything eventually seems to go back to normal, down to the smallest details—a sure sign that something will go wrong, of course. Then one of the eight tells a lie—a joke really—and thereby brings a biblical plague of locusts down on his head. Soon after that a prayer murmured unthinkingly instantly gets granted. The survivors are faced with the fact that the rational world is coming apart: superstitions have superseded the laws of physics; prayer now has all the effective power of action. Anyone who steps out of line is punished by heavenly fire.

What these people now realize is that they are stuck inside the Bevatron itself and that the energy released by the accident has transformed the personal universe belonging to one of them, probably the person closest to consciousness, into a collective mental universe in which everyone else is being held prisoner. As one of the protagonists exclaims, "We're subject to the logic of a religious crank, an old man who picked up a screwball cult in Chicago in the thirties. We're in his universe, where all his ignorant and pious superstitions function. We're in the man's *head*."

Phil immensely enjoyed creating the religious fanatic's universe, though he had no intention of devoting the entire novel to it. The whole point of putting the eight people inside the Bevatron was to explore each character's *idios kosmos*. From religious extremism, we enter the world of a war veteran not unlike Phil's father, then the puritanical utopia of a sweet little old lady. Here is a world not unlike what Phil might have imagined his mother's to be, filled with fine feelings, the love of art, purity, and all things beautiful—the world of a woman who hates disorder, sex, and anything organic and who is convinced that one can separate the wheat from the chaff and, more important, eliminate the chaff altogether. The old woman banishes from her universe not only particular objects and beings but entire categories of offending entities: car horns, noisy garbage collectors, door-to-door salesmen, meat, poverty, genitalia, asthma, drunkenness, filth, Russia, and atonal music.

Thus improved by an increasingly frenetic subtraction of everything she deems undesirable, the old lady's world dissolves into the still more fearful world of a young paranoiac—a woman whose world is frozen and insidious, unassailably normal yet deeply ominous. Everything in it is dangerous and deceptive—even inanimate objects. The people in the Bevatron begin to panic. Until that point, each character's universe has been more terrible than the one before it. What will come next—if there is a next? The three people whose worlds the group has just inhabited had seemed to be so normal: an ordinary, conventional guy, a society lady, and a secretary. Yet they turned out to be a religious fanatic, a maniacal puritan, and a psycho. What sorts of dangers are the others concealing? Worse still, the more intelligent among the group wonder, what sorts of dangers lurk inside themselves? What nightmares will each of their universes pose for the others, once it becomes everyone's reality?

Among the eight Bevatron visitors is a married couple. The husband has long suspected that his wife, Marsha, is a Communist, but she has sworn to him that she isn't. Now he begins to have doubts again. Once the secretary's paranoid universe has in effect self-destructed—transforming the husband and wife into giant insects that devour the others—the world changes again . . . into one governed by the vision of a militant Communist. Obviously recalling the stories Olive Holt had told him when he was a child and what Kleo's socialist friends had been telling him, Phil threw himself into this chapter body and soul: it is a capitalist nightmare, with bloodsucking industrialists, fascist gangs, blacks lynched on every street corner, towns ruled by gangsters, hordes of starving children rummaging through the garbage—here was how a card-carrying Communist viewed America.

But which one of the group is the Communist? From which of them does the grotesque and terrifying vision emanate? Naturally, suspicion falls on Marsha, whom the chief of security at the Bevatron facility had accused of being a Communist from the very beginning. Even her husband becomes persuaded that she has been lying to him all these years.

Here Phil exaggerates things more than a little; his political differences with Kleo were never quite so dramatic as this. Still, he wanted the book to turn on the identification of the mysterious Communist. As he typed out the last chapter (a mere two weeks after he had begun the novel), he imagined George Scruggs reading it. Phil wondered whether Scruggs would guess how the story turns out. Would he suspect that the Communist proves not to be Marsha, who is basically a good-hearted left-wing activist, but instead the very man who had been so ready to accuse her of being one—the chief of security, the head witch-hunter himself, a man who only pretends to be obsessed with rooting out Commies?

When *Eye in the Sky* was published the following year, in 1957, Phil sent one of the three copies his editor had given him to his friend in the FBI. Joe McCarthy had recently died of cirrhosis; a series of Supreme Court decisions had put an end to the witch-hunts. George Scruggs had not been to see Phil for some time, but after he received the book he came for a visit, to thank Phil and to tell him what he thought of it. Apparently Scruggs didn't understand a fair number of even the more obvious political references, to say nothing of the novel's philosophical dimensions. Phil tried to explain the difference between *koinos kosmos* and *idios kosmos*, to no avail. The only thing that interested Scruggs was the scientific plausibility of the premise: was this kind of psychological domination really possible? Phil couldn't resist the temptation to pull Scruggs's leg one last time. Recalling the naive attempt he had made a few years earlier to communicate with the Russian physicist, he declared that he was engaged in a correspondence on this very subject with Professor Alexander Topchev of the Soviet Academy of Sciences.

Scruggs said he knew.

Now it was Phil's turn to wonder who was taking whom for a ride.

CHAPTER 4

WHAT HE WAS REALLY DOING

The first warning signs came one evening after Phil and Kleo had eaten some lasagna she had made. She and Phil were talking and listening to music when Phil suddenly developed a stomachache. He got up and said he was going to find something to take for it, then walked down the long, dark corridor to the bathroom.

He reached the door and started fumbling for the light cord. Kleo called to him from the dining room, asking if he was all right. He replied that he was fine. But he still couldn't seem to find the light cord, even though he knew perfectly well that it hung inside the door on the left. It was getting ridiculous. His fingers spread wide, he made wide circles in the air with his arms, trying to snag the end of the cord. A wave of panic descended on him—it was as if everything had fallen away around him. In his flailing about, he banged his head against the corner of the medicine cabinet. The glasses on the shelf rattled. He swore.

Kleo's voice came again, as though from far away. "Are you all right?" Then, "What's wrong?" He groaned, though not loud enough for her to hear, and mumbled that he couldn't find the goddamn light cord.

And then it hit him. There wasn't any cord to pull. The switch was on the wall—it had always been there—just to the right of the door. He found it easily and flicked it up. The bulb hanging from the ceiling went on. He looked around the bathroom, expecting it would somehow look different, but it didn't. Undergarments were still hanging from the shower curtain rod, a cockroach was scuttling across the tiles. Phil lifted his foot to squash it, then stopped himself.

He opened the medicine cabinet, trying not to look at his face in the mirror, picked up a bottle that had fallen over, found the one containing his stomach pills, and swallowed one of the pills with a glass of water. Then, having gently turned off the light switch so that it would make no noise, he went back into the dining room. Kleo had cleared the table and was in the kitchen doing the dishes. He thought again about the light cord, wondered where the memory of it had come from—it was a specific light cord, of a specific length and in a specific location. He knew he hadn't been fumbling around for it randomly, as he might have done had he been in someone else's bathroom. He had been looking for a cord that he had used before, on any number of occasions—often enough, he thought, to create a reflex in his nervous system.

"Has that ever happened to you?" he asked Kleo. "Have you ever felt around for a light cord that wasn't there? Instead of the wall switch?"

"Oh, so that's what took you so long," she replied, looking up at him from the dishes in the sink.

"Where would I have gotten into the habit of pulling on a light cord?"

"I don't know. It's hard to find them anymore. Most lights work with wall switches these days. Maybe it's a childhood memory coming back to you."

Then Kleo went off to bed, leaving Phil with Magnificat, the cat, in the dining room, which in the evenings became his study. He put on Schumann's *Liederkreis*, opus 39, a new recording by Fischer-Dieskau, and sat down at the table. Kleo had already put his typewriter back in the usual place, in front of his chair. A car drove by, but after the noise had receded there was absolute silence. This was his favorite time of day. The first lied on the record, the most beautiful one, was about a man who has taken a trip and is now trudging through the snow, thinking nostalgically about his homeland. Actually the poem that Schumann had set to music said nothing about snow, but the lied was part of a collection that also contained a recording of Schubert's *Winterreise*, and the album cover showed a frosty winter landscape, putting the listener in the mood for snow. Phil laughed to himself. He wondered whether it would be possible to write a poem, and then a song, based on what had just happened to him: a guy goes into the bathroom, and instead of flipping a light switch he gropes for a pull cord that isn't there. Phil improvised some lyrics. He was almost tempted to wake Kleo up and sing them for her, to the melody of the lied that had just finished and in his best imitation of Fischer-Dieskau. *"Es gab keine Lampenschnur".* . . ."There was no light cord."

He considered writing a story about the incident. He had already written several stories in which someone is struck by some small, utterly insignificant detail, perhaps some little thing out of place, and realizes that *something is not right*. In one of these stories, a man goes to his office and notices that everything has been altered ever so subtly. He finds it hard to say what, exactly, is different—whether it's the furniture, or the arrangement of the furniture, or something about his secretary's face. But the more he thinks about it, the more positive he is that everything has changed. And in fact, he's right: a secret organization has been routinely recomposing his reality—in something of the same way one might renovate a building—all for vague reasons of national security that Phil doesn't take the trouble to develop in any detail. In another story, a man, his family, his friends, and everyone around them think they are residing in a small American town circa the 1950s; in reality they are living in an immense stage set, part of a historical exhibit in a museum in the twenty-third century. The townspeople are fenced in like Indians on a reservation, except in their case they have no idea where they really are. A sophisticated system of optics prevents them from realizing that they are being observed by the people of the future, who come to the museum in droves to get a glimpse of what life used to be like. At a certain point, the hero of the story suddenly understands what's going on and tries to convince the others. They think he's crazy, of course.

Phil adored writing this kind of scene, spelling out the arguments of the hero who speaks the truth and is believed by no one and who knows that if he were one of his listeners, he wouldn't believe himself either. One might expect these scenes to be tedious, given their obligatory nature and the formulaic character of the stories themselves, but they are extremely successful. In the story about the 1950s historical reconstruction, for example, Dick does a nice job presenting the encounter between the hero and his psychiatrist, who by definition is the worst possible interlocutor, since he is interested not in the truth or falsehood of what his patient is telling him, only in determining the mental state that the man's "symptoms" indicate. Phil hated psychiatrists' smug certainty. He joked that had Galileo gone to his psychiatrist and informed him that the earth moved around the sun, or had Moses repeated to his what Yahweh had told him, the doctors would have smiled benevolently and started asking them about their childhoods. At bottom what pleased Phil most about these stories, and about such scenes in particular, was that he got to have the last word. He could show that the psychiatrists were wrong, that the patients they dismissed as delusional were actually right. He delighted in being able to make the psychiatrist in the story an unwitting part of the historical reconstruction. The museum visitors double over in laughter when they hear the good doctor explain to his hapless patient—the only one to have figured out what is really going on—that he's avoiding reality by retreating into his imagination. An escape mechanism, the psychiatrist intones sagely, which is precisely how Phil's friends might have accounted for his writing stories about little green men instead of holding down a real job with adult responsibilities: obviously he felt guilty or feared authority or simply refused to grow up. Science fiction was an escape mechanism. Maybe they were onto something.

Several months earlier, reading Freud's *Five Lectures on Psycho-*

analysis, Dick had learned about the case of Daniel Paul Schreber, the judge whom Freud uses as the model of the paranoiac. Dick decided that, retold slightly differently, the case would make great science fiction. *The Man Whom God Wanted to Change into a Woman and Penetrate with Larvae in Order to Save the World*—sure, it was a little long as titles go, but if science fiction, as Anthony Boucher argued, consisted of asking the question "What if?," then clearly this was something he could have some fun with. What if Schreber was right? What if his supposed delusions were in fact an accurate description of reality? What if Freud was just another self-righteous know-it-all, pathologizing a man who understood better what was really going on? The whole idea that the only man who *knew* was locked away in an insane asylum wasn't all that crazy, but unfortunately it probably wasn't all that marketable either. No science fiction editor would be interested in a novel featuring Freud or Schreber. On the other hand, nothing prevented the writer of the light-cord lied from styling the protagonist after himself. After all, the light-cord incident was real and had actually happened to him.

So that's what he decided to do—he would tell the story of a science fiction writer who tries to turn on a bathroom light that is not there and realizes that *something is not right.* And if the publishers wanted mainstream, he would pile it on: a small town, little white houses, pretty little gardens, the neighbors' dog, a fat garage mechanic with a corncob pipe, the smell of a homemade apple pie baked by that nice lady next door. Except that it would be science fiction, meaning, first and foremost, that Phil would get it published and, second, that the main character would be right: something really *is* amiss; the world is not what it seems to be. It's a stage set, nothing but props and backdrops and special effects, all cleverly designed to fool the inhabitants and keep them from finding out the truth. But what is this truth that someone is concealing from them?

When he sat down to write the novel, *Time Out of Joint,* Dick gave the hero a different name and a different profession. The main character,

Ragle Gumm, has been earning a living for the past several years by participating in a daily mail-in contest organized by the local newspaper called "Where Will the Little Green Man Be Next?"

The entry forms are always the same—a blank grid on which the little green man appears in one of the hundreds of empty squares. From one day to the next, the little green man changes squares, and each and every day the newspaper publishes a series of apparently meaningless phrases, something along the lines of "A swallow is as great as a mile"—which supposedly offers a hint to where the little green man will next turn up. Operating under the assumption that these apparently meaningless phrases contain hidden messages, Ragle begins by free-associating, though he also uses his previous results, which he has carefully recorded since he started playing the game. Ragle's method, a combination of deduction and sheer inspiration, turned out to be oddly effective: he wins each and every time and manages to live off the modest prize money. What begins as a whim, a way of bringing in a few extra bucks playing little guessing games, soon becomes a chore. The game is his ball and chain. People don't understand this; they imagine that all he does is sit at his kitchen table, pick a square by intuition or at random, mail in the reply, and deposit his checks. They think he is a lazy bum leading the good life, thanks to a talent he doesn't deserve, while honest folk go out and work for a living. No one appreciates how stressful his life is—the toll taken on him by this occupation fit for no one but an arrested adolescent, and, even as he congratulates himself on the autonomy it affords him, he is plagued by the envy and suspicion that he arouses in those around him. He sometimes dreams of changing his life, of giving up the contest and doing something else—sweating under a hard hat in the shadow of oil derricks, perhaps, or raking leaves, or pushing a pen behind some desk. Any occupation has to be more rewarding, more grown-up, more *real* than this stupid game he can't seem to let go of. But then the next morning the newspaper arrives, and after eating breakfast, without even clearing the table, he opens to the page where the contest appears and gives the wheel of his life another spin. It must be his karma—at least that is what he has read in the Vedas.

Ragle Gumm has one consolation: he knows he is needed. The contest organizers have built their advertising campaign around his long tenure as undefeated champion. In fact, they *want* him to win. By secret agreement, they allow him to send in several entries a day to increase his chances of winning.

One day, Ragle works up the courage to ask Lowery, the man in charge of the contest, whether the puzzles actually mean anything.

"Not literally."

"I know that. I mean, do they mean anything at all, in any way, shape or form? Or is it just to convince us that somebody up at the top knows the answer?"

"What does that mean?" Lowery said, with a shade of annoyance.

"I have a theory," Ragle said. "Not a very serious theory, but it's fun to toy with. Maybe there's no correct answer."

Lowery raised an eyebrow. "Then on what basis do we declare one answer a winner and all others incorrect?"

"Maybe you read over the entries and decide on the strength of them which appeals to you the most. Esthetically."

Lowery said, "You're projecting your technique on us."

Then comes the business with the lamp cord, reinforcing Ragle's vague impression that something is wrong. He comes across some kids playing in an empty lot who have found an old telephone directory in which the prefixes correspond to no exchanges he has ever heard of, and when he tries dialing some of the numbers, no one answers. He is beset by strange impressions of disconnectedness, by feelings of déjà vu. He notices that everyone recognizes him on the street, even total strangers. They've probably seen his picture in the local paper, he tells himself; he is, after all, the perennial champion of the little-green-man contest, but still . . . Later, fiddling with an old radio set, he picks up messages that seem to come from planes circling constantly overhead. No one in town seems to know anything about these planes, or at any rate nobody mentions them. Maybe I'm the only one, he thinks, who's not in on this. Maybe I'm the center of something without even realizing it. No, no. Got to keep calm. I already suspect I'm the focus of some conspiracy, that the universe spins around me, without any other purpose than to torture me. I'm becoming paranoid. But no sooner do these thoughts cross his mind than the radio starts picking up messages again. They're about him:

> "It's fine. You're passing over him now."
> *Him*, Ragle thought.
> ". . . down there," the voice said. "Yes, you're looking down at Ragle Gumm himself."

In Dick's earlier stories of this sort, the hero typically uncovers a secret that involves nothing less than the fate of the world and vainly attempts to tell those around him what he knows. In *Time Out of Joint* Dick turns this plot on its head, creating something even creepier. The story line is no longer about the hero's being the only one to know the great secret; now it's about everyone *except him* knowing, about everyone conspiring to prevent him from finding out what's really going on. Ragle struggles no less mightily than Dick's earlier protagonists to convince others of his dawning revelation and receives the same incredulous response from those around him. The difference is that this time his "incredulous" fellow citizens are in on the secret and are waiting to see where his suspicions will lead him.

Pursuing his investigations—as surveillance teams look on—Ragle tries to leave town, but escape proves impossible. It is as though the world stops just beyond the outskirts of town and everything must be done to keep him in ignorance of this. If he is driving a car, the engine dies. When he tries to catch a bus out of town, the bus depot disappears in the middle of the night. He panics. If I turn on the radio, he thinks, I'll hear them talking about me. Because I am the center of this universe. They're working like crazy to construct a fake world all around me, to keep me quiet and happy. Buildings, cars—an entire city. It all looks real, but it's not. What I don't get is, why me? And what is this contest really about? Obviously it's very important to them, because this whole illusion has been built around it. When I figure out where the little green man is going to appear next, I must be doing something else. They know what it is. I don't.

I'm not going tell the story to the very end, but I will give away the secret on which the novel turns. Ragle eventually cuts through appearances and gets to the truth. One of his first discoveries is an issue of *Time* magazine dating from 1997—some forty years in the future—with a picture of him on the cover, under a banner reading, "Ragle Gumm: Man of the Year." And here is what he learns: at the close of the twentieth century, war broke out between the earth and its rebellious lunar colony, whose forces relentlessly bombarded the mother planet. Happily, the earth's defenses were led by a strategic genius—none other than Ragle Gumm, who, thanks to his superior intelligence, his experience, and, most of all, his almost infallible intuition, was able to predict where the next missiles were going to hit, so that people could be evacuated from the targeted towns before catastrophe. But one day, overcome by the weight of this crushing responsibility, he retreated into an imaginary world of peace and tranquillity—to the 1950s, the carefree years of his youth. An escape mechanism, the agonized psychiatrists declared; there was no way to draw him out of this mental universe he created for himself. The authorities came up with the idea of adapting his environment to his psychosis, and they built a world in which Ragle could feel safe and secure. In a top-secret military zone they constructed an entire little town, like those that existed on earth before the war, and peopled it with actors. Then they gave Ragle a hobby that allowed them to continue to exploit his talent. Believing that he has been solving a kid's puzzle in the daily newspaper—picking the square in which the little green man will appear again—he has in fact been telling the authorities exactly where the next missile will hit and thus continuing to defend the earth's population against the lunar rebels. Up until the day, that is, when a number of little incidents make him suspect that something is not right and he begins to recover his memory. The lamp cord triggered everything.

————

With this chapter, the apprenticeship years of Philip K. Dick come to a close, and I propose we now take a little break and play a game. Here are three exercises to help the reader guess where, in the pages that follow, the little green man will pop up next:

1) At thirty, when he had written the novel I have just summarized, Philip K. Dick thought he was a poor, struggling working-class writer, condemned to earn a meager living banging out stories for pimply teenagers, stories that kept him from writing the more serious works that he believed would make his mark. Yet at the same time, he sensed that this estimation of his activities was not the whole truth—and that he was actually, without knowing it, doing something else. The question is, what did he think he was really doing?

2) You are holding in your hands an issue of *Time* magazine from the year 2007, with a picture on the cover of Philip K. Dick, "Man of the Year." Describe what the article says.

3) Variation: the issue is dated 2004, which means that it comes not from the universe in which you are reading this book but from a parallel universe. Redo exercise number two with this in mind.

CHAPTER 5

THE RAT IN THE HOUSE

Berkeley, the peaceful little college town of Phil's childhood, was getting busier and noisier. A Montessori school had opened across from Kleo and his house, and he complained about the noise from the playground. He also complained, every time they went across the bay, about the damage being inflicted on old San Francisco by the Embarcadero Freeway, which was rising from the waterfront in a deafening din of jackhammers and cement trucks. The Dicks dreamed of moving out to the country. They could picture themselves as members of a rural community in which everyone knew everyone else, said hello, helped out—a place where life rolled along peacefully, unchanging, punctuated by fishing seasons and pumpkin harvests. They bought a small house in Point Reyes Station in Marin County. Located forty miles north of the Golden Gate Bridge, this village of two main roads and a few businesses attracted weekend visitors because of its proximity to Point Reyes National Seashore, famous for its dramatic cliffs where some three hundred different species of seabird nested. During the week, however, Point Reyes Station was deserted.

Unlike in Berkeley, where eccentricity was commonplace, the lifestyle of the new arrivals attracted the attention of their neighbors.

Three times a week, Kleo took the car and drove to Berkeley, where she worked part-time as a secretary. Phil, who still wrote at night, gave the impression of someone out of work. Locals didn't know what to make of this big, taciturn man with the gawky gait and beatnik look about him; they couldn't decide whether he was shy or arrogant. When word began to spread that he wrote science fiction, a local group interested in UFOs approached him. Out of politeness and curiosity, he attended one of their meetings, where he found a dozen or so fairly normal-looking people standing around a coffee urn eating homemade cake, among them a man who worked at the Point Reyes hardware store, the owner of a dairy farm, the wife of the man who ran the local cafe, and the wife of the technician who operated the local RCA transmitter. A landscape painter and long-time resident of Point Reyes Station, a man who sported a bolo tie with a silver tie clip in the shape of some sort of esoteric symbol, was about as eccentric as this bunch got. Ordinary people though they were, they firmly believed in extraordinary things. They were convinced, for example, that Jesus Christ had come from another planet the inhabitants of which—highly evolved beings who directed the evolution of our own planet Earth—had contacted them and let them know that the world's spiritual salvation was going to require its total material destruction. In other words, the world was going to end on April 23, 1959. There were only three months left to prepare.

When Phil told Kleo how he had spent his afternoon, they had a good laugh and wondered how on earth people could actually believe such things. But then they stopped laughing, for now they had a problem on their hands. How was Phil going to avoid his new friends? Point Reyes Station was a village, after all, and now that he had socialized with these people, he couldn't just ignore them when he passed them on the street. And what if they started dropping by? Under the circumstances, he and Kleo decided, he would just have to come out and tell them he did not believe in extraterrestrials. This would be hard for him, for he hated directly contradicting people, but he would do his best to tell them what he thought they should know. The reason he was skeptical about UFOs was that he wrote about UFOs, he said at the next meeting. What would happen if a science fiction writer started believing his own stories? A dazed silence, then open hostility, greeted this declaration of apostasy. Not knowing what to say next, Phil giggled nervously. Go ahead and laugh, they told him. We'll see who's laughing on April 23.

A few days after their arrival in Point Reyes Station, Kleo and Phil had received a visit from a neighbor named Anne Rubenstein. Having found the garden gate stuck, she simply climbed over it, then came barging in without the slightest apology. A nervous blond-haired woman who kept raising and lowering her sunglasses, Anne was abrupt yet at the same time charming. The young couple found her disconcerting. When she shook your hand her grip was a little too firm, a little too earnest; even the most innocent remark out of her lips seemed heavy with sexual innuendo. Though they were nearly her age, Phil and Kleo felt like awkward adolescents in the presence of this thirty-one-year-old woman who had already buried a husband and was raising three daughters on her own.

They were required, rather than invited, to come have a drink at her house. Anne lived outside of town in a large modern house with a bay window overlooking a patio, a circular fireplace in the middle of the living room, and hi-fi speakers built into the impeccably white walls. A horse trotted along the fence of an adjacent paddock. The house had three bathrooms; the kitchen was like the cockpit of a spaceship. It embodied the latest in interior design, or what all the magazines were featuring, at any rate—just the sort of thing the average Berkeleyite was quick to scorn, lest he envy it. Phil, who until now had professed precisely such disdain and, like Kleo, thought it was quaint and unbourgeois the way the fuses blew every time they plugged in the toaster, suddenly decided their bohemian lifestyle was actually pitiful. It was not so much the material comforts of Anne's house that fascinated him as her style. When she walked through the room—dressed in a silk blouse and shorts—he followed her with his eyes, drawn by her litheness, her tanned muscular legs, and her energy.

She had the grace of a dancer with none of the affectedness; she swore and used crude language. When she talked to him, she held his gaze with her green eyes, almost defiantly, then suddenly she would relax her stare and turn and leave the room, her flip-flops clacking.

He came to see Anne alone one day when Kleo was out. She took him down to the cliffs to show him a secret cove—the most westerly point in the United States, she said. To reach it, he had to climb down a rope, which terrified him, but she coaxed him down. He had never met a woman with such agility or determination. They combed the beach for whalebone that had washed up on the shore, then climbed onto the rocks and sat and talked as waves crashed behind them. They talked about Jung, for whom she said she felt such passion that she sometimes dreamed about him. They also talked about the UFO crowd.

Anne dismissed them as a bunch of lunatics. They think superior beings are trying to get in touch with them, she said, but what they really need is to get in touch with their own subconscious.

Phil wasn't so sure. He pointed out that prophets and saints are always regarded as lunatics by their contemporaries.

Anne agreed, but sided with the contemporaries. Then she asked him whether he himself believed in prophets and saints.

He said he didn't—at least not really. In any case, he told her, they would just have to wait and see what happens on April 23. Did she know they were going around saying the world was going to end on April 23? he asked.

Anne stared at him, then, in her usual teasing tone, said that lots of things could happen between now and April 23. Phil didn't dare to ask her what she meant, and she quickly changed the subject and started talking about her late husband, a poet who came from a wealthy family and had published a magazine called *Neurotica*. He had died the year before in a psychiatric hospital, following an allergic reaction to some experimental tranquilizers his doctors had put him on. Phil wondered how long one needed to remain respectfully silent after hearing such news, but she burst into raucous laughter and told him not to look so somber, that it wasn't necessary. Not to be outdone, he told her the story of his dead twin sister and followed it with an anecdote about Mark Twain.

Asked about his youth by a journalist, Phil said, Twain told the man about his twin brother, Bill. He and Bill looked so much alike as babies that they had different-colored ribbons put on them so people could tell them apart. One day, they were left alone in the bath and one of them drowned. The ribbons having come undone, no one knew which had died. "Some think it was Bill," Twain said, "some think it was me."

That's your story exactly, said Anne, suddenly serious. And Phil realized that she was right; it was exactly his story.

They began to spend whole days together. She softened up; he became more confident. Before they actually made love they spoke to each other as if they had already made love: intimately, openly, feeling that charge of electricity that lovers feel when they think the same thought at the same time. At the end of two weeks, they decided to kiss, and when they found themselves in bed they felt they were simply continuing the conversation, their bodies following a connection that was both spontaneous and inevitable. Each admitted to having thought about nothing except this moment since the day they met. Knowing that, they wanted to revisit everything about those two weeks, to go back over the sequence of events and tell each other what they had felt at every point.

Never for a second did they plan on having an affair—which in any case would not have remained a secret long in a village like Point Reyes. They had fallen in love, and the exigencies of love defied social conventions. Anne let her psychoanalyst know, then her daughters, and Phil told Kleo. She was sad but calm and dignified about the whole thing; she simply withdrew herself from their life. She consented to a divorce with a disinterestedness that seemed to Phil as perfectly natural as his newfound love but that he later learned was not a reaction one could take for granted in a wife one was about to dump. She left him the house in Point Reyes, because he was staying, and

took the car, because she was leaving. She didn't ask for alimony, as
neither earned much money. She kissed him and returned to Berkeley,
whistling tunes from the International Brigades to keep her spirits up.

Anne and Phil lived their relationship with great passion. "There is a
direct relationship between my hearing you, and the religious person,
who after the traditional isolation and fasting and meditation, hears
the voice of 'God,'" Phil wrote to her when they had to be apart for
several days. "The difference is that I know you exist, and I have some
doubts about that fellow God."

They were married in April, two weeks before the end of the world.
When the clock struck midnight on the twenty-third and nothing happened, they felt a sense of relief, in spite of themselves. Phil moved
into the large bright house, bringing with him his record player and his
collection of records, books, and magazines. Family life was a new
experience for him. At first he displayed a touching zeal for it, playing
with Anne's youngest daughter, reading *Winnie-the-Pooh* to the middle
one and *Quo Vadis* to the oldest girl (as well as the works of Lovecraft), joining in the housework, learning to fix leaky faucets, preparing breakfast for his four girls and the ritual drinks that he and Anne
would share before dinner—a martini for her, a glass of zinfandel for
him. He adopted a nine-to-six work schedule, with an hour off for
lunch, which he would spend talking to Anne.

Both Phil and Anne set great store by their midday and late-night
discussions: they had gotten to know each other through talking and
believed the art of conversation, at its best, to be a kind of amorous
jousting. Anne would yield no ground without a fight. She had a
degree in psychology and talked about Freud and Jung as if she had
known them personally; she was inclined to consider her opinion on a
subject as revealed truth. But in Phil she more than met her match and
initially was taken aback. She took some measure of pride in having
seen this in him from the start. Whereas some people are exceptional
lovers, Phil was a remarkable talker and had been waiting, it seemed to
her, only for the right partner. Kleo had been too much of a comrade,

too honest and straightforward to eroticize the spoken word; Anne was different.

It wasn't just that he could speak with her about culture: one could always find people who could talk equally knowledgeably about Schopenhauer, Australian aborigines, or the Nuremberg trials. No, it was something else—the way he could pull the rug out from under you, in a friendly way, of course, by arguing radically opposing opinions with equal conviction so that, whichever position you took yourself, you felt that it was he who had steered you toward it, that somehow you'd been had. With Phil, nothing was ever absolutely determined, final, or fixed. And your strongest argument, the one you were keeping in reserve to confound him, he managed to use against you, turning it to his own advantage. Some people charm snakes; Phil Dick charmed ideas. He made them mean whatever he wanted them to mean, then, having done that, got them to mean the exact opposite. A conversation with Phil was less an exchange of points of view than a roller-coaster ride in which the other person played the role of passenger and he the car, the rails, and the laws of physics themselves. Or like his favorite game, the Rat Game.

He had introduced the girls to this variation on Monopoly, having persuaded them that the whole business of playing for houses and hotels and properties was boring. In the Rat Game, one player, the Rat, could change the rules whenever he pleased. He could issue a decree out of nowhere that applied to everyone but him. The Rat Game was a perpetual tabla rasa—an absolute dictatorship, the negation of the rule of law. The way to ensure a good game was to choose the least scrupulous and most inventive person to play the Rat ("Phil! Phil!" the girls would shout). A Rat worthy of the name meted out the torture in small doses, let the other players think there was some logic behind the arbitrary decrees; he lured the other players away from their habitual strategies by setting them up with false hopes and then knocked them down—though not so hard that they would lose all interest. The point of the game was to create utter chaos and confusion, and what Phil was beginning to learn was that he was a born Rat. Not content merely to contradict himself, he would sometimes, in the course of a

conversation, deny having said what you had heard him say only minutes earlier. If you pointed this out to him, he would give you a pained,
puzzled look, as though wondering whether you were deaf, willfully
obtuse, or just crazy. Anne's jaw would drop at these displays of
prowess, and they fascinated her for some time, until she finally grew
exasperated with them. "It's lucky you're a retiring type," she told him,
"or you'd be another Goebbels!"

Anne began to suspect that Phil had a genius of which he was himself
only partly aware. He still saw himself as a loser and an oddball; she
was the one with brains, he a diamond in the rough that she had
plucked from the mud, polished up, and put on display for an admiring public. Their conversations convinced her that he would be
famous, but he needed to work hard, seriously hard. First of all, he
needed to write real books, for grown-ups, not those silly books for
pimply teenagers he'd been writing. Phil agreed entirely; more than
anything, he wanted to become a famous writer. The thing was, he had
tried to become one and failed, and what that had taught him was that
writing silly books for pimply teenagers was the only way for him to
make a living, and not a very good one at that. Anne dismissed his
objections. That was then, this was now; now she was in charge. As for
money, she would take care of that. She and her daughters were
already living off income she received from her late husband's family;
as for him, surely he could count on getting a small advance on his
next book.

Phil, who had been working on the proofs of *Time Out of Joint*
when they met, protested that despite the book's mainstream aspects,
he had received a *smaller* advance for it than he had for any of his previous works; as far as royalties were concerned, they could go on
dreaming. All he had to do, Anne replied impatiently, was sell that
dump that he and Kleo owned and pay Kleo back once he had made
his fortune. That would give Phil two years to work full-time on a
mainstream novel. Then, of course, it would have to get published and
make the best-seller list.

Phil rose to the challenge and set valiantly to work, producing not one novel but four over the next two years. He gave Anne the manuscript of the first work, *Confessions of a Crap Artist*, a few months after they were married. She was pregnant and undoubtedly looked on the manuscript as yet another fruit of their idyllic honeymoon. It was, but not the one she had expected.

She tried to understand as she listened to the man whose muse she had decided to become explain that this prodigiously hellish depiction of marital life was pure fiction, not autobiography. But he hadn't made much of an effort to fictionalize their lives or even to transpose its elements. The fact is, he probably couldn't have even if he wanted to. Science fiction engaged all his inventive capacities, and when he set about writing a *real* novel he followed the advice he had gotten from Aunt Flo, his first editor, years before: write about what you know. If you live in Point Reyes, then you write about Point Reyes and its inhabitants; if you've made a mistake, such as falling in love with a castrating female when you were already married to a loving and faithful woman, then that's what you write about. Write about how you let yourself get taken in by a siren's song, had been fooled by the beauty of her white house, deceived by an illusion of intimacy into revealing your innermost thoughts—and how now there isn't enough life left in you even to kick yourself for having given her the weapons to use against you. And don't forget to talk about yourself, either. Tell everyone about the daily humiliation you endure because she has money and you don't, and even if you work yourself to death there's no way you'll ever earn enough for her family to live in the fashion to which it is accustomed. Talk about your deep bitterness, the anger and resentment that you've got bottled up inside, how you want to kill her when she sends you into town to buy Tampax.

Anne couldn't understand it. Where did all this come from—this desperation, this raging misogyny, this feeling of living a nightmare in which every action you take only immobilizes you further? Even now he seemed so happy; they still had their discussions, they made love passionately. He was like a father to her daughters. When she had told him she was pregnant, he had been ecstatic. His agoraphobia, which he claimed had poisoned his childhood, no longer seemed to bother him. When friends came to visit, he loved playing lord of the manor; he took them out to the pasture where the sheep were and pretended to be upset when Anne teased him about how unhinged he became when they had to slaughter one. Sure, they argued sometimes, and as she wasn't the type to let others walk all over her, things got heated now and then. Sure, she was worried about his career, about money, and about social status, and the arrival of her fourth child wasn't helping matters. And, okay, artists are tormented souls. Still and all, he had told her a hundred times that she was the one he was writing for, that when his first serious novel was picked up by a publisher, he would dedicate it to her and to their wonderful talks—the basis of everything he was writing.

Why didn't you tell me you didn't want to when I asked you to go to the store to buy Tampax? she said.

Phil continued to maintain that it was all just a book.

What do you mean, "just a book"? You live with me, you screw me, you get me pregnant, smiling innocently and telling me that you love me, and the second you're alone you write that you hate me, that you dream about me at night as your worst enemy.

That's just it, he replied. A book is like a dream. It has nothing to do with life. Even the Spanish Inquisition believed that you couldn't sin in your dreams. No one but savages live in dreams, you know. I read that in a book by Mircea Eliade.

Fuck you!

Laura was born on February 25, 1960. The moment mother and daughter came home from the hospital, Phil had to check into one. He was having chest pains—his way of participating in Anne's labor pains, he joked. It turned out he was suffering from pyloric spasms brought on by the assortment of pills he'd been taking for some time, and in increasing quantities: tranquilizers to overcome the anxiety of becoming a father, amphetamines to help him work longer and better. As soon as he got out of the hospital, he threw himself into an angry novel about the lives of two unhappy couples living in Marin County: one a self-made man and an alcoholic wife who prevents him from fulfilling his ambitions, the other a self-assured woman from a wealthy background and a loser husband whom she takes every opportunity to put down. Phil based the first couple on neighbors of theirs.

At the beginning of the novel, *The Man Whose Teeth Were All Exactly Alike*, the loser husband has had his driver's license taken away, which forces his wife to drive him to work in San Francisco every morning. Annoyed at this tedious waste of time, she schemes her way into a job in the same advertising company where he works as an illustrator and manages to show him up in such spectacular fashion that their boss fires him. Humiliated—and unemployed—he can think of only one way to get back at his wife, who is thriving in her new career. He forces himself on her one day when she isn't wearing her diaphragm, so that she'll become pregnant and will have to quit her job. It doesn't matter, she tells him triumphantly. She'll just get an abortion.

That fall, Anne became pregnant again. They hadn't planned on having another child, and certainly the timing was not good. Worried about the physical strain of a fifth pregnancy, the financial burdens, and her husband's state of mind, Anne decided to get an abortion. Phil, violently opposed, accused her of having less feeling than a robot. Anne pointed out that he didn't want the baby any more than she did, that what he really wanted was for her to be pregnant, deformed, dependent, so that he could control her. The battle raged for several days, at the end of which Anne left the house. When she returned, she told Phil in an emotionless voice that it was done and that she didn't want to hear about it anymore. Phil went into his office and slammed the door.

Because it is impossible to date to the month the composition of *The Man Whose Teeth Were All Exactly Alike*, it is difficult to establish with any certainty whether the plot was simply lifted from events in his married life—or, instead, whether it anticipated them or even whether Anne, having read the manuscript, decided to enact it point by point. In any case, not long after the abortion she decided to go to work, hoping to help with the family's finances and especially to escape from the increasingly tense domestic situation. Of course it had to be artistic work in some way or another. Her clay sculptures had drawn compliments, and, in the course of a discussion with a neighbor, she hit on the idea of opening a jewelry boutique.

Nothing could have pleased Phil less. Like the hero of his novel, he saw her new venture as a slap in the face, a stinging commentary on his failures. There are several versions of what happened next. According to Phil, Anne, having decided that the fun and games had gone far enough, wanted to steer him away from his unremunerative calling and turn the tormented artist into a respectable businessman. According to Anne, Phil was the one who wanted to start over in the jewelry business, as a way of dealing with his creative impotence. She had been the one, she said, who tried to get him to go back to his type-writer. One thing is certain, however, and that is that after a period of brooding he began working in the studio. He fiddled around with molds and stamps, trying his hand at the various tools of jewelry making. Even the menial work that she assigned him, like polishing the pieces, appealed to his love of craftsmanship. One by one, he picked them up as they came out of the kiln and tossed them in his palm. They felt full, compact. Next to them, he thought sadly, his novels seemed vulgar and hideously flawed. He aspired to perfection; he wanted to produce something that would weigh what it should weigh and result from a single pouring. A friend of Anne's had shown her some books on traditional Japanese art and Anne had drawn on them in crafting her pieces. It was all a matter of getting the opposites to balance out, of respecting the Tao. Phil had dreamed of a book with this kind of harmony, but he felt utterly incapable of writing it; indeed, he could hardly even imagine it. These were not good times for him. And the worse things became, the more unbearable he was at home. One day Anne made him a proposition: why didn't he rent that shack the local sheriff owned, the one that sat in an outlying field about ten minutes' walk from the house? She had done some asking around: it wasn't being used, it would cost almost nothing, and he could work there in peace. He hesitated, thinking that if he went along, he would effectively be up against the wall. There would be no more getting around it—if he didn't write a novel that was really and truly worth all the trouble, he would never write anything again. The sheriff's shack offered him his last chance. He would emerge from it victorious, a novel in hand, or he would die trying.

Phil had recently discovered the *I Ching* and had begun to use it as a system of divination. He used it now, tossing three brass Chinese coins onto the rug six times and holding his breath as he added the sum of each throw—three for heads, two for tails—and drew on a sheet of paper the stack of six broken and unbroken lines each number corresponded to. Nine, eight, seven, seven, six, eight: the resulting hexagram signified *Fêng*—"Abundance" or "plenitude."

"Clarity within, movement without—this produces greatness and abundance. The hexagram pictures a period of advanced civilization. However, the fact that development has reached a peak suggests that this extraordinary condition of abundance cannot be maintained permanently."

Phil resolved to rent the shack.

CHAPTER 6

CHUNG FU: INNER TRUTH

Jesuit missionaries returning from Beijing at the end of the seventeenth century had introduced the *I Ching* to West. Believed to be China's oldest book and to hold the key to all wisdom, it reduces the entire universe to the interplay of two complementary principles, yin and yang—sometimes interpreted as shadow and light, female and male, rest and movement, earth and sky, cold and hot, and so forth. The simple technique of throwing three coins six times produces a figure, a hexagram, whose structure reveals precisely how much of each principle resides in the world at a given moment, and one can adjust one's actions accordingly. In the sixty-four possible figures, life can be found in all its infinite diversity, its eternal ebb and flow modified at every second. That is why the *I Ching* is called the *Book of Changes*. It describes not fixed states but rather the tendencies within them that impel their transformation. It explains that every moment is fleeting, that every zenith heralds a decline and every defeat a future victory. To those who wander in the shadows, the *I Ching* teaches that the light will return; to those who vaunt their triumph in the noonday sun, it advises that twilight is already on its way; to the wise man, it teaches the subtle art of letting oneself be carried along by the flux of things, the way a rudderless boat is borne along by the river.

Various translations of the *I Ching*'s sibylline texts, usually with commentaries on each of the hexagrams, had been proposed in the two centuries following its discovery by the Europeans. Interest in the book, however, was limited to a small group of scholars until 1924, when Richard Wilhelm, a German cleric who had fallen in love with China, offered a rendering whose exceptional quality dramatically increased the *I Ching*'s audience. Jung numbered among Wilhelm's admirers, and one of Jung's students, Cary F. Baynes, published an American version in 1951. The book was an underground classic in the 1950s, and in the next two decades came to enjoy genuine popularity. The composer John Cage used it to plot out his chord progressions, physicists turned to it to explain the behavior of subatomic particles; during the beatnik days, hipsters would smoke a few joints, throw the coins onto their kilims, and then make what they could of sentences like "Perseverance is advantageous," or "Caring for the cow will bring luck," or "Free yourself of your big toe. Then a companion will come up to you and you can bond yourself to him."

Phil's own discovery of the *I Ching* in 1960 put him, so to speak, at the tail end of the avant-garde. He had first read about it in an article by Jung and immediately obtained a copy, and from that moment on the book never left his side. He initiated Anne, and soon the whole household was living by the ambiguous laws of the oracle, consulting it on questions of every sort and entrusting to it even the most prosaic decisions.

There are two ways of using the *I Ching*, as either a book of wisdom or a technique of divination. One can look to it for general guidance about how to live or for specific answers to specific questions, such as "Will I have enough gas to make it to the next gas station?" The first approach seems somehow more respectable, more reasonable; certainly it leaves one open to fewer disappointments than does the second. Unfortunately for Phil Dick, if there was one thing he was not seeking, it was wisdom. Everything that Taoism (for which the *I Ching* was the frame of reference) had to teach about the benefits of flexibility, patience, and detachment, or, more broadly speaking, any approach to life based on reflective experience and asceticism was of no interest to him. In this respect Phil was deeply esoterist: convinced that beneath the visible there lay a Hidden Secret, he could not imagine that life would offer up its secrets to him gradually and progressively. It was up to the intellect, he thought, to lay hold of the Secret and take it by force, and what he asked of culture, psychoanalysis, and even religion was not that they educate him but that they hand over the password that would permit him to escape from the cave wherein we are shown not the real world but only its shadows.

When he had first begun to write, Phil had a particular fondness for a story by a fellow SF writer, Fredric Brown. In this tale, scientists from around the world join forces to build an enormous computer into which they have input all the data constituting human wisdom, along with a program capable of synthesizing the information. At last comes the solemn moment when they turn on the machine. Trembling slightly, someone taps out the first question on the keyboard. "Is there a God?" The reply is immediate. "Yes, now there is . . ."

In a way, the *I Ching* is like that computer, and its set of sixty-four hexagrams like the computer program: they make it possible to comprehend—in all senses of the word—the universe. With his customary pedantry, Phil explained to Anne how in this combinatorial system of solid and broken lines Leibniz had recognized the precursor of his own system, based solely on the two digits 0 and 1, which itself prefigured the on-off binary operations of digital technology. To someone who was always coming up with ultimate questions or always looking for the opportunity to ask them, the *I Ching* must have seemed like nothing less than a gift from the gods.

The *I Ching* had advised Phil to rent the shack in which he would either write a truly worthwhile novel or else die trying. (Naturally, it was Phil himself who framed the choice in such dramatic terms. The *I Ching* would never have put it that way; in the event of failure, it would have simply suggested that the time had not been propitious or that the task had been undertaken with inadvisable rashness.) When he moved his things into the shack, he set the two black volumes of the Wilhelm/Baynes edition on the table next to his typewriter, along with the three Chinese coins that he used to construct the hexagrams. Then he sat and waited. The recommended practice was to rid one's mind of all thoughts before consulting the oracle, but try as he might, Phil couldn't manage. Images and familiar ideas floated to the surface of his consciousness. He figured that some of this mental flotsam would find its way into the book, but in any case it was important not to force or rush things. You simply let everything drift along, carried by the current.

One image, in the center of it all, was of a piece of jewelry—a pin or perhaps a pendant—something dense and compact that you could hold in the palm of your hand. It was not precious, but when you examined it closely, tossed it in your hand to feel its heft, something began to change inside you. The din of consciousness began to subside, old antagonisms either disappeared or else struck such perfect balance that you now experienced them as one. Calm, clarity. The piece of jewelry would have to go into his book. The book would need to resemble the piece of jewelry.

But how could it, given that it was probably going to be about Nazism, a topic he had been thinking about for the last few months? He had read numerous books on the subject, most recently Hannah Arendt's account of the Eichmann trial in Jerusalem, and knew that when it came time for him to write his first really serious work, it would in some way or other be about this. Anyone who lived in the second half of the twentieth century had to contend with, to live with, to cope with Nazism, with the idea that it had happened—just as he had had to live with the death of his twin sister. Just because you don't think about it doesn't mean that it isn't there. That would also have to go into the book.

Nothing could be further from the Tao than Nazism. Yet the Japanese, who venerated the Tao, were the Nazis' allies during the war. What if the Axis powers had won? Books of this sort had already been written, of course; Phil had read one himself in which the South defeats the North in the Civil War. He turned the question around and around in his head. What would the world be like if, fifteen years earlier, the Axis powers had won the war? Who would be leading the Third Reich? Hitler, or one of his lieutenants? Would it have changed anything had it been Bormann, or Himmler, or Göring, or Baldur von

Schirach? Would it have changed anything for him, Philip K. Dick, resident of Point Reyes, Marin County, California? What would be different?

It felt odd to be imagining not a hypothetical future but a hypothetical past. The more he thought about it, the more this past and the present that ensued from it seemed to take on substance: things actually could have happened this way. In fact, this past and this present he was now thinking about actually did exist some way; they were using his brain to exist. But they could have existed in a million different forms—it all depended on the choices he made. At every moment, millions of events were either going to happen or not going to happen; at each instant, variables transformed themselves into givens, the virtual became the actual. That was why at any given moment the world reveals a different state of reality. On a small scale, this is how all writers operate: since anything can happen, it is up to them to decide that *this* happens rather than *that*.

Phil sensed that it was time to seek the counsel of the *I Ching*. He threw the coins and got Hexagram 60: *Chieh*—"Limitation."

Water over lake: the image of limitation.
Thus the superior man
Creates number and measure
And examines the nature of virtue and correct conduct.

Commentary: "A lake is something limited. Water is inexhaustible. A lake can contain only a definite amount of the infinite quantity of water; this is its peculiarity. In human life too the individual achieves significance through discrimination and the setting of limits."

Amazing, he thought, how the oracle nearly always got it right. Detractors would have said that the advice the *I Ching* offers—patience, moderation, perseverance, and so forth—is merely common sense phrased in terms general enough to be appropriate for all circumstances. To a certain degree, Phil agreed. He didn't need it to help him come up with the exact structure for his novel, he maintained, but it did lead him to see better the organization he was already struggling to build by helping him understand the importance of structure. For example, the first thing the novelist must do is adumbrate the novel's limits.

Phil decided that after their final crushing victory over the Allies in 1947, the Axis powers divided up the world between them. The Third Reich has Europe, Africa, and that portion of America east of the Rocky Mountains, while Japan rules Asia, the Pacific, and America's western states. Chancellor Martin Bormann continues his predecessor's policies, turning an appreciable percentage of the Reich's subject populations into bars of soap and the African continent into . . . well, no one knows for sure, and no one really wants to know. The populations ruled by Japan, on the other hand, bear a more humane yoke of oppression—no concentration camps, no police terror. Americans living under the Japanese regime have come to internalize the social code of their occupiers: they fear losing face and breaking protocol above all things, and they make no decision without first consulting the *I Ching*. At any given moment, thousands of ordinary Californians throw the coins and watch in fascination as the hexagram—this product of pure chance whose roots are nevertheless sunk deep into the texture of the world—takes shape. Each variation created by the solid and broken lines provides a key, at once singular and universal, with which the individual can understand the present. If the individual has his place in the order of things, it is in relation to that of every other living creature, past or present, and to the entire cosmos.

To illustrate this cosmic interdependence, Phil chose to multiply the number of protagonists and points of view. In the beginning, he had only names—Frank and Juliana Frink, Nobusuke Tagomi, Robert Childan, and the young Kasoura couple, Paul and Betty—but all he had to do was write down those names and throw the *I Ching*, and the specters came to life. Without their necessarily knowing one another, connections sprang up between them. Tagomi, a highly placed official of the Japanese government in California, wants to buy a gift for a visitor from the Third Reich. He pays a visit to Childan, who runs an antique shop specializing in prewar Americana: comic books, Mickey Mouse watches, Glenn Miller records, Civil War–era Colt .45s, all sorts of objects coveted by the occupying forces. Childan vouches for their authenticity—mistakenly, it seems, for most of them are actually fakes produced in a secret workshop where Frank Frink has worked until recently. But now he has been fired from his job there, and is trying his hand at making jewelry. Juliana, his wife, lives in Colorado, where she works as a judo instructor, having left Frank sometime before the story opens. At this point Phil still didn't know what he was going to do with this character, but he wasn't concerned. Somehow Juliana would make her way from the margins of the story to its very heart. He was sure she would turn out to be the perfect heroine; for the moment, all he had to do was let her live her life—go for walks, take showers, eat burgers at the diner. "Waiting in the meadow," instructed Hexagram 5. "It furthers one to abide in what endures. No blame." Phil made no bones about the fact that he had invented Juliana so that he could fall in love with her.

He worked feverishly, sometimes nine or ten hours at a stretch. He was beginning to feel that the novel already existed somewhere and that all he was really doing was following the directives of the oracle to bring it to light. When one of the characters came up with a hexagram that suggested a choice at odds with the admittedly vague plans the author had formulated for him or her, Phil fought the temptation to start all over and wait for a more propitious outcome. He let it go and went with the flow, trusting the story would develop on its own. At the end of his workday he was having more and more trouble pulling himself away from his writing. Pensively he would make his way slowly along the path that led through the pastures back to the big white house. He could hear voices from within, music too, and the clinking of plates and silverware. He lingered outside the door, scraping mud off his combat boots. It was always with a sense of disbelief that he found himself coming home to this woman to whom he had promised to dedicate his first serious novel and who had no place in it yet, as though the book admitted only real people into its world and thus excluded her. Juliana was dark and had jet-black hair; how could he have married a blond, and someone so shrill? She was always cursing and swearing, like the Russian pilgrim who mutters the name of Jesus over and over until it becomes part of his very breathing. Except with her it was "shit" and "fuck"—he felt as if toads were jumping out of her mouth. He tried not to rock the boat: he helped set the table; he played with the girls and with the baby. Then he would go into the bathroom to take the pills that enabled him keep his mental balance. Sometimes, late in the evening, when he knew he would be alone, he went into the jewelry workshop and sat down at the workbench. His fingers lingered on the brushes, tongs, metal shears, polishing wheels, and all those tiny precision tools he wished he knew how to use. That he didn't know didn't sadden him, however, for that part of his life had found its place in the world of the book he was now writing. Frank Frink worked in a place like this, except what he produced weren't the innocent baubles like those Phil was now looking at. For without anyone's conscious intervention, the objects that emerged from Frank's kiln, objects without historical or even aesthetic value, took on a spiritual value: they were in balance, in harmony with the Tao. They offered a portal to the real world, the world that lay beneath the surface of things, and one needed only contemplate them to gain access to that world. There were no objects like these in Anne's workshop, but in his novel there were, and it was even possible that the book itself would become such an object: a creation that might prove undistinguished from a literary standpoint but that, mysteriously, would give access to the truth. More and more, it seemed to Phil, something was wrong with his world, with Anne's world. The book would be like a small tear in the surface of the painting through which those who knew how could pass to the other side. Few would know how. Certainly not Anne.

By one of those natural but circuitous routes that the book seems to favor, one of Frink's jewelry creations finds its way into the hands of

Tagomi. He is a man with much on his mind. To save one life, he has had to take two others, a decision that a Buddhist would have a hard time defending. Sitting on a bench in a public park in San Francisco, a thin outline of a man in a dark suit, Tagomi distractedly takes the piece of jewelry, a silver triangle, out of his pocket and begins to rub it, then examines it. The silver catches the sun's rays.

Tagomi leaves the park, lost in thought. He tries to hail a bicycle taxi—a "pedicab"—and is surprised to find none around. On reaching the waterfront, he is amazed by the spectacle before him: a gigantic swath of concrete stretches as far as the eye can see along the edge of the bay. It looks like a midway ride on a monstrous scale, swarming with strange-looking vehicles. At first Tagomi thinks he must be dreaming. He has passed here on any number of occasions and never seen this futuristic-looking structure that must have taken months, perhaps years, to build. He shuts his eyes and opens them again, but the apparition remains. In a panic, he stops a passerby and asks him to explain what this monstrosity before them is. The man's reply, that Tagomi is looking at the Embarcadero Freeway, fills him with confusion and dismay. He goes into a coffee shop to seek solace, but the lunch counter is full and none of the people there—all Caucasians—will give up their seats for him, even though as a Japanese, a member of the ruling race, he should be shown more deference. He feels as if the earth is giving way under his feet. What nightmare has he fallen into? The silver triangle has disoriented him, yanked him from his universe, his space, his time. He stumbles through a twilight zone where there are no familiar landmarks to guide him, and he cannot decide whether what he is experiencing is objective reality or the sign of some internal breakdown—perhaps he has an inner-ear infection, or else he's sleepwalking or hallucinating.

Then the bicycle taxis reappear, with Caucasians pedaling Japanese fares to their destinations. The world looks familiar again. Tagomi's absence could have lasted no more than ten minutes. But until his dying day he will wonder where he spent those ten minutes. Never again will he dare to look at this strange piece of silver jewelry that opened the door to a strange world. Nor will he ever again flip through that scandalous science fiction novel *The Grasshopper Lies Heavy,* which seems to be on everyone's mind. Written by Hawthorne Abendsen, a reputed recluse, the book has been banned in the Reich-controlled lands but circulates openly in the Japanese zone; it is a source of endless controversy, for it describes an imaginary world in which the Allies won the war.

Dick puts Abendsen's novel in the hands of each of his characters and observes their reactions. Some of them find it fairly pointless, more so even than stories that try to predict the future; for whereas the future is anyone's guess, the past is a foregone conclusion, so why go to all the trouble trying to imagine it differently? Others find the novel troubling yet instructive. "Interesting book. . . . Odd nobody thought of writing it before. . . . It should help to bring home to us how lucky we are. In spite of the obvious disadvantages, . . . we could be so much worse off. Great moral lesson pointed out by that book. Yes, there are Japs in power here, and we are a defeated nation. But we have to look ahead; we have to build."

The most vivid reaction is Juliana's. In creating this seductive, slightly neurotic brunette, Dick was not only giving vent to an erotic fantasy but also suggesting the outlines of the ideal reader; for him it was the same thing. And Juliana doesn't let him down. She doesn't think Abendsen's novel is strange or weird or provocative; she thinks it's *true*. "Am I the only one who knows? I'll bet I am; nobody else really understands *Grasshopper* but me—they just imagine they do."

When he decided to complicate his novel by inserting Abendsen, Phil still did not know if his characters should actually set eyes on this writer who, in the world of the novel, has written its complement. He thought it might be better if they didn't know whether he existed or not. The idea of portraying Abendsen was both appealing and terrifying at the same time. It was a lot like looking at oneself in the mirror.

There are those who sense that every mirror conceals a depth within it, that on the other side of the mirror's flat, smooth surface lies a world as fully formed and as real as their own—maybe even more so. And for someone who believes that the hallway that starts on this side of the mirror continues on the other side, it's not an enormous leap to the conclusion that the real world lies not on this side of the mirror but on the other. This side—the side we live on—is the reflection. Phil had known this since he was a small boy, and he also knew something else, something that no one else knew: he knew who lived on the other side of the mirror—it was Jane. In the world on this side of the mirror, the one people called the real world, Jane had died and he had lived. But on the other side of the mirror, things were reversed. He was dead and Jane had survived and was now peering anxiously into the mirror world inhabited by her poor twin brother. Perhaps Jane's world was the real one; perhaps he was the one living in the reflection, in a world that had been re-created for him to obscure the terrifying fact that he was surrounded by the dead. Phil believed that one day he would have to write a book about that: the story of someone who discovers that all of us are actually dead.

The oracle had guided him into describing the hidden world on the other side of the mirror, and he had obeyed. He had described the novel that Hawthorne Abendsen, in that mirror world, had written in his place. He had described this dark-haired girl—the mirror opposite of Anne, she was just as he had imagined Jane would be—and this girl had understood, just as Jane would have understood, as Anne would never understand, that Abendsen's novel wasn't about some imaginary world; it was about the real world. So now Juliana wanted to meet Abendsen. It seemed to Phil that, in Abendsen's place, he would have been both terribly drawn to the idea of meeting her and terribly afraid at the same time; it would be like meeting Jane, or death itself. But the decision wasn't up to him.

The end of the novel was approaching. Phil knew this as surely as any reader who flips through the thinning number of unread pages left to read. He has Juliana, now in her old Studebaker driving through the Rocky Mountains, pull over to the side of the deserted road. Her black hair is wet. Her breasts swing freely beneath her dress, a gift from a Nazi whose throat she slashed with a razor blade just a few hours ago. Out of her purse she takes the two worn black volumes of the

Wilhelm/Baynes edition and right there and then, with the car engine running, throws the three coins. "What'll I do? She asked it. Tell me what to do; *please.*"

She gets Hexagram 42—"Increase"—with moving lines that transform into 43, "Breakthrough."

> *One must resolutely make the matter known*
> *At the court of the king.*
> *It must be answered truthfully. Danger.*

One can imagine Phil biting his lips, hoping for one of those usefully equivocal replies the *I Ching* sometimes makes, the kind you can interpret as you see fit. The reply Juliana gets is frightening clear. She will have to go to "report to the prince." She puts the car into gear and drives on.

Up until this point, Abendsen has been described by one character after another as living in an isolated mountain fortress—hence his sobriquet, the Man in the High Castle—but Phil was no longer interested in pursuing this aspect of the story; what's more, he knew it wasn't true. Juliana's quest ends in a suburb of Cheyenne, Colorado, in front of a single-story stucco house with a nice lawn and a child's tricycle parked in the long cement driveway. The house is lit up; you can hear music and the sound of voices. Someone is having a party.

She makes her way up the flagstone path to the front steps and walks in the door. Just a few more pages, Phil must have thought, and a little bit of dialogue and it'll all be over. I'll know what story this damn novel is supposed to be telling.

Danger.

She is greeted by Abendsen's wife, who points out the master of the house to her, then guides her over to him to make the introductions. So this is what the author looks like, Juliana is thinking: a tall, solid-looking guy with dark curly hair, holding an old-fashioned. They start to chat. He asks if she wants a drink, and she takes him up on the offer. What can I get you? Oh, an I. W. Harper over ice would be fine.

She tells Abendsen why she's come, then asks why he wrote his novel. He resists her questions, but Juliana presses on. "The oracle wrote your book. Didn't it?" she asks, and finally Mrs. Abendsen answers for him, telling Juliana that he used the oracle for every decision involved in the book—the setting, the characters, the plot, all those thousands of choices that go into making up a story; that he even consulted it to find out how the book would be received and was told it would be a huge success. The first great success of his career.

Knock on wood, Phil must have thought, tapping his knuckles on the tabletop.

But Juliana shakes her head impatiently. She has not come all this way to find out that Abendsen and the oracle collaborated on the novel; she's known that for a long time. What she wants to know is— why. Why did the oracle choose to write a novel through the intermediary of Abendsen? And why *this* novel? Why *this* subject rather than some other?

Abendsen has no answer to that question. Nor, for that matter, did Phil. Perhaps the oracle could tell them. The two black volumes are brought out again, along with three Chinese coins, a piece of paper, and a pencil to draw the hexagram. Juliana asks the question: "Oracle, why did you write *The Grasshopper Lies Heavy*? What are we supposed to learn?"

Phil held his breath, then threw the three coins six times. He drew the hexagram.

"Sun at the top. Tui at the bottom. Empty in the center.

61: *Chung Fu*—'Inner Truth.'

"The wind blows over the lake and stirs the surface of the water. Thus visible effects of the invisible manifest themselves." A moment of silence follows. Finally, Juliana speaks. "And I know what it means," she says.

Raising his head, Hawthorne scrutinized her. He had now an almost savage expression. "It means, does it, that my book is true?"

"Yes," she said.

With anger he said, "Germany and Japan lost the war."

"Yes."

Hawthorne, then, closed the two volumes and rose to his feet; he said nothing.

"Even you don't face it," Juliana said.

Then she leaves.

Confused, Phil followed her. Was that it? Was the novel finished? No publisher would take it on. They would want him to explain the ending, to at least add another chapter to justify it. Even he, the author, felt disconcerted by the way the book now ended. In *Time Out of Joint*, he didn't just say that Ragle Gumm had been right all along and leave it at that; he explained why and went to a hell of a lot of trouble coming up with that whole business about the antimissile defense requiring the fabrication of a retro world around the hero. It was part of his responsibility toward his public. Now it dawned on him that he hadn't worried about any of this while writing *The Man in the High Castle*. He had been going along like the detective novelist who waits until the last chapter before figuring out who the murderer is going to be and dealing with questions of means and motives. He had been counting on the *I Ching* to show him the way out. And now the *I Ching* had left him with nothing but this ambiguous nonending, this lousy Zen koan.

The letdown was all the more exasperating because had he caught himself in time, had he laid the necessary groundwork, a revelation like this one would have fit in almost perfectly in a novel that was at least in part about Nazism. He had understood from Hannah Arendt that the goal of a totalitarian state is to cut people off from reality, to give them a make-believe world to live in instead. If the notion of a parallel universe is a chimera, then totalitarian states give substance to it. They exercise what Saint Thomas Aquinas denied was possible, and what Saint Peter Damian believed was the province only of the Almighty Himself: the ability to alter the past. This privilege—to make what happened not have happened—the Nazis and the Bolsheviks arrogated to themselves by rewriting history, foisting on it their own apocryphal versions. Trotsky had never led the Red Army; Beria disappeared from the Soviet encyclopedia, replaced by an alphabetically contiguous entry less compromising to those in power—the Bering Straits. And as for the victims of the German concentration camps, the object had been not simply to kill them but to make it seem as if they had never existed in the first place. In one extraordinary passage in *The Origins of Totalitarianism*, Arendt describes how the czarist secret police reportedly mapped out the acquaintances of every person deemed unfit to live: around the name of each person a circle was drawn; around those of his political friends, his nonpolitical friends, and people in contact with those friends more circles were drawn; then, between those circles, lines were drawn to show all the cross-relationships. Had the sheet of paper been large enough, all of humanity would have found its place on the chart.

Phil had once read about social psychologist Stanley Milgram's "small-world study," which had concluded that everyone living on the earth was separated by five or six handshakes. The idea delighted him. What that means, he told Anne, is that you have shaken the hand of someone who has shaken the hand of someone else who has shaken the hand of someone else who has shaken the hand of someone else who has shaken the hand of, let's say, Richard Nixon or such and such a resident of Benares. This principle of universal contamination, the nightmare and engine of the totalitarian utopia, logically entails the deportation of everyone, including those doing the deporting. Nonetheless, given that even a totalitarian state is not exempt from the reality principle, it had to find another solution, which was to erase the disappeared not just from the documents but from the memory of those who were, for the time being at least, spared. And one of the most horrific discoveries totalitarian states revealed to humanity is that such a thing can be done. If the Third Reich had still ruled Europe, thought Phil, not only was it likely that it would have had to exterminate dozens of millions more people; it was also likely that the survivors, their throats made raw by the smoke bellowing day after day from the crematoria smokestacks, wouldn't have even known. If the price of survival is ignorance, you simply choose not to know.

Phil had also read in a popular psychology magazine about Solomon Asch's famous experiment on social conformity. A group of people, all but one of them confederates of the experimenter, were shown three lines of varying lengths and asked which of the lines was the same length as a fourth they were shown. The confederates, as instructed beforehand, all replied incorrectly although the correct answer was obvious. With astonishing frequency, the one real subject, who went next to last, ended up disregarding what his own senses told him was true and joined in with the others. Totalitarian states were nothing if not an experiment of this kind on a vast scale. They had found out how to show a chair to people and get them to say it was a table. More than that, they got people to *believe* it as well. Looked at from this point of view, what Phil, under the prodding of the oracle, had described in his novel was not all that absurd. He had even touched on a profound truth.

The hypothesis was obviously even more plausible, he thought, if you flipped it around. There is really no reason for a democracy, even one as compromised as America's had been by a Communist witch-hunt, to lead its citizens to believe that they are living under a totalitarian regime. But one could easily imagine that had Germany and Japan won the war, they might have tried to convince Americans that the opposite was true, in order to control them more completely. The poor deluded Americans could then have gone on living their little lives in their quiet suburbs, taking as much pride as they ever did in their God-given constitutional rights, never realizing that they were subjects of the Third Reich, with no rights at all. Year after year, millions of their fellow citizens would disappear without a trace, and no one would notice or ask questions—so strong is man's instinct *not* to know. But in this case it would be up to Phil Dick, inhabitant of a supposedly free America, and not Hawthorne Abendsen, his specular double, to formulate these suspicions and weave them into a novel.

That, of course, was exactly what he had done.

Whoa. Wait a second.

Phil shook his head, trying to find his way out from under this absurd line of reasoning. He read through the commentary of the hexagram he had just drawn, hoping it might show him how to end the novel.

"This indicates a heart free of prejudice and therefore open to the truth."

Phil chuckled. Imagining trying to tell that to an outraged publisher. He threw the coins again.

Meng—"Youthful Folly."

It is not I who seek the young fool;
the young fool seeks me.
At the first oracle, I inform him.
If he asks two or three times, it is importunity.
If he importunes, I give him no information.
Perseverance furthers.

Okay, okay, he thought, irritated. I get it.

So Juliana had said everything there was to be said. He typed "The End" and walked back to the house, thinking he himself would have been curious to read the last pages of *The Grasshopper Lies Heavy*. He would have liked to find out whether the novel was about him and what kind of ending the other guy had managed to come up with.

CHAPTER 7

IDIOCY

As the oracle had predicted, *The Man in the High Castle* became the first big success of Dick's career. It won the Hugo Award, the most prestigious prize in the American science fiction community.

Several weeks later, he received a large box in the mail. Inside were the manuscripts of eleven of his "mainstream" novels, along with a letter from his agent explaining that though he had done everything humanly possible to find a publisher for them, no one would take them on; moreover, he would no longer be able to promote the fruits of Phil's efforts at mainstream fiction. Phil was disappointed but hardly surprised. He had come to believe that an incomprehensible and insurmountable obstacle—like a force field—stood between him and the Promised Land of respectable literature. Now the die was cast: he would be king of his village and not play second fiddle in Rome. This, he told people half jokingly, was his karma.

This seemingly definitive double verdict—science fiction success and mainstream failure—was a blow to his vanity, as well as to Anne's, but he was beginning to realize that if he was ever going to prove his mettle, it was going to have to be as a science fiction writer. But more than winning the Hugo (which he expected to unleash a shower of material rewards that were not forthcoming), it was the feelings of jubilation and mastery he had experienced playing the part of Hawthorne Abendsen from behind the mirror that persuaded him that he had found his path. Maybe what he had written could only be marketed as science fiction, but it was something no one but he had the capacity to write. Too bad if he would remain poor and obscure, or famous only among a circle of readers he knew would never be large: he wasn't happy about that, but he figured he might one day count himself lucky that he hadn't had any choice in the matter.

And so, with a five-thousand-year-old oracle guaranteeing its "inner truth," he plunged methodically into the labyrinthine ways of his *idios kosmos*. His personal "idiocy" would henceforth be organized around the conviction that reality could not be apprehended directly, because it gets filtered through each individual's subjectivity. What seems real is a deception. What rational beings agree on as constituting reality is merely an illusion, a simulacrum created either by the few in an effort to mislead the many or else by some external power intent on misleading everyone. Reality is not reality.

All this provided fertile ground for a notion that had been making its way up and down the West Coast on the winds of the Zeitgeist— namely, that certain modes of altered consciousness offered direct access to Reality with a capital *R*.

In 1954 Aldous Huxley had published *The Doors of Perception*, an account of an experience he had had with mescaline; he took his title from a line by William Blake: "If the doors of perception were cleansed, everything would appear to man as it is, infinite." Huxley had begun as a brilliant satirist; his drift toward the study of mysticism and the universal fundaments of all religions surprised and even dismayed many of his admirers. Mescaline had had a profound effect on him. Even as he ostensibly acknowledged that the drug did not bring mystical enlightenment, he nevertheless argued that

> the mescaline experience is what Catholic theologians call "a gratuitous grace," not necessary to salvation but potentially helpful and to be

accepted thankfully, if made available. To be shaken out of the ruts of ordinary perception, to be shown for a few timeless hours the outer and inner world, not as they appear to an animal obsessed with survival or a human being obsessed with words and notions, but as they are apprehended, directly and unconditionally, by Mind at Large—this is an experience of inestimable value to everyone and especially to the intellectual.

In short, Huxley offered mescaline as a means to take a quick spin around the Buddha's or Meister Eckhart's *idios kosmos*, as a round-trip ticket to ultimate reality. It was easy (almost distressingly easy), well within reach of just about anyone, and risk free. Well, almost risk free. Huxley also described the darker side of the drug, a looming abyss that even he, someone without psychological problems, had glimpsed. He felt obliged to point out that immersion in reality was a feature not only of the mystic state but also of madness and thus that tendencies in the user of which the user himself might be unaware could lead him as easily to hell as to heaven. Like Henri Bergson and other vitalist philosophers on whose theories Huxley drew, he believed the brain was a mechanism for filtering a reality that was too rich for the humble receptors with which human beings are equipped. Drugs could temporarily disable this mechanism, and mental illness could damage it more or less permanently. And if reality could give itself over to the serene contemplation of those like Huxley who thrilled to the recognition of the dharma-body of Buddha in the crease of their flannel trousers, it could horrify others, to the point where they might "interpret its unremitting strangeness, its burning intensity of significance, as the manifestations of human or even cosmic malevolence, calling for the most desperate countermeasures, from murderous violence at one end of the scale to catatonia, or psychological suicide, on the other." Once one had "embarked upon the downward, the infernal road," Huxley continued, there was no way to stop taking everything and anything as proof of a conspiracy against one. To the question of whether this meant that he now understood madness, Huxley's answer was "a convinced and heartfelt 'yes.'"

————

The first experimenters with LSD-25, which Albert Hoffmann synthesized in 1943 while working for the Sandoz Laboratory, had not imagined that this substance, so similar in its effects to mescaline, could be used for anything other than exploring madness. Psychiatrists for the most part, they considered LSD a "schizophrenia simulator," permitting them to experience firsthand for a brief moment what their patients experienced. It was only later, when, under the influence of Huxley and small religiously oriented scientific groups in Los Angeles, a movement arose around the drug, that people started to think of using it to gain knowledge of absolute reality. Some even began to refer to it by the most ancient of its secret names: LSD, they said, was God.

Phil felt a kinship to the ideas Huxley expounds in *The Doors of Perception*, which, by the beginning of the 1960s, was enjoying a wide readership in California. He had always embraced some of the same ideas, though he had not yet taken either LSD or mescaline—he hadn't even smoked a joint—and it would be absurd to speak of him in this period of his life as a doper, let alone an acidhead. If one had spoken of him that way, he probably would have shrugged and pointed out that he wasn't one of those fancy writers with Dürer drawings hanging on the walls of their wood-paneled studies and the time and money to experiment with their brains. He was a working stiff with a family to support. Sure, he was taking pills nonstop—Serpasil for a heart murmur, Semoxydrine for agoraphobia, Benzedrine to stimulate his brain, and a few others to counteract all the side effects. And yeah, sure, the pills sometimes left him in a weird state of mind—sometimes making him think he could see through things and people as if he had X-ray eyes, right through to their insides, which happened to look like the insides of a radio or television set, a tangle of wires and plastic and metal components. There was nothing pleasant about these visions. Nor did he find it pleasant to learn one day, when out of curiosity he decided to read the label on a bottle of medicine of which he had been taking the maximum recommended dosage for years, that abuse of the drug could lead to "hallucinations, delirium, serious vascular problems, and *death*." But he couldn't do without the pills; his work rhythm depended on them. He wasn't taking them for the fun of it or to help him see the dharma-body of the Buddha in the crease of his two-hundred-dollar flannel trousers. He always wore jeans, for one thing.

On the other hand, he saw himself as something of an authority on mental illnesses, and nowhere does this comes through more clearly than in his 1963 novel *Clans of the Alphane Moon*, in which, with nearly parodic exhaustiveness, he paints a psychopathological portrait of an entire society. Originally intended as a receiving station for colonists from Earth with psychiatric woes, the Alphane moon has been cut off from the mother planet by war, leaving the patients to their own devices. In just two generations, they construct their own, clan-based society, with a caste system like India's, presided over by maniacal, dominating, and aggressive Manses who, from their city, Da Vinci Heights, exercise their imperious authority over everyone else— the politically and strategically astute yet paranoid Pares, who live behind an array of protective devices inside their bunkerlike city, Adolf- ville; the manic-depressive Deps, who mope around in their grim little community of Cotton Mather Estates; the obsessive-compulsive Ob Coms, who staff the planet's bureaucracy; the polymorphous schizo- phrenic Polys, who brighten their hamlet of Hamlet-Hamlet with their whimsically creative genius; the Skitzes, who wander from place to place writing poetry and having visions; and finally, at the very bottom of the Alphane social heap, the psychotic, vegetative, hebephrenic Heebs, some of them saints with psychic powers, who crowd together in the filth of Gandhitown. Phil wanted to compare the survival advantages the var- ious psychoses conferred, and, in keeping with the spirit of the times, he came up with a positive conclusion: Alphane society, he found, functions more or less successfully and in this respect is hardly differ- ent from our own society, in which any individual, though nominally healthy, can nevertheless be slotted into one clinical category or another. On the Alphane moon, however, the classification is official and takes place as soon as an earthling arrives, as part of the customs formalities, with the test results showing just how unaware of his true mental con- ditions a supposedly normal person can be.

Subjecting people to ad hoc psychological tests had been a favorite game of Phil's when he was a boy. He used to go around observing his friends and relatives, noting their reactions and responses to questions that he took pains to toss off in a natural manner. Of course, his tests were not nearly as elaborate as the ones the psychiatrists of his novel would have at their disposal; he relied mainly on his intuition, later adding a bit of the *I Ching* to the test battery now and then to fine-tune his diagnoses. Anne's daughters loved it when he played the game with them, asking them questions like, "If you were a nut what kind of nut would you be? One who thinks he's a mouse, one who thinks he's Abraham Lincoln, or one who thinks he's director of an asylum?" The kids played the game endlessly and even got their friends to join in. It became a big hit at their school, much to the cha-grin of the girls' teacher, who soon grew exasperated when her young charges would suddenly burst into the uncontrollable giggles pro-voked by such exchanges as,

"But tigers don't eat doormats!"

"Yeah, but I'm not sure that the principal knows that."

When the teacher discovered that the Rubenstein girls had started the whole thing, she decided she needed to pay a visit to their parents. Anne happened to be away but Phil met with her. He showed a lively interest in her ideas about teaching and he assured her that he would try to get the girls to settle down. But while seeing her out he couldn't help himself. With a mad gleam in his eye—the one that used to make Laura weep with laughter—he whispered to her conspiratorially. I'm Phil Dick, the famous writer, he told her, but don't tell anyone.

The poor teacher stared at Phil. His expression reverted to that of the responsible father who earlier had listened with such concern as she spelled out her complaints about the girls.

She decided that she must have imagined what she'd heard.

Anne didn't entirely appreciate these antics. Her daughters' father had died in a psychiatric hospital, after all, a fact she preferred the girls not be reminded of. She had no qualms, however, about going after Phil about his own family, a topic he had loved to discuss with her at the beginning of their relationship. Anne, who had a strong sense of family, regularly invited over Dorothy, who told her all the indiscreet little stories a mother tells a daughter-in-law to exasperate her son—about how sweet he was when he was little and how shy, and what the psychiatrist had said about Phil's dead sister, and how old he was when he finally stopped wetting his bed. She talked freely, too, about her own sister, Marion, who had also given birth to a set of twins but, unlike Dorothy, had not let one of them die and had seemed for all the world to be a warm and loving mother. In the late 1940s, however, when Phil was still in school and living at home, Marion had suddenly and without warning started having serious mental problems, which eventually were diagnosed as catatonic schizophrenia. Dorothy visited her sister in the hospital often. She also put her up in her home between hospital stays, particularly after Phil had moved out and she had an extra room. She showered Marion with devoted, if unconventional, care, turning from one fad miracle cure to another, from Dianetics to sensory-deprivation chambers to Reichian orgone therapy. Dorothy had a rather romantic notion of her sister's illness, and while Marion, toward the end, suffered from a horrible sensation of not being able to breathe, Dorothy claimed her sister was experiencing marvelous visions. One day, with great solemnity, Dorothy read to Phil and Anne the funeral elegy she had written in her diary when Marion died, ten years earlier:

> I do not believe we shall ever know what happened to her physically, and we already know what happened psychically: she decided not to live. The attraction of that other world of hers, which contained all that we recognized as the creative one and much more besides, was so strong . . . she meant to keep it at any cost, but she thought she could do that and keep the actual, physical world around her, too. . . . But the more I learn of other people's thoughts the more universally true it seems that each person has another world in him and that no one really belongs to the world as it is. In other words, we are all aliens. None of us belong to this world; it does not belong to us.

Phil found this performance disturbing. Anne gave him a conspiratorial wink that seemed to say, "Now I know: it runs in the family."

(Apparently, "it" extended to in-laws, for not long after Marion's death, her husband claimed he had received messages from his dead wife, ordering him to marry Dorothy—with whom, until then, his relations had been cool at best. They were married in 1954, and Dorothy began raising her sister's twin daughters—a detail Phil would often bring up when he wanted to show just how interesting a case he was.)

Soon after finishing *The Man in the High Castle*, Dick wrote a novel called *Martian Time-Slip*, in which, with considerably more earnestness than Huxley had after his mescaline trip, he asked himself the question, What does it feel like to be psychotic?

The story, which begins with a suicide whose effects ripple outward and touch every character at some point in the course of the novel, turns around land speculation on Mars, Earth's somewhat neglected colony, where labor union fiefdoms and United Nations concessions vie for control and influence. In an effort to get the jump on the competition, the chief of Mars's powerful Water Workers Union, an erstwhile plumber, would like to take a peek into the future. An ingratiating psychiatrist tells him of a new theory that holds that autism, and schizophrenia in general, is a derangement of the individual's sense of time. What distinguishes the schizophrenic from other people, according to the theory, is that the schizophrenic gets the whole picture all at once, whether he wants it or not: the entire reel of film that normally passes before people's eyes frame by frame unravels in a rush. Causality doesn't exist for the schizophrenic; he lives in a world governed by a principle of acausal connection that Wolfgang Pauli called "synchronicity" and that Jung, replacing one enigma with another, tried to use to explain the phenomenon of coincidence. Like someone on LSD or like God—insofar as one can know the nature of His *idios kosmos*—the schizophrenic dwells in an eternal present. All of reality comes rushing headlong at him as though he were in a never-ending car wreck. Accordingly, the psychiatrist tells the plumber, the schizophrenic has access to what we call the future. With this the ex-plumber has heard all he needs to and turns to that staple of Dick's fiction, the genius misfit, in this case a recovering schizophrenic and jack-of-all-trades capable of repairing everything from toasters to helicopter blades—a highly valued skill on Mars, where spare parts are exceedingly hard to come by. The plumber wants him to rig up a machine that will let him enter into mental contact with an autistic child named Manfred and extract precious information about the future from the boy's mind.

The repairman accepts the job reluctantly, fearing it will bring back painful memories of his own schizophrenia and force him to confront the question he has been trying to repress for years, ever since he left Earth: what was it he really saw that day he sat across the desk from his company's personnel manager and the man appeared to him as an assemblage of gears and electric circuitry? A hallucination or a vision, a psychotic breakdown or a sudden glimpse of true reality, stripped of its facade? Nevertheless, he grows attached to Manfred, eventually deciding, in the plumber's words (and with the same optimism that Dorothy felt with regard to her sister, Marion), that "it must be like fairlyland, in there, all beautiful and pure and real innocent."

A serious mistake, of course. Soon strange things start to happen. A Bruno Walter recording of a Mozart symphony becomes a hideous jangle of sound; the bodies of other people seem to split open as if in an accelerated process of organic decay. The entire objective universe in which the characters move about becomes progressively invaded by that of Manfred, who sucks them into his nightmarish reality, a place of absolute entropy, a land of death. The concept of the "tomb world" had fascinated Phil ever since he first came across it in essays by the Swiss psychiatrist Ludwig Binswanger. The schizophrenic, Binswanger believed, lives (if one can call it living) in a world of eternal death in which everything has happened and at the same time is still happening, in which nothing more can ever happen. This "tomb" swallows up anyone who approaches it; it is waiting there to engulf everything and everyone.

All the characters in the novel become Manfred; no one can speak except to produce the desolate noises that are his response to the world. "I kept on going," the horrified repairman tries desperately to explain, "looking for someone who I could still talk to. Who wasn't like—him." The ex-plumber gets his wish and travels through time, but it's Manfred's time that he travels through, the time of the tomb world, and the voyage turns hellish. His once-faithful secretary has become a predatory monster, everyday objects have taken on sharp, angry edges, the coffee he drinks tastes bitter and poisonous. A mask of empty darkness hangs in the air above his face and begins to descend on him. Now he realizes that never again will he see the living world he so foolishly left behind; he knows he will die in Manfred's autistic world—which he does.

It is hard to imagine anything more horrific than dying in someone else's nightmare, and Dick, merciful creator that he was, rescues the ex-plumber from this fate and grants him a kinder, and at the same time more ironic, demise. The hideous spell is lifted and the ex-plumber emerges from the tomb world, only to be killed by a minor character from one of the novel's subplots. As he is being rushed to the hospital in the throes of death, he can't believe what's happening to him and starts to laugh, because now he figures he knows the routine: he is still trapped in one of those fucked-up schizophrenic universes where first you get killed for no reason and then you wake up. That's what's going to happen to him, he thinks: he'll wake up and find himself back in his own reality. And as he's lying there thinking all this, he dies, this time for good.

Perhaps it's better this way, the repairman concludes. Phil thought so too, for two reasons: first of all, the ex-plumber dies consoled by the thought that he is not dying and, second, he dies in the real world, not in a place where things far worse than death can happen.

Phil liked writing the end of this novel. It reassured him. Illusion and reality were clearly separated; the survivors walked on the terra firma of the koinos kosmos. The repairman continues to have his doubts, for no one is ever cured of schizophrenia. "Once a person becomes psychotic," he tells himself, "nothing ever happens to him again. I stand on the threshold of that."

Me too, Phil thought. Perhaps he was standing on that same threshold. Perhaps he had always been there.

He had thought that before—on that unforgettable day at the movie theater when he became sick watching a newsreel of U.S. marines burning Japanese soldiers alive. Dorothy had told the story to Anne, to prove how precociously antimilitarist and sensitive her son had been. But she didn't know what was actually going on with Phil that day. Sitting in the theater in the red plush seat, a bag of popcorn in his hand, he had been looking all around him: at the walls of the giant box in which he was trapped along with a hundred other people, mostly strangers; at the beam of light from the projectionist's booth, an expanding cone that went all the way up to the screen, filled with dancing motes of dust; at the rip in the carpet underneath his feet. And suddenly, before the newsreel even started, he *knew*. He knew with utter certainty that nothing existed but this: the four walls, the ceiling, the torn carpet, and the other prisoners. What he had thought he knew about the outside world and his life in it had been nothing but a collection of false memories, an illusion that someone or something implanted in his brain, out of either malice or kindness—there was no way of knowing which. He had always been in that box watching that film which he had believed was his life. Any minute now, he would believe he was getting up and leaving the theater, walking with his mother along the streets of a place called Berkeley, returning home and putting on Schubert records; yet none of that actually existed—not Berkeley, not his mother, not Schubert, not America, not Germany, perhaps not even the other moviegoers shut up in the room with him. Maybe they were extras in his film. Phil swore to himself that when he left the theater (or thought he had left it), he would try never again to be fooled; he would try to remember that he was still in that room and that there was no other reality. He could already sense that this thought would soon lose its certainty, that it would soon feel to him like a seductive paradox rather than a living truth. He wished he could be who he would be several hours later, so that he could warn himself not to be taken in. To make that moment happen sooner rather than later, to ensure that when he reentered the world of illusion it would be with as much lucidity as possible, he pretended to be ill. His worried mother led him toward the exit, holding him so he wouldn't fall. They found themselves back on the street, in the bright sunlight, and for a moment or two he savored the joy of knowing that this street, this sun, this skinny woman with the furrowed brow who was earnestly asking him how he felt—none of them existed and in reality he was still inside the theater, where he had always been and would always be. If he could only come and go as he pleased, moving in and out of the world of illusion, and continue to play his role in it but without losing this precious clarity and insight, it would be . . . How *would* it be? Nice? Definitely not. But who cared about what was "nice"; what he wanted was to *know*, to not be fooled. Yet already he could feel that what he had foreseen was now happening: illusion was crowding out reality and it was no use fighting it—he had already stopped believing what he knew to be true. His last conscious wish was that the clarity and insight would return someday, if only briefly.

They did come back to him, in flashes: at the door to the bathroom when he couldn't find the light cord, and later in another bathroom, one of three in the house with bright white walls that he shared with a blond woman who bossed him around. From behind the locked bathroom door, he heard her coming and going and swearing like a sailor. All an illusion. A new episode in the film. In this episode he was a thirty-five-year-old man with a beard who wrote science fiction—a cultivated man, a lover of dizzying paradoxes. And he could never shut himself up inside the bathroom without smiling to himself, thinking of Martin Luther's moment of revelation *in latrinis*. He knew the various forms his intuition had assumed over the centuries—Plato's cave, for instance, and the dream of Chuang-tzu, who, some four hundred years before Christ, had wondered whether he was a Chinese philosopher dreaming he was a butterfly or a butterfly dreaming he was a Chinese philosopher; and the darker version of this question, posed in 1641 by Descartes when he asked, "How do I know that I am not being deceived by an infinitely powerful evil demon who wants me to believe in the existence of an external world—and in my own body?" Phil had made a professional specialty out of such speculations and had learned how to bring back on command the flash of insight he had in the movie theater. Now, alone in the bathroom, all he had to do was look at his face in the mirror, look at his body, at the tiles on the floor, at the dead cockroach lodged in the hem of the shower curtain, and the certainty that everything was unreal returned with disconcerting ease.

He had always been there.

CHAPTER 8

CRAZY DAYS

The literary breakthrough Phil had achieved with *The Man in the High Castle* brought about no change in his material and social conditions, in spite of the Hugo Award. The publication of *Martian Time-Slip*, of which he had also expected much, went nearly unnoticed. Despite the income from the wealthy family of Anne's dead husband and despite the jewelry sales, Phil needed money, lots of money by Berkeley standards, to maintain his family of six in a middle-class lifestyle. He had to work incredibly hard to earn what Anne thought was still only barely sufficient. With the help of amphetamines, he could turn out a novel in a few weeks—in two years he published a dozen—but he paid for the boost they gave him with terrible bouts of depression. He felt incapable of measuring up to his responsibilities. He looked haggard. The face behind the beard was blotchy and puffy. Large black insects buzzed on the periphery of his field of vision. He began to regard Anne as his enemy. He was certain that she considered him a failure and that the advice she gave him—to work less and earn more, the way other men somehow managed to do—was designed merely to rub it in. She despised him for being a loser but it seemed to him she needed a loser to despise, and he, for his part, was happy to oblige her, having discovered a certain dark pleasure in acting according to the role he figured she wanted him to play. He had dedicated *The Man in the High Castle* to her, just as he had promised, but she had blanched when she read the way he had worded the dedication: "To Anne, my wife, without whose silence this book never would have been written." A small masterpiece of churlishness, the cheap vengeance of an underling—but after all, he reasoned, she had brought it out in him. She may have looked like the model American wife, but there was something of the Nazi inside her: a cruelty born of the absolute certainty of being right, of believing that the natural order of things, indeed nature itself, was on her side. When he had come up with that caste system for *Clans of the Alphane Moon,* he'd wondered where exactly he would have fit in and decided he would have been either a Skitz (a flattering idea, since the Skitzes possessed visionary powers) or a depressive Dep (the more likely possibility, he felt, and one that was growing likelier with each passing day). But he had no doubt about Anne: she was pure Mans—overbearing, predatory, and utterly without empathy.

Phil amused himself turning that novel into a psychodrama of Anne and his relationship. Chuck Rittersdorf, the hero, has a job not unlike Phil's, programming CIA simulacra—humanoid robots that the agency uses for delicate or dangerous missions. The job carries no prestige whatsoever and it doesn't pay well either, but Chuck takes pleasure in the secret knowledge that, when the simulacra speak, the words coming out of their mouths are his. It gives him a feeling of power and usefulness that his wife, Mary, apparently cannot fathom. She thinks what Chuck does is pathetic hackwork ill-befitting the man to whom she gave the honor of marrying her, and she thinks Chuck is pathetic too. An attractive, ambitious, and utterly uncompassionate woman, she specializes in other people's problems and is convinced she has none of her own. Phil had a great time developing this character, and was nearly jubilant the day he figured out what he would have her do for a living. It was too delicious—Mary would be a marriage counselor, and of that particularly offensive breed: garrulous and self-assured, continually lacing her pronouncements with liberal doses of Freud and Jung.

Chuck is unhappy with their relationship, and his wife's being a marriage counselor doesn't help matters—quite the contrary. He leaves home and holes up in a rundown apartment house in a seedy part of town, hoping to elude Mary for as long as possible. Phil must have derived vicarious pleasure from his protagonist's flight. How many times had he imagined doing exactly the same thing? But there were the girls to think about, and now his own daughter, and then that devastating paralysis of will that overcame him as soon as he stepped out the door—actual physical shakes. And where could he go? Those times he did make it to the car and managed to drive off—his hastily packed suitcase in the trunk and with no particular destination in mind—he always ended up at his mother's, where, after a few hours, Anne would come find him and bring him home. He would stand there outside his mother's door like a man on the lam who knows the jig is up and is waiting for the police to arrive. It was no use trying to look for a better place to hide: Anne would find him anyway, just as, at the beginning of the novel, Mary finds Chuck. Phil didn't bother explaining how; this kind of woman always finds you, and she doesn't take her time about it. And now, having found him, Mary lays down the law: Chuck is going to have to earn some real money, she tells him, so that he can pay the colossal alimony the court will award her at the divorce.

> "You can have everything," he told Mary, all at once.
>
> Her look said, But what you can give isn't enough. "Everything" was merely nothing, as far as his achievements were concerned.
>
> "I can't give you what I don't have," he said quietly.
>
> "Yes you can," Mary said, without a smile. "Because the judge is going to recognize what I've always recognized about you. If you have to, if someone makes you, you can meet the customary standards applied to grown men with the responsibility of a wife and children."
>
> He said, "But—I have to retain some kind of life of my own."
>
> "Your first obligation is to us," Mary said.
>
> For that he had no answer; he could only nod.

Having issued this warning to her husband, Mary takes off for Alpha III M2, the madhouse Alphane moon, as field psychologist on a government mission. This one detail aside, Phil suspected that his life with Anne would play itself out in just this way. She might make him her doormat, but she would never let him go. Like Chuck, he felt starved for sympathy and compassion and had no one to turn to. How alone he was! In drawing him into her web, Anne had created a void around him. Their friends were her friends. Their pets were her pets. Even their psychiatrist was her psychiatrist. If only he had a mistress . . . He wanted to call Kleo, to hear her voice and that ringing laugh that used to get on his nerves but whose honesty and uncalculating cheerfulness he now missed terribly. But he didn't dare. She had gotten remarried, to another salesman at University Radio. She probably hated him. Perhaps she had found out that he had sold their house without telling her about it or sending her a penny. Anne, of course, had pushed him to sell it; she told him that they would pay Kleo back when their finances were in better shape, but he knew very well that they never would. He had been a coward to give in, a coward and a fool. As he always did when he felt guilty, Phil felt sorry for himself.

But there wasn't time for him to feel sorry for himself. He needed to keep typing, one eye on the page and the other riveted to the calendar on the wall that was telling him that this novel which he had barely started was going to be finished in three weeks. He still needed to find a way of connecting the two plots that he had set up: the war between Chuck and Mary and the one on the Alphane moon.

Thank goodness for robots. Chuck's bosses at the CIA order him to program a simulacrum that will join the mission Mary has signed on with. This robot, whom Mary will no doubt take to be just a handsome travel companion, will actually be operating under her husband's guidance via remote control. From a marital standpoint, the situation is scandalous, but Chuck immediately sees how to turn it to his advantage. A jealous man might have seized the chance to seduce his own wife in the guise of another. But Chuck isn't a jealous man; he's a man oppressed, married to a hateful woman who is bent on his destruction, and now he has been handed the opportunity to kill her. He can say that the robot went berserk, and although he'd certainly be a prime suspect in the murder, no one would have anything on him.

Perhaps it's not the perfect crime, but the idea is too good to let go, and Chuck is obsessed with it. Phil was, too. For two weeks, everyone at home found him in a far better mood, a remarkable thing since, when he was busy writing, he generally crammed himself with pills and didn't sleep. Anne accused him of playacting, of pretending to be the model husband. And in fact he *was* playacting, but at a different role: that of a lookalike robot whose mission was to kill Anne. At the same time, he played a second role, that of the robot's programmer, who, having launched the "model husband" program, was now waiting for the right moment to strike. The dual roles added spice to the most mundane activities, such as drying the dishes when Anne was washing them. He watched her move, listened to her hold forth about this or that, her speech punctuated by all those "shits" and "fucks," and took great pleasure in the thought that he knew something that she didn't, which was that at any second he was going to strangle her.

Two weeks later Chuck and Phil staggered off the field of battle together, leaning on each other for support. They had managed to transform the planet of the lunatics into a slaughterhouse, but without having accomplished the one thing they had set out to do. Sitting at the bottom of a trench, they went over what had happened, trying to find some meaning in their failure. "Maybe some day when it doesn't matter," Chuck thinks to himself, "I can look back and see what I should have done that would have avoided this, Mary and me lying in the dirt shooting back and forth at each other. Across the darkened landscape of an unfamiliar world. Where neither of us is at home, and yet where I—at least—will probably have to live out the remainder of my life. Maybe Mary too."

In fact, Mary and Chuck both remain on the Alphane moon, and, as they will be living among the mental patients, they must undergo tests to determine which clinical family they should be assigned to. Phil now roused himself from the dazed stupor into which the carnage of the penultimate chapter, his feelings of inadequacy, Anne and his own marital troubles, and the general messiness of the plot had plunged him in. He decided that Mary would run the tests since she is after all a psychologist, but he reserved for himself the right to announce the results. To everyone's surprise, Mary, who thinks herself the only normal person on the moon and whom her husband thinks is a Mans, turns out to be a Dep, profoundly depressed and destined to wallow in the depths of Cotton Mather Estates. As for Chuck, the Dickian flipped-out hero, whom his wife has pegged as a latent hebephrenic, he suffers from no pathologies whatsoever. He is completely normal. As the only one of his kind on the Alphane moon, he will found the clan of the Norms, with its capital in Thomas Jeffersonburg, and dedicate himself to the task of making others well. His wife looks at him with respectful gratitude. The end.

It would be hard to imagine a more perfect illustration of wishful thinking than this triumphalist ending. Yet the strangest part of the whole business was that an actual psychiatrist—not just one of Dick's fictional creations—had come round to his view.

For two years Phil and Anne had been going separately to San Rafael, a suburb just north of San Francisco, to see a doctor whom they had come to consider the arbiter of their differences. By this point, they were no longer hoping to understand each other so much as trying to convince him that the other one was at fault. Anne had been his patient originally and was banking on her seniority, as well as on what she considered the obvious validity of her grievances: her husband was refusing to face up to his responsibilities and had withdrawn into an infantile stubbornness; he had no sense of reality; his Oedipus complex, his inferiority complex, and his guilt complex had made him impossible to live with and quite possibly dangerous. Phil didn't pull his punches either. He accused Anne not only of harboring deep feelings of aggression behind a facade of friendliness and civility but also of acting on those feelings. In fact, Phil told the doctor, she might already have actually committed a murder. Phil had become persuaded that Anne had managed to kill her first husband, and now Phil lived in fear that his turn was next. If she had managed to have Rubenstein committed to an institution, she could get him committed

too. That was actually the best-case scenario. More likely she would
simply kill him with her own two hands. She had tried to run him over
once while backing the car down the driveway. Another time she had
threatened him with a knife. When the doctor broached the possibility that Phil himself might be harboring unacknowledged emotions—
feelings of insecurity, perhaps?—he laughed and shook his head
ruefully: Wouldn't you feel insecure, doctor, if your life was in danger?
Sure, okay, maybe he was paranoid, but paranoids can get themselves
murdered too. One of these days they'd find him on the floor of the
garage, asphyxiated by car exhaust, or floating facedown in the bathtub, and the coroner would rule his death an unfortunate accident;
and maybe then the doctor would remember what Phil had told him
and regret not having acted while there'd still been time.

One evening in the fall of 1963, while Phil and Anne and the girls
were having dinner, the sheriff—the man from whom they rented the
shack—came to the door. He had with him a court order committing
Anne to a psychiatric hospital for three days of observation. When she
realized that the order was signed by *her* psychiatrist, she flew into a
rage, convincing the sheriff that the poor guy he had been renting his
shack to had been telling him the truth all this time: he really was married to a crazy woman.

It was a painful scene. Anne had to be dragged away by force. The
girls were in tears. Philip immediately took charge, ministering to the
girls with the sad gravity of the responsible father who continues to
keep the family clothed and fed even as their world is crashing down
around them.

The three days of psychiatric observation turned into three weeks.
Phil and the girls were at the hospital every morning as soon as visiting hours began. Anne's shock and rage at her forced internment had
been deadened by massive doses of tranquilizers, and she received her
family calmly, as if they had come to see her after an appendix operation. She wore a pink bathrobe whose buttons she toyed with inces-
santly. Her movements were slow, her expression vacant.

Phil felt uneasy about what he had done, yet it wasn't exactly
remorse that he felt, for he had truly believed that his life had been

in jeopardy. Somehow he couldn't quite shake the notion, though, that by having Anne committed he had brought about one of those nightmarish reversals in which the lunatics take over the insane asylum and tie the staff up in straitjackets. The classic scene has the "director" of the asylum showing around the policeman who's heard rumors about strange goings-on there. As they pass in front of one of the padded cells, the policeman is informed that the patient inside is one of their oddest and most interesting cases. He thinks he's the director, the visitor learns, and that the inmates of whom the "director" is supposedly the ringleader have locked him away.

Now that Anne—zoned out on tranquilizers—couldn't tell him he was wrong, Phil was less sure he was right. Lacking an enemy against whom to hone his arguments, he began to feel that they were losing their edge. Anne had been in the hospital a few days when Phil went to see the psychiatrists to try to explain that the whole thing had been a terrible misunderstanding, that he was the one who needed to be locked up: he had schizoid tendencies, he told them, because his mother had let his twin sister die from hunger when they were six weeks old; he had the diagnostic tests to prove it. The resident psychiatrists curtly suggested that he take his concerns to his *own* psychiatrist.

By now, however, Phil had lost confidence in his doctor: he had revealed his weakness by taking Phil's side. As for the doctor, he was beginning to fear he had made a grave mistake, and when Dick showed up at his door, agitated and suspicious, his fears were only confirmed. Not daring to go back on his diagnosis, he could do nothing but try to shore up his patient's defenses against the forces of self-doubt. He told Phil it was perfectly natural to have feelings of guilt; in fact, he would have been surprised had Phil not had them. But what Phil needed to do now, the doctor advised, was to face reality and stop trying to run and hide behind fictions.

The doctor must have known his patient well, for Phil never felt more reassured than when someone told him he wasn't facing reality or that there was something wrong with the way he looked at things. It was easy to get him to admit that his mistake—his unforgivable mistake—had been in not realizing that he was perfectly normal and that his wife was desperately ill. He understood that he had been behaving like someone who tries to start a car that doesn't have a motor, then gets angry with himself for not being able to.

It wasn't Phil's fault that there was no motor, the doctor explained with insinuating persuasiveness. It was his fault, though, that he believed it was his fault. That was a case of refusing to face reality. His wife, not he, was sick, and he would have to deal with that. Not admitting it was crazy.

Phil left the doctor's office feeling nearly convinced. He may not have completely bought the doctor's assessment of the situation, but he held out the hope that one day Anne would be well enough to recognize its truth. He imagined her confessing to him with a sad smile—exactly as Mary does in the last scene in *Clans of the Alphane Moon:*

"I'm not a Mans at all. In fact I'm just the opposite; I reveal a marked agitated depression. I'm a Dep." She continued to smile; it was a worthy effort on her part and he took note of it, of her courage. "My continual pressing of you regarding your income—that was certainly due to my depression, my delusional sense that everything had gone wrong, that something *had* to be done or we were doomed."

Rereading these lines in proof, Phil experienced a powerful surge of tenderness for Anne. Tears rose to his eyes. She had looked so fragile, so helpless in her pink bathrobe. What an idiot he had been: here was this unhappy, frightened little girl who needed his protection, and he had been able to see her only as a shrew intent on crushing him like an insect. All he could think about now was taking her in his arms and telling her that he would never leave her, that he would help lead her through these rough waters and back to the shores of reason. Yes, he would lead her out of the cold, desolate world of madness and back to the soft and welcoming warmth of the real world.

Anne came home from the hospital a zombie, thanks to the powerful drugs that, according to the doctors, she would probably have to take for the rest of her life. It would be Phil's responsibility to make sure that she took her pills as prescribed. Because the medicines didn't so cloud her mind that she ceased to aspire to complete recovery, she would sometimes pretend to swallow them and then spit them out when Phil wasn't looking. Suspecting this subterfuge, Phil would hover around her while she took the pills and would rifle among the leaves of the houseplants for the ones she had spat out. He felt sorry for himself for being married to someone so seriously ill. One day, while he was on the phone with his mother complaining about Anne, she overheard him making the magnanimous concession that "it must have been hard for her too." She nearly choked with rage.

Phil wondered what he would do if Anne didn't get better. Divorce her and marry someone else, or carry this ball and chain for the rest of his life? How long would he have this burden to bear?

While Anne was in the hospital, an attractive if somewhat odd woman came to his aid. Maren Hackett was of Swedish descent, athletic, and hard-drinking. She had been a policewoman and a truck driver, and was a member of Mensa. Although she didn't fit Phil's idea of a religious fanatic, she was in fact active in Saint Columba's Episcopal Church in Inverness, the village not far from Point Reyes where she lived. At her suggestion, Phil began to read the epistles of Saint Paul, and in particular those passages concerning charity. In them Phil recognized what until then he had called empathy and, like Paul, held to be the highest of the virtues. He saw himself as a self-denying caregiver who for his wife's sake sacrificed the brilliant life and gratifying love affairs that would otherwise have been his due. Eric, the hero of *Now Wait for Last Year*, the novel that Phil wrote that autumn, faces a similar dilemma and finds the same courage and comfort Phil had found in Maren Hackett in a talking taxicab:

To the cab he said suddenly, "If your wife were sick—"

"I have no wife, sir," the cab said. "Automated Mechanisms never marry; everyone knows that."

"All right," Eric agreed. "If you were me, and your wife were sick, desperately so, with no hope of recovery, would you leave her? Or would you stay with her, even if you had traveled ten years into the future and knew for an absolute certainty that the damage to her brain could never be reversed? And staying with her would mean—"

"I see what you mean, sir," the cab broke in. "It would mean no other life for you beyond caring for her."

"That's right," Eric said.

"I'd stay with her," the cab decided.

"Why?"

"Because," the cab said, "life is composed of reality configurations so constituted. To abandon her would be to say, I can't endure reality as such. I have to have uniquely special easier conditions."

"I think I agree," Eric said after a time. "I think I will stay with her."

"God bless you sir," the cab said. "I can see you're a good man."

CHAPTER 9

THE REAL PRESENCE

One November afternoon in 1963, Phil was making his way through the horse pastures, which relentless rains had turned into vast muddy lakes. In the hollows, tree branches broke through the surface of the water; soon, he thought, he would need a boat to get from the house to the shack. The floods reminded him of one of his favorite passages from *Winnie-the-Pooh*, but on this particular day even a memory of that beloved book from his childhood couldn't cheer him up. Now that Anne had stopped taking the medications prescribed by her psychiatrist, she had become her old self again, to Phil's chagrin. In fact she was worse than ever, for now she hated him with such murderous venom that he could no longer flatter himself with the notion that he was saving her life. He was back to putting up with her. On the question of whether it would be better for him to stay or to go, the *I Ching* had rendered an uninspiring response: *Ku*, "Work on what has been spoiled."

The hexagram represented a plate crawling with worms—a rather accurate reflection of his state of mind, his marriage, and his life in general. The interpretation was obvious: if someone puts a plate like that in front of you and you have the least trace of a survival instinct,

you give it a good swift kick and run like mad, before your brain liq-
uefies and you spend the rest of your life watching worms devour one
another. But with the *I Ching* nothing is final. Everything changes.
Hexagrams of victory contain the seeds of decline, and those that
announce the most crushing devastation, like the one he had just
drawn, harbor within them the germs of renewal. Phil continued on.
"It furthers one to cross the great water," read the judgment, which the
commentary explained as follows: "The conditions embody a demand
for removal of the cause. What has been spoiled by man's fault can be
made good again through man's work."

In other words, instead of fleeing Anne, he had to keep trying to
save their marriage. Perhaps the passage across the great waters was
nearing its completion and the farther shore lay just ahead. It would
be stupid to give up at the last minute; it would be as if Christopher
Columbus had decided to turn back only a few leagues from the
American coast.

Overhead a bird screamed. He looked up.

There in the sky above him, a gigantic face peered down. Robotic
and horrible, it filled a quarter of the sky. And it was watching him.

Terror-stricken, Phil closed his eyes, but the vision persisted. It was
not the face he saw—that was no longer there—but the look the thing
had given him, one of sheer malice, as if all the evils of the world were
concentrated in it, in the hateful gaze that poured from the empty
horizontal slots of the face's eyes. Phil instantly understood that this
was what he had been afraid of seeing his entire life. His father's gas
mask, the one that had so frightened him as a child, had heralded this
vision long ago. And now here it was. He would never forget it. Never
again would he sleep peacefully.

Slowly he opened his eyes and found himself staring at his boots,
solidly stuck in the gluey mud. They were a comforting sight, a welcome dose of reality. He looked up again.

The face was back.

It grinned at him—a sneer of malevolence and death. Phil took off
running, heading straight for the house, not even trying to avoid the
puddles that splattered his clothing with mud. He didn't dare look up

again at the sky, having lost all hope that the face would not be there if he did.

For several days the face in the sky played hide-and-seek with Phil, disappearing when he worked up the courage to look up to see if it was there, insinuating itself into his field of vision the moment he stopped expecting to see it. Even the dots and flecks that danced behind his closed eyelids either contained the face or presaged its appearance.

At the end of his rope, Phil drove out to San Rafael to see his psychiatrist. The doctor eyed him suspiciously and asked if perhaps he had taken that hallucinogenic drug everyone was talking about. Every day another story seemed to come out in the press. Phil's doctor was particularly interested in reports that for two hundred dollars a session the more fashionable L.A. psychoanalysts were offering their well-heeled patients LSD-based therapies. Cary Grant had confided to a reporter from *Time* that he had been taking LSD every week for over a year and that the experience had changed the way he looked at the world, even his approach to comedy. Reading this, the doctor had gone to see the actor's latest film, *Charade*, wondering if he would be able to detect a difference. And indeed, he felt there was one, though you could tell only if you knew about it beforehand. The craze for LSD extended beyond Hollywood and had reached even the most respectable academic circles. Timothy Leary, who liked to say that LSD had blown his mind, had been fired from Harvard for recommending its use to his students.

Phil shrugged. Yes, he had heard about it, he told the doctor, and he had read what Huxley had to say about mescaline—which was more or less what Leary had been saying about LSD—but he himself had never taken it. You couldn't get ahold of it in Point Reyes. Besides, as far he could tell, what he had seen in the sky wasn't at all like what this Harvard professor had been going on about. If this Leary character had seen this malevolent and horrible face in the sky while tripping on LSD, he would have had to be a real bastard to encourage his students to copy him; either that or he was the devil's disciple looking for new acolytes to serve his master. In fact, maybe he *was* the devil's disciple. It was a dreadful thought, but if that's what Timothy Leary was really up to, then Adolf Hitler was a choirboy next to him.

The doctor tried to calm Phil down. His patient was making him more and more nervous. Feeling that perhaps he should move the discussion back to more solid ground, he told Phil that the hallucination could have been caused by exhaustion, anxiety, and Anne's terrible problems. But Phil wasn't about to let him off the hook. First of all, he took cold comfort in the possibility that the horror he had seen existed in his head rather than in the world. If the doctor hoped his explanation would placate him, he was mistaken. Second, insisted Phil, he knew very well what had happened to him and it was no hallucination—just the opposite. For all sorts of reasons—fatigue, amphetamines, his unhappiness, and maybe a certain predisposition—the inner psychic mechanism whose function it was to filter reality had shut down. The screen that shields us from the unbearable sight of reality as it truly is had torn. He had seen what he had seen, and now his problem was to survive his vision.

He told the doctor what John Collier, the British writer of fantastic fiction, had said—that the universe was a pint of beer and the galaxies nothing but the rising bubbles. A few people living in one of the bubbles happen to see the guy pouring the beer, and for them nothing will ever be the same again. That, said Phil, is what had happened to him.

In reply, Phil's doctor asked him if he thought he had seen God.

On his way back from San Rafael, Dick stopped off in Inverness, at the church to which Maren Hackett belonged. A pretty wood structure, it stood beside a gorge, and although it was an Episcopal church that followed the Anglican rite, for Phil it evoked austere Nordic serenity, like Maren herself. He went inside and asked to have his confession heard. The priest seemed far less obtuse than his psychiatrist had been and was at least willing to listen to what Dick had to say. More than once the man winced in pain, as if he truly understood. He seemed to Phil like an old hunter who long ago came face-to-face with a monstrous wolf and, after a difficult struggle, believed he had rid the world of it forever—but who, when a terrified young man comes running out of the woods many years later and tells him what he has seen, understands that his old enemy has returned and that he now must go out and take up the fight once more. At the end of Dick's confession, the priest said simply, "You have met Satan."

Dick was comforted. The Church took him seriously; it understood the problem. He knew, to be sure, that the Church, for its own sake, preferred not to consider the possibility that it was God himself he had seen, that the whole nightmare was the hand of the Lord rather than of some evil underling. After all, was the world so well designed that one could simply assume it was the work of a benevolent deity? Phil shared this thought with the priest, who looked at him with sorrow in his eyes but not a trace of surprise. Nothing surprised him, so far as Phil could tell. You could utter the most repugnant blasphemy and he would probably shake his head sadly, the way an experienced doctor might react to an alarming but not uncommon symptom. His attitude rankled Phil, but he found it reassuring too. He was no longer alone to confront the robotic face that filled the sky. Someone else, though he might not see the horror himself, knew it existed and prayed with him and for him.

When he told Anne of his intention to undergo baptism and join the Church, she did not respond as expected. Kleo would have burst out laughing at the news, and everyone in Berkeley would have joined in; only a few months earlier, he himself would have laughed at the idea. But Anne was moved. She took him in her arms and murmured that she would be baptized with him and so would the girls. Misery has a way of blunting one's sense of the ridiculous and turns the sufferer to God—that was what misery was supposed to do, according to Christians. In any event, Phil realized that in Anne's eyes the conversion was a last-ditch effort either to save their marriage or to survive its breakup. He promised himself he would not spoil the chance.

To prepare for the baptism, they attended classes in catechism. Neither Anne nor Phil had had much of a religious education, but their ignorance sat far better with the priest than did Phil's vague yet profuse theological speculations, his inclination to find some merit in even the most patent heresies, and his favoring the apocryphal texts over the canonical scriptures, which he had yet to read.

The girls couldn't grasp the principle of Communion. They found it revolting that Jesus had exhorted his followers to eat of his body and drink of his blood; that was cannibalism. To reassure them, Anne said it was an image, sort of like the expression to "drink in someone's words." Phil objected. He saw no point in becoming a Christian, he told her, if you were going to rationalize all the mysteries and turn them into platitudes.

Anne replied that she saw no point in becoming a Christian if it meant treating religion like one of his science fiction stories.

But that was just it, Phil said. If you took what the New Testament says seriously, then you had to believe that a little over nineteen centuries ago, ever since Christ departed and left us with the Paraclete—the Holy Ghost—humanity had undergone a kind of mutation. You couldn't see it, but it had happened, and if Anne didn't believe him, then she simply wasn't a Christian, and that was that. This wasn't something he had made up—it was Saint Paul who had said it—and it wasn't Phil's fault it seemed like a science fiction story. The Eucharist was the agent of this mutation and shouldn't be explained away as some kind of silly commemoration.

Phil gathered the girls around him and told them he would tell them his cat joke. "It's very short and simple," he began. "A hostess is giving a dinner party and she's got a lovely five-pound T-bone steak sitting on the sideboard in the kitchen waiting to be cooked while she chats with the guests in the living room, has a few drinks and whatnot. But then she excuses herself to go into the kitchen to cook the steak—and it's gone. And there's the family cat, in the corner, sedately washing its face."

Hatte, the oldest, asked if that meant the cat had eaten it.

Phil complimented her on her perspicacity and told her to wait and hear the end of the story. "The guests are called in," he continued, and they argue about it; there sits the cat, looking well-fed and cheerful. 'Weigh the cat,' someone says. They've had a few drinks; it looks like a good idea. So they go into the bathroom and weigh the cat on the scale. It reads exactly five pounds. They all perceive this reading and one guest says, 'Okay, that's it. There's the steak.' They're satisfied that they know what happened, now; they've got empirical proof. Then a qualm comes to one of them and he says, puzzled, 'But where's the cat?'"

Christmas came, and the rains finally stopped. The face in the sky disappeared. Under a Christmas tree, Phil and Anne exchanged little volumes of pious teachings. Hatte got a Barbie doll equipped with several outfits, hair ornaments, makeup, and a boyfriend—Ken. Once he suppressed his initial impulse to make fun of these risible caricatures of the American dream in good ex-Berkeleyite fashion, Phil found Barbie and Ken an endless source of fascination. He tried to imagine what future archeologists—or Martians—would make of them and how they would reconstruct our civilization based on these artifacts alone. Like a connoisseur hunched over a miniature, he marveled at the details, delighting in their precision and amused by what the dolls' designers chose to leave out. Barbie's hair dryer seemed more sophisticated and, all things considered, more realistic than Anne's did. Her bra hooked in the back just like a real one—and was no easier to unhook—but the breasts it held lacked nipples. And if (he waited until Anne had turned her back) one dared to pull down her panties and give her a quick look—nada, there was nothing there, no pubic hair, nothing at all. The archeologists of the future would scratch their heads trying to figure out how twentieth-century humans managed to reproduce. On the other hand, maybe they would find nothing odd at all about Barbie and Ken, for the simple reason that they would look exactly like them. Ken and Barbie prefigured the humanity of tomorrow, those who would replace us. Or else maybe—why not?—they were the vanguard of an extraterrestrial invasion.

This idea of Earth being taken over by toys from outer space appealed enormously to Phil; he had used it a number of times already, notably in "War Game," a short story published in December 1959. It is about wary customs inspectors holding up the entry of a shipment of toys from the planet Ganymede until it can be subjected to a careful examination. The toys seem harmless enough and reputedly are even educational, but you can never be too careful with these Ganymedeans, whose expansionistic tendencies are legendary throughout the galaxy. The earthlings are worried that the Ganymedeans will do to them what they have done to other planets and take over Earth without ever firing a shot. The easiest thing to do would be simply to block entry to all Ganymedean exports, but the law prevents that. Hence the inspectors are always on the lookout for a Trojan horse. Of the three toys tested, two are clear-cut cases, while the third is less certain. You don't have to be a genius to reject out of hand a cowboy outfit that "scrambles" the appearance of whoever wears it and gives rise to multiple personality disorder. On the other hand, there was no reason not to allow in a silly variation of Monopoly that isn't remotely a weapon of war. What catches the attention of the inspectors is an odd-looking fortified castle that comes with a set of little robot soldiers whose role is apparently to lay siege to the citadel. Every three hours the drawbridge lowers and a soldier approaches and crosses over the moat; then the drawbridge is mysteriously raised and the soldier is never seen again. It is impossible to see inside the castle, and when the inspectors weigh it they find that its weight hasn't increased by a single ounce, even after the castle has swallowed up dozens of the little soldiers. How anyone could find this complex and seemingly pointless process fun or even educational is the true mystery. It just doesn't make sense. And where does the danger lie, assuming that the toy is dangerous—but what else can one assume? The inspectors wonder what is inside the castle and, since there seems to be no other way the "game" can end, what will happen once there are no more soldiers left for the castle to swallow up. There is nothing to do but wait and find out. But while the poor customs inspectors wait, I propose to return to our story. (The outcome of the inspection will be revealed at the end of the chapter.)

Four years later, Phil came up with an idea for using Barbie and Ken—a Martian idea. As in the two or three novels he had already set on Mars, Phil imagined the red planet in bleak terms, conceiving of it as a particularly inhospitable colony of Earth to which no one emigrates entirely of his own free will. In the novel he now began, small teams of unhappy colonists huddle together in boredom, neglect, and listless promiscuity, passing their days in underground bunkers, called "hovels," scattered across a desert landscape whose most appealing native fauna are hordes of telepathic jackals. Naturally, any form of diversion, even religion, is welcome under such circumstances, and terrestrial industries are urged to supply whatever amusements might distract the colonists from their grim conditions and offer them a feeling of connection to Earth. On Mars, the opium of the masses is a pair of accessorized dolls—Perky Pat and her boyfriend, Walt.

Clones of Barbie and Ken, Pat and Walt supposedly live on Earth, in California. In addition to the dolls themselves, the homesick colonists can purchase Perky Pat Layouts—kits complete with miniaturized accessories to help them represent the dolls' enviable existence with maximum realism. Once they acquire the basic components—houses, gardens, automobiles, sexy bathing suits, lawn mowers—the hovel dwellers, encouraged in their feverish consumerism by a pair of interplanetary disc jockeys in the pay of the doll manufacturer, spend all their time expanding and improving the dolls' little universe. They order mock-ups of streets, diners, and hair salons, as well as high school pals of Pat and Walt and places where they can all hang out together. They can buy a shopping district, a beach with palm trees, and a psychoanalyst, complete with his own miniature couch, pipe, and bound works of Freud—a fabulous little item that is in particularly great demand. The official line on the kits is that it gives the Mars colonists an unparalleled sense of well-being to be able to activate that pricey automatic garage-door opener they've bought or to take Pat into town behind the wheel of her new Ford convertible and have her slide a miniature dollar coin—which lists in the catalog for ten dollars; miniaturization doesn't come cheap—into a miniature parking meter. But they aren't stupid, these colonists. They don't really believe they are being transported to Earth by means of these childish games. Perky Pat Layouts are merely a legal cover for an illicit though tolerated trade. The company that markets them also sells a drug made from a lichen found only on the planet of Titan, called Can-D, which gives its users the illusion of *really* being Pat or Walt, of being transported out of their own miserable bodies and into those of the gloriously gorgeous dolls. While they languish in the corners of their sordid Martian bunkers, inert, their fingers clutching a naked doll without body hair, their spirits are free to soar. At worst, a dim memory of the personality they have left behind persists—like a feeling of déjà vu, an intuition of having lived a previous life. But once free of their Mars-bound chrysalis and having taken on the gratifying identity of Pat or Walt, they can enjoy with their partners any sort of experience they desire, without moral compunction. There is no better, no fuller way to appreciate adultery, incest, or murder than in this dream state, in this state of pure desire. The problem is that their dreams are mitigated dreams, their desires are desires fulfilled in another dimension. And that isn't the only complication: if you take the drug with other people, you inhabit along with those other people a single body and share its sensations with them, for better or worse. Thus one of the first scenes of the book that Phil was writing that winter has six people—residents of the same hovel—participating in the languorous kiss that Walt and Pat are exchanging on a sun-drenched beach: "The waves of the ocean lapped at the two of them as they silently reclined together on the beach, two figures comprising the essences of six persons. Two in six. . . . The mystery repeated; how is it accomplished?"

The mystery of "translation," which users face each time they take Can-D, causes something of a rift among the colonists, separating "believers" from "unbelievers." For the unbelievers, the layouts are merely symbolic, a representation of the universe from which they have been banished; identifying with Pat or Walt is an illusion that helps the colonists hold up under harsh circumstances. The believers, on the other hand, maintain that what the Can-D user experiences is real and hold sacred the moment when the miniaturized elements of the layouts stop acting as a stand-in for Earth and *become* Earth.

Is the Eucharist merely a commemoration, or does it literally sub-
stantiate the real presence of the savior? A few weeks earlier, Phil
would have treated the question as a pretext for playing off two different ways of thinking against each other. But now things were different. Something else was on his mind and the thought of it terrified
him: what would happen, he wondered, if the "real presence" was that
being whose face he had seen in the sky, the one he had become too
afraid to make sure did not exist?

"Whosoever eats of my body and drinks of my blood remains with
me and me with him" (John, 6:56). What happens to those who,
thinking there is no harm in it, eat of the body and drink of the blood
of Palmer Eldritch?

In the stories of H. P. Lovecraft, which Phil had devoured as a child
and which I like to believe determined his choice of a career—for they
determined mine—things happen that are so horrible that the author
refuses to describe them. Among the numerous adjectives that Lovecraft ritually musters up to justify this effective and emphatic reticence, there is one that is more idiosyncratic than *eerie, uncanny*, or
hideous, and that is *eldritch*. In Dick's eyes, *eldritch* encompassed the
sense of unsettling strangeness that Freud captured in the word
unheimlich but added to it another dimension, that of panic. *Eldritch*
could refer to perfidious betrayal or to the falsely familiar but also to
engulfing horrors, to the shocking revelation that makes you scream,
the way you scream in order to wake from a nightmare, only to realize
that you are already awake and that thus there is no escape.

When Phil started the novel, he knew where it was going but he
was afraid of going there—truly and profoundly afraid. Between
Christmas and New Year's he wrote the first hundred pages, establish-
ing the Martian setting—the bunkers, the dolls, the Can-D. To run the
Perky Pat Layout monopoly and the drug trafficking network for
which it provides the cover, he invented a likable crook named Leo
Bulero, whose second-in-command was one Barney Mayerson, a depressive character consumed by self-reproach. Barney still regrets decisions

he made at critical crossroads in his life, like dumping his pregnant wife rather than lose their apartment in their no-kids-allowed complex at a coveted address. Phil could have left things at that, playing with only these elements—the paradoxes created by the "translation" mystery provided enough material on their own for a respectable SF novel. But here and there in those first pages, he also slipped in disquieting rumors about the return of someone, or something, named Palmer Eldritch.

Palmer Eldritch is an adventurer who ten years earlier left for the Proxima Centauri system and has not been heard from since. It is assumed that he is dead, or worse. But now witnesses were coming forward to say that they have seen him again, that he has returned, recognizable by his triple prostheses: an artificial arm, gleaming metal teeth, and eyes that aren't actual eyes but narrow horizontal openings—like gun slits—fitted with wide-angle cameras. From his journeys beyond the known worlds, Eldritch—or, as people soon begin to suspect, the thing that has taken Eldritch's place—has brought back a new drug that can run circles around Can-D and is going to make it a thing of the past. The new drug is called Chew-Z, and its advertising slogan is "God promises eternal life. We can deliver it."

On the tenth day, Phil wrote the scene in which Leo Bulero arrives on the moon to meet with Palmer Eldritch, thinking—naively—he can cut a deal with him to divide up the drug market between them. Phil left the typewriter at dinnertime, knowing that when he returned to it, it would be in order to have his hero take Chew-Z. When he went to bed that night, he wondered what would happen if he died in his sleep. How would Eldritch manage without him? Phil didn't die that night, but he didn't sleep either. Eventually, he got up quietly from his bed and went to the bathroom, where, pausing before the medicine cabinet where he kept his pills, he took a long, hard look at himself in the mirror, to be sure that later he would be able to remember his own face. Then he got dressed and went out. As he passed the horse in the paddock, it whinnied weakly and approached the gate, steam coming from its wet muzzle. Phil stroked it gently, then disappeared into the night. As though he were two people at once, he watched himself walking to the shack in a sort of stupor. Fragments of a dream from his childhood came back to him. In the dream he had built a toboggan and made his way with it up to the top of a hill, and then the moment came when he had to let go, when he would fly faster and faster into the starless night, all the way down to the bottom, where Palmer Eldritch was waiting to devour him.

In a white, empty room Leo Bulero sits strapped to a chair. From a suitcase next to him comes the voice of Eldritch; he is announcing his plans to invade the solar system, but in a way no one has thought of before. Leo couldn't care less. He has come to talk business, to find out whether he can strike a deal with this guy, or whether he and Eldritch will fight a turf war over this extraterrestrial peyote. He's growing testy.

Suddenly the room explodes in his face.

He finds himself on a grassy embankment. Nearby, a little girl is playing with a yo-yo. Everything seems normal and strange at the same time. The setting could be something out of *Alice in Wonderland*. Except something else is in the air, something far less pleasant.

Eldritch.

In some way that is both obvious and inexplicable, the little girl playing with the yo-yo is Eldritch. The grass is Eldritch, and so is the yo-yo; the very air Leo breathes is full of Eldrich. The little girl tells him he's "where you go when you're given Chew-Z" and he realizes that somehow he must have been given the drug without knowing it, probably in that empty white room where he was being held on the moon. On the other hand, maybe that room was already part of the hallucination. So when was he given the drug? Before he even got to the moon? He has no way to prove that he wasn't already under the effects of the drug before that moment, perhaps long before, and that Eldritch hasn't simply been toying with him by having him believe that all this time he has been living his own life, in the normal world. Perhaps now, like a fisherman playing a fish he has hooked, Eldritch has decided to bring him back with one final, decisive jerk. And that is exactly what Eldritch has been doing. Now he stands before Leo in person, with his three prostheses, at the entrance of a labyrinth into which he is trying to lure Leo, and very civilly—in the way a fisherman might explain to the fish the ground rules of pole fishing—he lays out the details of the "real thing," compared with which Can-D is but a cheap imitation.

> "When we return to our former bodies—you notice the use of the word 'former,' a term you wouldn't apply with Can-D, and for good reason— *you'll find that no time has passed.* We could stay here fifty years and it'd be the same; we'd emerge back at the demesne on Luna and find everything unchanged, and anyone watching us would see no lapse of consciousness." . . .
>
> "What determines our length of time here?" Leo asked.
>
> "Our attitude." . . .
>
> "That's not true. Because I've wanted out of here for some time, now."
>
> "But," Eldritch said, "you didn't construct this—establishment, here; I did and it's mine. . . . Every damn thing you see, including your body."
>
> "My body?" . . .
>
> "I willed you to emerge here exactly as you are in our universe."

What people experience on Chew-Z isn't fantasy, Eldritch explains. "They enter a genuine new universe."

> "Many persons feel that about Can-D," Leo pointed out. "They hold it as an article of faith that they're actually on Earth."
>
> "Fanatics," Eldritch said with disgust. . . . "And you better believe me, because if you don't, you won't get out of this world alive."
>
> "You can't die in a hallucination," Leo said. "Any more than you can be born again. I'm going back."

Whereupon, taking a stairway he has willed into being, Leo leaves Eldritch's booby-trapped universe and finds himself back on Earth, in his office, surrounded by his employees and associates. He starts to tell them excitedly about his experience with the rival drug, which he says is not as good as Can-D:

"You can tell without a doubt that it's merely a hallucinogenic experience you're undergoing. Now let's get down to business. . . . What is it, Miss Fugate? What are you staring at?"

Roni Fugate murmured, "I'm sorry, Mr. Bulero, but there's a creature under your desk."

Bending, Leo peered under the desk.

A thing had squeezed itself between the base of the desk and the floor; its eyes regarded him greenly, unwinking.

"Get out of there," Leo said. . . .

The thing from beneath the desk scuttled out, and made for the door. It squeezed under the door and was gone. . . .

Leo said, "Well, that's that. I'm sorry, Miss Fugate, but you might as well return to your office; there's no point in our discussing what actions to take toward the imminent appearance of Chew-Z on the market. Because I'm not talking to anyone; I'm sitting here blabbing away to myself." He felt depressed. Eldritch had him and also the validity, or at least the seeming validity, of the Chew-Z experience had been demonstrated; he himself had confused it with the real. Only the malign bug created by Palmer Eldritch—deliberately—had given it away.

Otherwise, he realized, I might have gone on forever.

Spent a century, as Eldritch said, in this ersatz universe.

Jeez, he thought, I'm licked.

The baptism, which had been planned for weeks, took place the following day. The entire family went to the church, all decked out in their Sunday best. Phil wore a tie and a tweed jacket with leather elbow patches, which, Anne told him, made him look like a real writer. Phil, who had no idea how religious ceremonies were supposed to go, thought everything went just fine. The priest spoke the soothing words of the liturgy. The girls, Anne, and Maren Hackett, who had agreed to serve as sponsor, all looked very serious. Little Laura did fine. It was nice there in the little wooden church; one felt sheltered and safe. But Phil was still nervous. The whole scene struck him as a sacrilegious parody. At any moment, whether quietly or spectacularly, Eldritch might manifest his presence. He might make some minuscule, barely perceptible alteration in the set decorations that he had brought into being in the first place or he might lift the priest up into the air and smash him against the walls or turn the baptismal water into hydrochloric acid. Or perhaps he would simply give Phil a wink, like an old friend, without anyone else's noticing. For this, he would use the priest's eye, of course. Phil was afraid that if he looked at the priest he would see the face in the sky.

They chanted Psalm 139:

O LORD, thou hast searched me, and known me.

Thou knowest my downsitting and mine uprising, thou understandest my thought afar off.

Thou compassest my path and my lying down, and art acquainted with all my ways.

For there is not a word in my tongue, but, lo, O Lord, thou knowest it altogether.

Thou hast beset me behind and before, and laid thine hand upon me.

Such knowledge is too wonderful for me; it is high, I cannot attain unto it.

Whither shall I go from thy spirit? or whither shall I flee from thy presence?

If I ascend up into heaven, thou art there: if I make my bed in hell, behold, thou art there.

When they got home, Phil affected the Mephistophelean pose the girls found so funny and said that he had seen someone standing behind the baptismal font, someone whom their visit to the church had clearly disturbed. It was a little devil with horns and a long forked tail. But he was joking. For all intents and purposes, he had been baptized.

As Phil plunged back into his novel, he felt the need for fresh reinforcements. He needed something to bear witness to his baptism, some minister of the God of love in whom he had just been reborn from the water and spirit to accompany Barney Mayerson, his alter ego, who would now come to the fore. Though it was in principle a little late to introduce a new character, he had Barney, whom he has sent off to Mars, meet a young "New Christian" named Anne on the way there. Anne, a model of integrity and Christian virtue, is convinced that a sordid reality is better than the most exalted illusion and that drug taking among the colonists is a sign of their spiritual hunger, of their need for that which only the Church can provide. Alas, if there was one thing that Phil simply could not do as a writer, it was to create positive heroes and heroines. With Anne Hawthorne, he did the next best thing, and made Barney's new companion a saint. As soon as she gets to Mars, though, the galactic missionary breaks down and before long there's nothing she wants more than a dose of Can-D to escape the despair rising in her. It is either that or dark and lonely depression. And when faced not much later with the even more terrible temptation to try Chew-Z, she knows that her prayers will be of no use and that she will succumb. She has already been taken in by Eldritch's slogan, "God promises eternal life. We can deliver it." She knows that it is all a lie; were the slogan true, it would be even worse:

An evil visitor oozing over us from the Prox system . . . offering us what we've prayed for over a period of two thousand years. And why is this so palpably bad? Hard to say, but nevertheless it is. Because maybe it'll mean bondage to Eldritch; Eldritch will be with us constantly from now on, infiltrating our lives. And He who has protected us in the past sits passive.

Each time we're translated . . . we'll see—not God—but Palmer Eldritch.

And that is what begins to happen. Now it's Barney's turn to take Chew-Z, and since it was with Barney rather than with his boss, Leo, that Phil identified, the entire novel falls under the thrall of Eldritch. Barney struggles, stumbles, and argues with himself in a pandemonium of nested universes that are constantly renewing themselves and yet are ceaselessly refractory, in which you have only to trust someone to see that person slough off his or her familiar appearance and reveal the gun–slit eyes, the mechanical right arm, and the steel jaw—the three stigmata of Palmer Eldritch. Barney eventually emerges from this nightmare to find Anne, the neo-Christian, at his side, silently laughing, her teeth agleam, and then he knows for sure that the nightmare will never end. Whoever takes Chew-Z lives for all eternity in Palmer Eldritch. Once you're in, there's no escape; it's a one-way street. The worst is that everyone roils around in his nets; if you're caught, it's already too late to warn anyone else. No one on the outside suspects anything. Eldritch will devour every last human being, every last living creature, one by one. He will become a planet and all of its inhabitants at the same time. He will be the spirit of their civilization and the soul within each of them. He will be their civilization, and he will be each and every individual, and there will be nothing else. Maybe there already is nothing else besides Palmer Eldritch. Maybe these panicked thoughts that haunt Barney Mayerson, that Phil Dick transcribes, that I am paraphrasing, and that are now forging a path into what you believe to be your brain all exist only within Palmer Eldritch, who is using us, equivocal creatures that we are, to populate his never-ending puppet theater.

Barney, Anne, and their fellow Martian colonists, believing the translation is finished, trade impressions of it, although it could be that their conversation is taking place in Palmer Eldritch's mind, under his control. They all have found the experience fascinating, but at the same time they agree that they sensed something—how to say this?—strange or untoward, a creepy presence somewhere, like a shadow across a photograph.

> "That thing," [Barney] said, speaking to all of them, . . ."has a name which you'd recognize if I told it to you. Although it would never call itself that. We're the ones who've titled it. From experience, at a distance, over thousands of years. But sooner or later we were bound to be confronted by it. Without the distance. Or the years."

Anne Hawthorne said, "You mean God."

It did not seem necessary for him to answer, beyond a slight nod.

"But—*evil?*" Fran Schein whispered.

"An aspect," Barney said. "Our experience of it. Nothing more."

Phil was now a Christian—freshly minted and after his own fashion, to be sure—but a Christian nonetheless. Having typed this exchange, he felt that he couldn't finish the novel there, and so he added a strange and lovely theological discussion between Anne and Barney. Both of them know that from now until the end of what they will believe to be their lives, and perhaps beyond, Eldritch will live in them. Everything seems back to normal, but he is there, and he will always be there. Perhaps that's what God is, Barney ventures, this nightmare of Eldritch's abiding presence. Still, they also know that there is a difference between this presence and the presence with which mankind was visited two thousand years earlier. The difference is that Eldritch increases human desire instead of diminishing it; he stokes the fires of our shortsighted, animalistic, aggressive preference for ourselves over others. This predatory God is, when it comes down to it, simply a thing of nature. The other God, the one who came two thousand years ago, sweet and humble of heart, was not a god of self-aggrandizement but one of restraint and renunciation, who sought to give instead of take. He even gave His own life.

Phil was now a Christian but he was also still Dick the Rat, who could never resist the impulse to give his fiction that one last turn of the screw and always had a terrible time ending a story. There was nothing wrong with concluding the story of Palmer Eldritch on a Christological note, but having finished the chapter, Phil found himself beset by a nagging temptation to give the last word to Eldritch. This temptation stemmed both from a properly philosophical horror of concluding and from an older, more juvenile, and more perverse predilection of his for loss-of-innocence tales, for the rhetoric of horror films that seem to offer a final scene in which the monster is dead, life is returning to its normal course, and everyone—survivors and spectators alike—heaves a sigh of relief. Everyone, that is, except those who understand the conventions of the genre and know that any horror-film director worth his salt is going to sucker punch his audience with one last scene that will nail them to their seats and turn the happy ending on its head. Christian though he was, Phil had to give the last word to the monster, to the darkness, to the horror. And so Leo, now in a rocketship heading toward Mars, notices that all the passengers, himself included, bear the three stigmata of Palmer Eldrich, that even without the drug, the contagion is winning. "And suppose it reaches our minds?" he asks himself. "Not just the anatomy of the thing but the mentality as well . . . what would happen to our plans to kill the thing?"

Dick concludes things there, but I think the outcome of the customs inspection discussed several pages back might offer a subtler ending to this chapter. That mysterious castle, once all the soldiers have been swallowed up, doesn't explode or turn into something else; it doesn't do anything at all. The game is over, it seems, but the mystery remains unresolved. The customs inspectors still have no idea what to make of the toy, and, figuring they ought to play it safe, they deny it entry to Earth, along with the schizophrenia-inducing cowboy costume. On the other hand, they let through that harmless variant of the Monopoly game, which people soon discover is played according to the rule that "to lose is to win." The game enjoys a spectacular success among young earthlings, who willingly fall under its spell, converting to and living by its message. The worrisome castle and the crazy-making cowboy suit are only decoys; the real weapon of conquest is the Monopoly game. When they are attacked, the earthlings will turn the other cheek, marvelously consenting victims of an utterly original type of conquest that consists, essentially, of making Christians out of them. Yet the message comes not from a God of love but from a race of warrior conquerors. It may well be that Jesus, too, was an agent of Palmer Eldritch.

CHAPTER 10

KO: REVOLUTION (MOLTING)

That spring Phil fled Point Reyes and returned to Berkeley. Emerging from the awful interlude, from the suburb of life that every unhappy marriage is in some way, he discovered that the world had changed while he was gone, and he liked what he now found. In the boondocks, he had been only vaguely aware of the changes sweeping the country during the early 1960s. He had heard about the first student sit-ins, about Caryl Chessman and Martin Luther King Jr., and about those new drugs his psychiatrist had suspected him of experimenting with; he had wept when he learned that John Kennedy had been shot. But it had all seemed to be happening only on the radio, where you could hear the piercing, twangy voice of a twenty-year-old genius proclaiming that "the times they are a-changing." For Phil, it was as if those times belonged to some other era and the changes had taken place somewhere else, in a parallel universe, a theater of real life to which he would never gain access so long as he was rusticating in Point Reyes. His newfound freedom altered all of that: the show would not go on without him, he realized. There was a part in it for him.

A noncommissioned officer I once knew divided recruits, and by extension all humanity, into two distinct groups: Good Kids and

Punks. Whatever the limitations of this classificatory scheme, I for my part continue to find merit in it. Consider the picture of Bob Dylan on the jacket of the record containing the song I mention above: skinny, arrogant, and stubborn, with his girlish eyelashes, he looks like someone who will say no to whatever you ask of him. There you have the Punk in all his perverse splendor. In the great cultural upheaval that was turning such people into the heroes of the day, Phil's handicaps became so many advantages. So what if hadn't finished college and was on an FBI watch list? To be a dropout, someone who rejected the system and its values, was a mark of distinction; to have an FBI file was a badge of honor. So what he if he worked in a fringe genre, turning out pulp novels and short stories for a second-tier audience? That merely showed what integrity he had in refusing to court the suit-wearing zombies of the literary establishment. If he couldn't make it as a Good Kid, he'd shine as a Punk.

And so it was that in 1964 Phil Dick, maladjusted scion of the lower middle class who had never overcome his adolescent shyness, discovered to his absolute delight that he was completely in synch with the Zeitgeist. He who had always felt marginalized by life had landed smack into the middle of those handful of years when the margins took center stage. He easily inserted himself into the little circle of Bay Area science fiction writers who seemed to have made a collective decision to wear their hair long, sport ethnic jewelry, and smoke dope. And the best thing about this milieu, as far as Phil was concerned, was that it was strongly endogamous: the novelist Avram Davidson had just gone through an amicable separation from his young wife, Grania, who admired Phil and, despite a fairly serious weight problem, managed to charm him handily. Consulting the *I Ching* together, they drew *Pi*, signifying "solidarity and union," and thereupon decided to share a small house in Oakland that soon became a meeting place for neighborhood science fiction buffs. After his exile in Point Reyes and the claustrophobia of family life, this new sociability delighted Phil. It also revived his sense of self-respect, which had suffered rough treatment at Anne's hands over the previous five years, devoted as Anne was to the cause of "great literature."

Now he lived as he pleased, among his peers, people who also saw science fiction as a royal road to the uncharted regions of the soul and who believed Phil Dick to be the boldest of the new adventurers. He could do as he pleased—sit cross-legged on the floor if he wanted or sprawl out on old, coffee-stained couches without worrying about spilling on them. He no longer had to bother with trimming his beard. Once upon a time, when he worked at University Radio, he had refused to sell anything but classical music and considered rock 'n' roll a waste of time—except for Elvis, who had earned Phil's respect for having survived a stillborn twin. But now he became an expert on what was beginning to be called pop music, snapping his fingers to the beat, jiggling his hips, and throwing his considerable heft into a studious effort at being cool. Finally, he thought, he was starting to live.

The audience of admirers that would henceforth surround him brought out the ham in Phil, and he played to their expectations, loath to compromise the little legend that had sprung up about him. His books, his reclusiveness during his Point Reyes period—together with the few public appearances he had actually made—had conferred on him the reputation of a strange, drugged-out, paranoid genius. He was all that, and without even trying.

His new friends spent their time visiting one another, hanging out at one another's houses, but Phil, playing up his agoraphobia, didn't budge from his. His car would only run between home and his psychiatrist's office, he said; take it anywhere else and it would steer itself right into an accident. So people had to come and see him, and this new role, that of Old Man of the Mountain, brought out the Rat in him.

As far as his paranoia was concerned, his fears seemed on the face of it to be well-founded. He was in the middle of a nasty divorce, and all his friends who had gone that way before him—and there were quite a few of them—sympathized with his overly vigilant behavior: it was a matter of not giving legal ammunition to a woman who, by general consensus, was a complete harpy. Thus, even though he and

Grania were sharing a tiny house, he tried to hide his relationship with her—which for him meant letting anyone and everyone in on the secret and then swearing them to silence. His friends were even willing to believe that Anne had hired a private detective to have him tailed and had had a tap put on his phone line, but even their indulgent credulity must have cracked under his insistence that they help him look for microphones in the kitty litter. When he didn't find any he decided that he was up against his old enemies at the FBI, who, ever since the publication of *The Man in the High Castle*, had sworn his downfall. Phil asked people to prove their identity when he talked to them on the phone—were they really who they said they were?—and, once satisfied with the proof, he would pepper the conversation with comments directed toward eavesdroppers ("Hey, guys, I know you're listening to us and that you can't answer. So fuck you. Do you hear me? I said fuck you!"). His friends didn't know whether to laugh or to feel genuine concern, and in the end they concluded that this was just Phil Dick being Phil Dick, as nuts as his novels and as fascinating.

And he *was* fascinating; about this everyone agreed. His obsessions were fueled by an artistic imagination always at the boiling point. Anything might happen in a conversation with Phil, for he had all the furious energy of the paranoiac but without the monomania. Thus, his enemies, their methods and aims, and especially the degree of seriousness with which he denounced them could vary depending on the circumstances, the inspiration of the moment, and the person he happened to be talking to. Phil was a chameleon, an actor adept at reading his audience and figuring out their expectations, and if he overshot the mark from time to time, it was because he was trying too hard to please them. One evening he might go on a rant about being a victim of a global conspiracy and the next day he might have forgotten all about it or else calmly refer to his monologue of the previous evening as a manifestation of his legendary paranoia and give you to understand how surprised he was that you had taken him seriously. And if indeed you had taken him seriously, that meant either that you were paranoid as well or that you had good reason to believe that he was right, which meant you were in cahoots with his enemies.

Except in his work—which he had to turn out as quickly as possible before he became disgusted with what he was producing—he could be erratic to the point of pathology. With great solemnity, he showed Grania the little revolver he had bought when he was afraid Anne might attack him. He was ready to use it, he said, against Anne or, if necessary, against himself. Grania was worried and told their friends, who feared the worst. One Sunday morning, Anne showed up at the house with baby Laura in her arms. She wanted to talk to him. Panicked, he refused to open the door and ran from room to room waving the pistol, eventually shoving Grania into a closet, as in some vaudeville routine. She stayed there for several hours, expecting at any moment to hear the gun go off. But all she heard was Laura babbling, the sound of bacon and eggs frying on the stove, and Phil singing some Schubert lieder in his fine deep voice, then the sounds of a peaceful family get-together around an amply laden dining room table. The brunch went on until early afternoon, when Anne and her daughter left and the heroic and half-asphyxiated Grania emerged from the closet. Phil seemed surprised to see her. Why hadn't she come out and said hello? In the face of Grania's protests, he decided that his memory must have been playing tricks with him; the drugs he had taken must have had something to do with it. The next day he brought his revolver back out while talking about Anne and again started subjecting his friends to complicated tests in order to find out if they were spying for her—or for the FBI, or the Nazis, or whomever.

After several months, Grania found a calmer, more peaceful roommate and moved out. Hoping to get her to stay, Phil asked her to marry him, but to no avail; then, because he couldn't stand to be alone, he invited a couple of friends to move in with him. They lasted three weeks, during which time he dropped acid for the first time in his life.

Through the newspapers, Phil had followed Tim Leary's goings-on at Harvard, which struck him as something out of 1950s-style science fiction, like *Invasion of the Body Snatchers*. Distinguished academics had started a research program to study a drug considered useful to the field of psychiatry. As soon as they took the drug, their colleagues found them changed: their pupils were dilated, they looked ecstatic and mysterious, and though all had been confirmed empiricists, they now spoke only of love, ecstasy, and becoming one with God. When pressed for details, they turned evasive. What they had experienced couldn't be described; it could only be . . . experienced. Those who, their curiosity piqued, decided to try the drug for themselves were transformed in turn. And unless you followed suit and took the drug yourself, you couldn't talk with them. Rumors began spreading across the campus as more and more students came knocking on Leary's office door, asking to be initiated, then returned from their "trips," eyes aglow, and held forth in singsong voices about the wonders of acid. The dean was at his wits' end. He had an epidemic on his hands.

At first Leary had been regarded as a benign eccentric. Then he began to speak out, to organize conferences and seminars, to explain to journalists that a decisive moment in the history of humanity was at hand. It was no coincidence that Albert Hoffmann had synthesized LSD at the very moment that Enrico Fermi split the atom. One had given man the means to destroy the entire species, and the other the opportunity for reach a higher evolutionary level. If man embraced the latter gift, if he plunged into the unexplored oceans contained within the human brain, he would leave Homo sapiens behind and enter into a wise and joyful communion with the cosmos. He would know God; indeed, in a certain way, he would *be* God.

By themselves these pronouncements would have won few converts. But unlike previous illuminati, Leary had the means—thanks to Sandoz Laboratory—to have them substantiated. Indeed, whoever subjected himself to the overpowering effects of LSD emerged from the experience either terrified or, as seemed more often the case, converted. Prominent intellectuals and artists and even businessmen become followers, including the head of the Ford Foundation. Leary got permission from the Massachusetts state penitentiary board to offer LSD therapy to inmates at the state prison in Concord. This new Eucharist filled even hardened criminals with mystical inspiration that amazed the wardens.

Terrified by the association of Harvard's august name with flaky experiments so at odds with the rigors of the scientific method, the administration fired Leary, and, in doing so, confirmed him in his new vocation as prophet. He called his detractors dried-up relics of a bygone age, citing Niels Bohr's formula, according to which a new truth triumphs over its opponents not by persuading them but because the opponents die off, to be replaced by a generation that takes the new truth as a given. In a mansion lent to him by a patron, Leary brought the faithful together in a community that under his leadership—and to the accompaniment of Indian ragas and the wafting odors of incense—devoted itself to the methodic exploration of the new worlds that acid opened up to them. They had a guidebook for these voyages of discovery, the *Bardo Thodol*, also known as *The Tibetan Book of the Dead*. This Baedeker of the inner spaces had been a farewell gift from Aldous Huxley to the rising generation; he had read it, it was said, on his deathbed and, several hours before the end, had asked for an injection of LSD, not out of cowardice but, on the contrary, so that he could fully experience his voyage to the beyond.

According to Leary and his friends, this ceremonial antecedent would soon be common currency. They saw themselves as twenty-first-century anthropologists living in a time capsule during the dark, waning years of the twentieth century, but they felt certain that a general conversion was at hand. They were counting on an exponential growth in the use of LSD: 25,000 users in 1961 meant 4 million in 1969—a critical mass that would force society to change. They convinced themselves that, as the drug-induced mental deconditioning worked its way through the ranks of the middle class, by the mid-1970s the president of the United States himself would be an acid user and leaders would drop a tab or two at international summits. And the world, of course, would be the better for it.

This messianic vision seemed plausible in 1964, more plausible at any rate than the idea that in thirty years' time the man sitting in the Oval Office would admit that he had smoked marijuana but claim he hadn't inhaled. Newspapers followed Leary's activities and reported what he said. The word *bardo* was suddenly in vogue. People spoke of "bardo experiences" and of "bardo music" and "bardo films." Lots of people who had no connection to the worlds of art, science, or high society, people who were not Cary Grant, who didn't think of themselves as drug users were trying acid and acknowledging that it opened the doors of consciousness: one acid trip was worth about three years of psychoanalysis, according to one popular formulation. In Berkeley a standard dose of 250 micrograms could be legally obtained for about ten dollars. Phil's friends dropped acid regularly and praised it to the skies.

Thus there was no way Phil could not try LSD—especially since he was now regarded as a seasoned trailblazer of this new frontier. When *The Three Stigmata of Palmer Eldritch* was published, readers it saw it as the great LSD novel, and the notion of Dick as acid guru did a lot for his reputation. As Phil hated to contradict people, he let himself be taken for an expert in psychedelia, offering sage advice to those who turned to him to glean the fruits of his experience. The truth was, he was frightened of the drug.

He was right to be, for the first time he took it, with a group of friends, things didn't go well for him. After an hour, he seemed to have lost all contact with his friends and found himself "where you go when you're given Chew-Z": in the world of Palmer Eldritch. He made his way through a dark tunnel full of hostile shadows, traversed a frozen landscape with steep cliffs, catacombs, and then found himself in a Roman amphitheater in which he would suffer the fate of the early Christians. He felt certain he was lost and despaired of ever finding his way out. He tried to reassure himself: what was happening to him, he told himself, could be explained by the fact that he had ingested a psychotoxin. It would continue to act on him for a few hours—nine or ten hours, people said—and then its effects would wear off. The problem was, he was not at all convinced he would still be alive in nine or ten hours, and in any case hours could last centuries in the world in which he found himself. As a child, sitting in the dentist's chair, he felt the ordeal was taking forever, and now he knew he had been right—it really *had* lasted an eternity. He had always been there. He would be there forever. Everything else was merely an illusion and, like Leo Bulero, he could only pray that, mercifully, the illusion would return.

Those around him, whose presence Phil was no longer aware of, thought they heard him speak in Latin. No one understood Latin; all they could understand was the phrase *"Libera me, domine,"* which Phil repeated over and over, as sweat rolled down his neck, his face a mask of terror.

Eventually, having seriously worried his companions, Phil rejoined the *koinos kosmos* and slept for an entire day, and when he awoke he told his friends what the trip had been like. He had been in hell, he told them, and it had taken him two thousand years to crawl out.

They were surprised, naively perhaps. During these euphoric times bad trips were rare. People who took LSD invariably talked about swimming in iridescent oceans, about feeling capable of understanding everything, of doing anything. The drug had something for every taste and temperament: to contemplative souls, the world on acid seemed like a calm epiphany, a Vermeer painting quietly pulsing to the rhythm of their nervous system. To the more active, the world became a giant pinball machine, generous with its free games, its lights flashing up to the vaulted heavens. But for Phil it was different: he found himself in the nightmare world of his novels and afterward could never stop wondering whether he had encountered Ultimate Reality or merely a reflection of his own mind—hardly a comforting alternative.

Ever faithful to his binary logic, Phil concluded that there were but two kinds of minds: those for whom the reality of reality is light, life, and joy and those for whom it is death, entombment, and chaos; those who in the deepest, darkest depths behold the figure of Christ the savior and those, like Dostoevsky's Svidrigailov, who, when they think of eternity, imagine it as a dirty outhouse covered with cobwebs; those who, despite Auschwitz, believe in love and God's infinite mercy and those who, in the presence of blue skies and life's pleasures, still perceive the basic horror of the universe. Of course, a person's mental makeup, which LSD exposes unmercifully, explains much of one or the other reaction. But such drastic differences cannot simply be a matter of opinion or temperament: the truth must necessarily belong in one of these two camps, Phil felt, not in both. Compromise was out of the question. In Christian terms, terms that Phil had recently embraced, only one of two things could be possible: either Christ was resurrected or he wasn't.

He knew what he wanted to believe, but he also knew—and acid had confirmed it for him—what he believed in the depths of his psyche. Knowing which camp he belonged to, despite himself, he would have given anything to be wrong, or at least to be convinced that he was wrong.

It hadn't been the best time for him to drop acid (as if for him there ever could have been a best time). Celibacy wasn't good for him. Even when he lived with Grania, he couldn't stop himself from hitting on any woman who came through the door. On his own, he lost all restraint, adding to his legend with pathetic anecdotes. Every woman he met he fell in love with, more or less platonically and never discreetly. With his social world as small as it was, most of these women were the wives or girlfriends of his friends. Some of these men took umbrage at Phil's ardent attempts at courtship; others were amused, rightly persuaded they had little to fear from a rival the likes of Phil. As brilliant a writer and conversationalist as he was, this overgrown baby with his unkempt beard and premature middle-aged paunch made emotional demands too excessive to inspire anything more than tender curiosity. In the winter of 1964, at least four or five wives of science fiction writers he knew received passionate, hilarious, plaintive letters in which he told them about his sister Jane or copied out verses from the Metaphysical poets or lines from Schubert's *Winterreise* so they would know the extent of his solitude and melancholy. He phoned them late at night, usually stoned, and was surprised at their lack of eagerness—not to mention that of their husbands when it was they who answered—to listen to his monologues. The transported romantic could then become a total boor, calling his *ferne Geliebte* a slut in public, dropping her for the most recent newcomer to the scene while letting his hand fondle the knee of yet a third. After such exhibitions, he would inevitably sober up and realize that he had made a fool of himself, that he had traded on his status as a stormy genius only to be regarded as a colorful crank. The only way he could think of to redeem himself was to write more letters and make more phone calls, which were as unwelcome as the earlier ones. Or else he played up his outlandishness and tried to project the image of a boisterous, randy old Falstaff, which could not have been further from the truth.

Realizing that he probably wouldn't find a woman in his present circles, Phil figured he ought to spread his net wider and went through his address book. He ended up getting back in touch with Maren Hackett, the friend from his Point Reyes days who had introduced him to the writings of Saint Paul and to the Episcopal Church. Maren had been married to an alcoholic whose daughters from a previous marriage had remained with her after she and their father broke up. The older one, Nancy, had just returned from France, where she had studied psychology and been hospitalized with a nervous breakdown. Nineteen, sweet, shy, with an almost inaudible voice, Nancy had a slender, graceful body and a face she kept hidden behind a curtain of long, straight hair. When no one was watching her, she would take a photo of herself out of her jeans pocket and stare at it, as if to reassure herself that she really and truly existed. Dick often went to see the three Hackett women, without anyone—including himself—really understanding why he went, whether it was for the pretty stepmother or for one of the two girls. Finally he settled his gaze on Nancy and not only told her of the love he had for her but also let her know how disastrous his life would be if she refused him. He would take more and more pills and wouldn't eat, or sleep, or write; he would probably die. After numerous awkward silences and nervous smiles, Nancy gave in and agreed to be his muse. In the spring of 1965, she moved in with him.

CHAPTER 11

WHAT IS HUMAN?

The year before, when Dick was leaving Point Reyes on the verge of a mental breakdown, he had consulted the *I Ching* and drawn Hexagram 49, *Ko.* "Revolution," it had told him, and "molting," and that is what he had observed both in the society around him and then in his own life. He had suffered and made others suffer, too, but now when he looked around him he felt certain that the wheel had turned and that he had entered a new and more favorable phase.

Every day he congratulated himself for having found Nancy and thus broken the pattern of failure that had governed his emotional life up until this point. Now he had someone to care for and protect, a child-woman who loved him in return without trying to change him. Their relationship respected the balance of the sexes. He was yang—corpulent and bearded, filled with creative energy—and she, frail, watery, a creature of the shadows, was yin. The Tao would smile on them. They laughed together, played jokes on each other, and had pet names for each other. Like the lovers in *The Magic Mountain,* who, instead of exchanging photos, trade X rays of their tubercular lungs, Phil and Nancy shared their phobias, diagnosing each other's psychiatric symptoms and marveling at how well they understood each other. He was constantly comparing his new life with everything he had known before. He vastly preferred the charming disorder of Nancy and his rundown place by the canal in San Rafael to the starched and paranoid whiteness of Anne's modern house at Point Reyes Station. That house was cold like Anne herself, who expressed her sensuality in fits of erotic furor that made him seize up in fear; it was cold like his mother, whose absurd notions of pediatric hygiene had made her afraid to touch Phil. Nancy was different. She was warm and innocent, given to infantile fits of giggling, which Phil approved of wholeheartedly, taking them as a sign of healthy polymorphous perversion. She liked to pull at his already graying beard, to jump into the bathtub with him and rest her head on his belly. In her hands, the body that he had watched, in consternation, spread and thicken over the past few years became something soft and warm, something to love, and therefore something lovable. After a wild (if sterile) yearlong binge, his life had stabilized and now, pampered and surrounded by friends who admired his work and let themselves be seduced by his ideas, he returned to his old routines. He started to write again, and since Nancy had shown him what it was like to be authentically human—tender, compassionate, vulnerable—his writing began to extol the glory of the human being.

But to extol the glory of the human being, Phil first had to define and flesh out the opposite of the human, which for Phil was not the animal or the thing but what he called the "simulacrum"—in other words, the robot.

From the earliest science fiction on, the robot—like the golem and Frankenstein's monster before it—had been cast in the role of villain, its human creator's most cunning adversary. In the fifties, Isaac Asimov had tried to impose a code of good conduct on robots and their writer-creators, to reduce the theme of robot rebellion to the scientific absurdity and cheap literary convention it was, but he did not succeed. As the fictions became more and more plausible and the possibility of "thinking machines" aroused interest not only among the visionary set, the writers and philosophers, but in the scientific community as well, fear of the robot grew in the popular imagination. The term *cybernetics*, coined by an American mathematician, Norbert Wiener, caused a great stir, and the ideas it represented raised two interrelated questions— first, whether it would one day be possible for a machine of man's creation to think like a human being and second, what exactly it meant to think "like a human being." Or, to put it another way, what was it about the way we think and act that could be called specifically and exclusively human? The debate over artificial intelligence had begun, with the materialists on one side and the spiritualists on the other. The former were convinced that at least in theory all mental operations could be broken down into their component parts and were thus reproducible, whereas the latter maintained that the human mind harbors, and always will harbor, something nonquantifiable, something that cannot be reduced to a set of arithmetic operations and that, depending on which church one belonged to, one might call the ghost in the machine, reflexive consciousness, or perhaps simply the soul.

Phil followed this debate as well as anyone could who divided his reading mainly between theological tracts and popular science magazines. Eventually, while leafing through a collection of essays, he came across a groundbreaking article written in 1950 by Alan Turing, the English mathematician. The book's introduction gave a bit of biographical information on Turing, whom Phil found fascinating: one of the founders of modern computer science, he was credited with helping win World War II by designing a machine for the British Secret Service that broke the Luftwaffe's secret codes. Later he committed suicide under strange and disturbing circumstances. But what interested Phil most was that Turing had thought a great deal about thinking machines, which were one of Phil's obsessions.

In that famous article, Turing takes up the range of objections that had been raised against the possibility of artificial intelligence—that what computers do is too specialized to be called thinking, that they lack spontaneity, moral sense, desire, and taste, and so forth. Turing dispatches these arguments one by one, and proposes instead a single criterion by which to answer the question of whether a machine can think. That criterion is whether the machine is capable of making a human being *believe* that it thinks as he does.

As Turing points out in his essay, the phenomenon of consciousness can only be observed from the inside. I know that I have a consciousness, and indeed it is because of it that I know this, but as to whether you have one or not, nothing can prove to me that you do. What I can say, however, is that you emit signals, gestural and verbal for the most part, from which, by analogy with those I emit, I can deduce that you think and feel just as I do. Sooner or later, Turing argues, it will be possible to program a machine to respond to all stimuli with signals as convincing as those emitted by a human being. By what rights, then, can we reject its bona fides as a thinker?

The test that Turing devised to implement his proposed criterion involves a human examiner and two subjects—one of them human, the other a computer—each in a separate room and thus isolated from the other two. The examiner, who communicates with the two subjects by typing on a computer keyboard, bombards them with questions intended to allow him to determine which is the human and which is the machine. For example, he might ask his subjects about the taste of blueberry pie, or their earliest memories of Christmas, or their erotic preferences, and so forth; alternatively, he might ask them to perform mathematical calculations that a computer would normally perform more quickly than a human could. Anything is fair game—even the most intimate or the most off-the-wall questions; Zen koans are a classic means of creating confusion. Meanwhile, each subject tries to convince the examiner that he, or it, is the human being. One of them does this in good faith, the other by recourse to the thousand and one tricks contained in its programs—for example, by deliberately erring in its calculations. In the end, the examiner must render his verdict. If he is wrong, the machine wins, and, Turing argues, one has no choice but to admit that the machine was thinking. If a spiritualist wants to maintain that what the machine has demonstrated is not *really* human thought, the burden of proof, says Turing, is now on him.

Phil loved the Turing Test, as Turing's thought experiment came to be called. As someone who prided himself on his ability to throw sand in the eyes of any psychiatrist who crossed his path, he would have been thrilled to play the role of the machine. He subjected his friends to endless variations on this theme, notably in the course of those complicated telephone conversations where they had to prove they were who they said they were.

The novel he wrote during his honeymoon with Nancy—they married in 1966—takes up the theme of robot intelligence in earnest. Setting the action of *Do Androids Dream of Electric Sheep?* in 1992, twenty-five years in the future, Dick describes a world in which the production of androids has advanced to such a point that there are as many different types as there were models of car in the United States during the 1960s. The androids are deployed mainly in the Mars colonization effort, and some are rather rudimentary—simple mechanical tools with human faces or else fake families of neighbors designed to make the colonists, scattered across the Martian wastelands, feel less isolated and alone. For a modest sum, you can buy an entire family of Smiths or Scruggs and have them installed next door to you: George, the father, steps out every morning in his bathrobe onto the front steps to pick up the newspaper and on weekends mows the lawn, while his wife, Fran, puts blueberry pies in the oven all day long and their two kids, Bob and Pat, throw sticks to be fetched by Merton the German shepherd, who comes as an optional accessory. Though they can produce only a dozen or so preprogrammed replies, these machines can at least give you the feeling that there are people around. Besides, the manufacturers point out, would you really be more involved with actual human neighbors?

But androids like those are strictly low-end merchandise, and people who can afford to do so go in for the most sophisticated models, the kind that can't be told apart from real humans. So long as these perfect imitations keep to their place and perform the tasks assigned to them, everything is fine. But every now and then, some of them rise up against their owners and flee Mars for Earth, where they try to live free. They are dangerous, and it becomes the job of specially commissioned bounty hunters (which in Ridley Scott's film adaptation of Dick's novel became the eponymous "blade runners") to track them down and destroy them. It's difficult, nerve-racking work, and the bounty hunters live in constant fear of making a mistake and "retiring" a human instead of an android. To minimize the risks, they submit suspected androids to tests that seem to combine the Turing Test, standard Psych 101 personality inventories, and that peculiarly American and long-discredited institution the lie detector. The problem is, the methods quickly become outdated, as the manufacturers of androids keep improving their models by incorporating the test parameters into the androids' computerized brain units.

Thus, he began with the proposition that the best-equipped androids of the 1992 model year would be capable of passing the Turing or any other test. He was not, however, about to welcome the androids into the human community, as Turing said one would have to do when a machine finally managed to pass his test, and so he did something that Turing would have considered cheating—exactly the sort of cheap trick that spiritualists were known to drag out when pushed against the wall: he added a new criterion, another ability that a subject would have to demonstrate in order to qualify as human.

This criterion was empathy—what Saint Paul called "charity" and considered the greatest of the three theological virtues. Phil, who liked to speak to God in Latin, preferred the term *caritas*, but whatever name it went by—empathy, *caritas*, or *agape*—it came down to the same thing: respect for the Golden Rule, for the commandment to "love thy neighbor as thyself"; the capacity to put yourself in the other person's place, to desire his happiness, to suffer with him and, if necessary, in his stead.

Turing would surely have found this additional criterion laughable, and with good reason. He would have pointed out that plenty of humans were incapable of charity and that in theory nothing prevented someone from programming a machine to carry out behaviors that one would normally attribute to charitable feelings.

But Phil was not the kind of man who, once the line in the sand had been drawn, was content to stand astride it spouting pious humanistic platitudes. On the contrary, his job, he felt, was to keep pushing that line forward and to ask the difficult questions that ensued, and it was precisely this attitude that turned a science fiction thriller like *Do*

Androids Dream of Electric Sheep? into a cybernetic theological tract of truly dizzying implications.

The first question that Dick grapples with is the following: If the simulacrum is the opposite of the human being, what is the opposite of empathy? Cruelty, pride, disdain? Those were merely effects. The source of all evil, he thought, was withdrawal into the self, into one's shell—a symptom, in psychiatric terms, of schizophrenia. The issue, then, was the troubling resemblance between an "android" personality and the "schizoid" state, which Jung describes as a permanent constriction of emotion. A schizoid thinks more than he feels. His comprehension of the world and of himself is purely intellectual and abstract, his awareness an atomistic aggregation of a number of disparate elements that never cohere into an emotion or even truly into a *real* thought. A schizoid speed freak would never say, "I need to take amphetamines in order to hold a conversation with someone," but rather, "I am receiving signals from nearby organisms, but I cannot produce my own signals unless my batteries are recharged." (Phil claimed to have heard someone utter this sentence, but it is possible he said it himself.) The schizoid is the kind of person who, like Jack Isidore, the protagonist of Dick's mainstream novel *Confessions of a Crap Artist*, can never quite shake the thought that his body is 90 percent water or that what he thinks of as his body is actually just a survival module for his genes. Whereas most people encounter the world through their feelings, apprehend these feelings through their thoughts, describe these thoughts in sentences, and use words to form those sentences, the schizoid spends his time endlessly combining letters and numbers—twenty-six letters if he is human or, if the schizoid is a machine, two numbers, zero and one. The schizoid does not even believe that he thinks; for him, cogitation is a matter of activating his neurons. But if he thinks about that, he will say that in fact his neurons are not activating but rather following the laws of organic chemistry. This must be what an intelligent machine thinks or believes it thinks: it is in any case the kind of thought that can be programmed into it and filed in the application folder called "Reflexive consciousness." In sum, the schizoid thinks like a machine. Phil would have been thrilled to have learned that one of the first artificial brains capable of passing a not too demanding version of the Turing Test was a program developed at MIT called "Parry," which simulated a paranoiac. There was no magic to it: like a psychoanalyst, Parry replies to all questions with other questions or repeats them. One wag proposed that without too much trouble the program could be rigged up to produce a flawless simulation of catatonia.

For the Blade Runner, the problem with such tests—what makes them so untrustworthy and therefore so agonizing to administer—is that even though schizoids think like machines, they nevertheless are human. Phil knew this firsthand, torn as he was between his keen need to empathize with others and the powerful paranoid tendencies that made it impossible to. These two poles of empathy and paranoia stood, in his mind, for good and evil; they were his Jekyll and Hyde, and thus he knew exactly what Saint Paul meant when he said that "the good that I would I do not: but the evil which I would not, that I do."

Phil delighted in having found in Nancy an empathetic spouse who provided him with warmth, joy, and attention and who had saved him from the clutches of a woman he considered schizoid—a hating machine who had made him, in turn, schizoid and full of hate, locking them both in a nightmare of self-involvement and mutual mistrust. Nevertheless, he was honest enough to recognize that he might not have been an innocent victim at all and if Anne was crazy, then it might have been he who had awakened the madness within her. He knew that Anne had suffered as much if not more than he had, and partly because of him. If she was the crazy one and not he, the principle of charity he had been making so much of demanded that, instead of vilifying her, he should put himself in her place and help her. As the church might say, sin is a sickness of the spirit, and those who are sick are to be comforted in their distress. Christ had come to redeem us, but most of all he had come to heal us. If the schizophrenic suffers, then perhaps so does the android. In Turingesque terms, if a computer program permits an android to simulate suffering convincingly, then how can we refuse to believe it is genuine and withhold our sympathy? Therein lies the second question.

It is the one Rick Deckard, the Blade Runner, faces when, for reasons more erotic than evangelical or philosophical, he comes to feel empathy for his quarry, or more specifically for one among them. It doesn't help matters that the androids' manufacturers have played a particularly vicious trick on their high-end models, implanting in their brain units a store of artificial memories that make them think they are human. They can recall their childhood, have humanlike emotions, experience moments of déjà vu. Not only can others not tell they are not human beings but even they believe they are human. They simply don't know they are different. And when they are suspected of being androids and are forced to submit to one of the Blade Runner's tests, they react as any human might, with a mixture of resentment at being forced to prove their humanity and fear that they may fail in their attempt. "You'll tell me the truth, right?" one of Dick's characters asks, while under suspicion. "If I'm an android, you'll tell me?" As it happens, that one passes the test, but naturally the greatest pathos in the book arises not from the moments of human self-confirmation but from those of android self-discovery, when the conscious machine that thought it was human finally realizes who, or what, it is. These moments offer a view into a void that lies within all of us, an experience of absolute horror that can neither be surmounted nor forgotten and that renders anything monstrously possible.

If empathy defines what it means to be human, then one day androids will be given this ability. If to be human means to have a sense of the sacred, then they will believe in God, will sense His presence in their souls, and with all their circuits firing will sing His praises. They will have feelings and doubts, they will know anguish and fear. They will express their fears in books that they will write. And who will be able to say whether their empathy is real, whether their piety, their feelings, their doubts, and their fears are genuine or merely convincing simulations? If the terrifying cry of an android at discovering its identity is simply a programmed response to certain verbal stimuli that is produced by the proper activation of a certain number of bits (a description that perfectly fits the workings of the human brain, though of course there it is a matter of organic cells rather than bits of plastic or metal) does that change (a) everything, (b) nothing, or (c) something, except that we don't know what?

Circle your answer.

As the Blade Runner notes with a certain unease, the best possible disguise for an android would be that of a Blade Runner.

Or, thought Phil, that of a science fiction writer.

CHAPTER 12

PORTRAIT OF THE ARTIST AS A HERETIC

Those days everything had to be new—France had its New Wave in cinema and its *nouveau roman;* America had its New Frontier. And if something couldn't be new, then at least it had to have a new name. The men who picked up your garbage were now calling themselves sanitation engineers and your barber was now a hair stylist. Not to be outdone, science fiction tried to become "speculative fiction," which didn't actually mean very much, or "new thing," which meant nothing at all, but at least said it with more panache.

The "new thing" had its most ardent champion in Harlan Ellison, who, by dint of hard work and force of will, had transformed himself from a mere fan into something of an impresario and a master of public relations. Ellison had big plans for science fiction and decided that something needed to be done to celebrate its elevation from a retrograde genre fit only for the likes of army privates and office drones, into the hip redoubt of inventors, iconoclasts, and avant-gardists. His manifesto cum SF anthology *Dangerous Vision,* the vehicle for his ambition, was going to revolutionize the bourgeois and moribund institution of American letters, which seemed to have spent the socially and intellectually turbulent 1960s on some other planet. Establishment stars—

writers like Gore Vidal and Thomas Pynchon—would come knocking on his door, hat in hand, asking to join the ranks of writers like Norman Spinrad and Samuel Delany and other members of Ellison's literary shock troops.

Ellison's glorious dream for SF never materialized, yet for that brief moment in history when everything seemed possible (including the notion that stories set in the future would perforce constitute the future of literature), it gave the helots something to live for. Believing that they had won their place in the pantheon, the thirty-two writers whom Ellison assembled into his celebratory volume wrote their short stories the way one might sit for an official portrait intended for posterity. Ellison, as master of ceremonies, wrote a rambling, effusive introduction to each piece, a mixture of hagiography and talk-show hype. And the writers were each asked to append to their contributions an afterword in which they could say whatever they liked—pay homage to their literary forebears if they so chose, display their modesty or vanity—in short, step into the limelight.

Few writers can resist this kind of temptation, and those who do are generally banking on the greater eloquence of silence. Contacted toward the end of 1965 by an enthusiastic Ellison, Phil was thus delighted to learn that if there was one writer whom the anthologist absolutely had to have among his band of dangerous visionaries, it was Phil Dick. Needless to say, he took great pleasure in rendering his self-portrait.

To read the afterword to "Faith of Our Fathers," Dick's contribution to the anthology, is to discover a man of happy contradictions: a sociable recluse who likes snuff and hallucinogens and whose tastes in music encompass Heinrich Schütz and the Grateful Dead, a captivating raconteur who holds forth to culture-deprived hippies on the medieval Irish Gnostic John Scotus Erigena, an unregenerate lady's man blessed with a very young, very shy, and very accommodating wife. The tormented denizen of Point Reyes Station who, under the harsh dictates of Palmer Eldritch and Anne Rubenstein, had thought he had lost his mind was now, on the threshold of his forties, a debonair guru. He took psychedelics, he let it be understood, but only so that he could confirm firsthand his theological theories and those of his glorious predecessors, whom he had begun to quote at every opportunity, transforming even the most modest science fiction novel into a patchwork of epigrams borrowed from Boethius, Master Eckhart, and Saint Bonaventure. He affected to be a veteran acid user in spite of the fact that he had never taken LSD again after that single terrifying experience, and he continued to maintain, as Timothy Leary had, that to follow a religious life in the twentieth century without LSD was like studying astronomy with the naked eye. He loved to tell people how Leary had phoned him one day from John Lennon's hotel room in Canada while the Beatles were on their North American tour. That's right, Phil said solemnly, delighting in the incredulous, fascinated reaction this tidbit always provoked from his listeners—Leary had called *from John Lennon's hotel room*. He and Lennon had just finished reading *The Three Stigmata of Palmer Eldritch* and couldn't contain their enthusiasm. That's it! That's it exactly! the stoned Lennon had managed to wheeze, after dragging himself across the floor to get to the phone. He was already talking about making the novel into a film, *the* psychedelic film of all time, the visual corollary to the album he was then recording. Caught off guard, Phil hadn't had the time to think up one of his tests to verify that he really was speaking to Leary and Lennon and not a couple of jokers pretending to be them. But when *Sgt. Pepper's Lonely Hearts Club Band* came out the following year, he recognized the title, as well as the paean to lysergic acid— "Lucy in the Sky with Diamonds"—that Lennon had talked about.

This episode left Phil with an aggravated tendency to name-drop, along with the idea that he exerted a special kind of influence—an underground, almost occult power. And as a matter of fact, the adjective *Phildickian*—a term used to describe strange situations or a twisted yet accurate perspective on the world—was becoming a counterculture shibboleth, at least in some circles, as his reputation spread beyond the small world of science fiction devotees. In their crudely printed magazines, underground writers and artists like rock critic Paul Williams and cartoonists Robert Crumb and Art Spiegelman spoke of Dick as one of the great unsung geniuses of the day.

The new role suited him. For one thing, it put some distance between him and his dangerous and terrifying religious obsessions; now these were simply his professional trademark, a part of his legend. God was, as they used to say, his thing. No one challenged him on what all agreed was his exclusive territory or reproached him for venturing into it, provided that he did so as a saboteur, a bomb thrower, a shatterer of traditions. He preferred not to recall the miserable weeks he spent writing *The Three Stigmata of Palmer Eldritch* or the abject terror he experienced when his acid trip hurled him back down into the dark, pitiless world of that novel; yet when people spoke of it as his "black mass" and compared it to Scriabin's work of that title, the chilling Piano Sonata no. 9 in F Major, he loved the flattery. He also loved being told that had he lived several centuries earlier the Inquisition would have burned him at the stake ten times over. He had recently discovered Borges, who, along with Tolkien and M. C. Escher, was riding the crest of worldwide acclaim. Phil greatly admired Borges's slick and mischievous dilettantism, the way he treated theology as a branch of fantastic literature, a seductive and ultimately inconsequential intellectual game. Phil tried to come up with Borgesian paradoxes of his own (America, he liked to say, harbors two superstitions—that God doesn't exist and that there's actually a difference between different brands of cigarettes) and imitate Borges's tongue-in-cheek casuistry. He even went so far as to undertake—along with Roger Zelazny, a fellow science fiction writer—an elaborate religious fantasy, *Deus Irae*, which they took ten years to complete, only to realize that what they had come up with made absolutely no sense at all.

Phil was not quite the detached intellectual that he would have liked to appear, however; the literary heretic was also a conscience-ridden parishioner who quaked at the idea of hell, of which his acid trip, he felt, had merely been a preview. If someone spoke of the biblical Apocalypse as allegory, not to be taken literally any more than, say, the Creation stories of the Book of Genesis, he would shake his head in rueful dismay, like a man whose fate it was To Know the Truth while his fellow men consoled themselves with false hopes and comforting illusions. Phil wanted to love God but he feared the devil even more. People forgave him his gothic religiosity, regarding it as an amusing provocation, one more example of his legendary deviancy. And in Phil's vaguely Buddhistic/agnostic milieu it was easy to be deviant. You didn't have to profess adherence to Pelagianism or Albigensianism; all you had to do was let people know you were a practicing Christian. It took Nancy some time to understand, back before his marriage to Anne had been annulled, that Phil wasn't joking when he told her how troubled he was that they were living together in sin, which meant that he couldn't take Holy Communion. More than his eventual divorce, he felt, this exclusion from the rite of the Eucharist—his sole protection in the battle for his soul being waged within him and all around him—was his punishment for the sacrilege he had committed in parodying the rite of communion in his "black mass." His nostalgia for the sacramental life led him to come up with various substitutes, none of them odder than the "empathy box," the device around which the major subplot of *Do Androids Dream of Electric Sheep?* revolves.

The empathy box is the principal ritual instrument in the quasi-religious cult to which Rick Deckard belongs, along with almost everyone else in the year 2021. Like a small television set with a pair of handles on its sides, which the viewer grasps while looking into the screen, the empathy box allows the follower of a cult called Mercerism to witness the constantly repeated scene of an old man, about whom we know nothing except that his name is Mercer, climbing painfully up the side of a mountain, pelted with rocks as he makes his slow and arduous ascent. To practice Mercerism is not merely to watch this scene unfold but to participate in it: it is *your* feet that drag their way up the gravel-strewn mountainside, *your* flesh that bruises under the hail of stones, *your* soul that bears a crushing sadness while you remain, inexplicably, joyful. You become one with Mercer and with all the others who at the same moment, on Earth and on the colonized planets, are also grasping the handles of their boxes. You sense their presence as they, too, suffer and exult. You incorporate all the others into yourself. The fusion with Mercer—a combination of a Via Dolorosa and a communion of saints—is the diametrical opposite of the "translation" that Palmer Eldritch inflicts on those who take the drug Chew-Z. Fusion with Mercer does not isolate but unifies; it does not damn but redeems. And it is constantly renewed. On reaching the summit of the mountain, Mercer falls to the ground in the throes of death; carried to the tomb, he then rises again. "Inevitably," marvels one character. "And us with him. So we're eternal, too."

Toward the end of the novel, the truth of Mercerism is challenged when Buster Friendly, a talk-show host who seems to appear live on television more hours a day than there are in a week, airs an exposé claiming that Mercerism is fraud, an opiate for the masses, perhaps fabricated by the government itself. Friendly has pictures and testimony proving that the scene on the mountain was shot in a studio; Mercerism is just another television show. As for Mercer himself, people used to wonder whether he was a man or a universal archetype put on Earth by some inscrutable cosmic dictate. Buster Friendly reveals him to be a mere Hollywood bit actor fallen on hard times— little more than a skid row alcoholic. The man happened to stumble into the role of a lifetime. All he had to do was get bombarded by stones made of rubber while ketchup ran down his face. The only drawback was that he had to lay off the booze during filming.

Buster Friendly's revelations would seem to spell ruin for humanity's religious hopes and dreams. And yet . . . they don't. In a truly magnificent scene, Dick's version of the walk to Emmaus, Mercer appears before one of his followers and calmly explains that everything Buster Friendly has said is true—everything, even the business about the drinking. Yet that doesn't change a thing, he says. Not a thing. "Because you're still here and I'm still here."

With this affirmation of blind faith in the face of all evidence, Dick staked his position in a debate that was roiling public opinion, or at least the segment of it that cared about matters of religious belief. The discovery in 1947 of the Dead Sea Scrolls had given rise to the scandalous notion that, if a sizable portion of the teachings attributed by the synoptic Gospels to Jesus could also be found in documents antedating his birth, those teachings might not be as original as previously thought and Jesus himself might be merely one of those garden-variety itinerant preachers Palestine was teeming with back in those days. Jesus, in other words, might well have been a fake. Nonbelievers who followed the debate believed the Dead Sea Scrolls offered a strong argument against Christianity. The clergy, naturally, were deeply distressed. Some among them came to question their faith, including James A. Pike, the Episcopal bishop of California.

An erstwhile lawyer and a gifted speaker, Pike was an important public figure, an exemplar of the progressive prelate. He had fought for civil rights, marching alongside Martin Luther King Jr. in Selma, and was a friend of the Kennedy clan. He oversaw the introduction of rock 'n' roll into the mass and presided over the completion of San Francisco's Grace Cathedral, on whose stained glass windows parishioners could behold not just the usual panoply of saints but also the realistic likenesses of Albert Einstein, Thurgood Marshall, and John Glenn. Pike had appeared on the cover of both *Time* and *Newsweek* magazines and had his own nationally syndicated weekly television show. The height of his ecclesiastical chic came when he was tried for heresy: he had made audacious claims—which he audaciously defended—about the existence of the Holy Spirit, who in his opinion had vanished from circulation around the time of the apostles.

Maren Hackett had met Pike in the fall of 1965, when she was head of a Bay Area feminist organization, and they became lovers. Not long after, Nancy and Phil were invited to dinner at the apartment where Hackett and Pike carried on their relationship in secret—at the time, the bishop was still married, though separated. Phil did not look forward to the dinner; he didn't like venturing onto unfamiliar turf and Pike's fame intimidated him. But by the end of the evening he was rolling on the floor, laughing, babbling, completely swept up in the good vibrations emanating from his mother-in-law's lover. Jim and Phil—they were on a first-name basis from that day on—began a conversation that would last for three years. Both unregenerate intellectuals, they loved controversy and trading volleys of learned citations. Like a couple of medieval realists, they believed that words were things and that any idea to which one could give verbal form must necessarily have a correspondent in reality. Deeply respectful of the printed word and deaf to the notion that books often contradicted one another, they had a tendency to give credence to whatever they happened to be reading and a talent for persuading others to share their beliefs. And as they were voracious readers, their beliefs often changed. Other people found their inconstancy irritating, but it seemed perfectly natural to them.

During their verbal jousts, Jim brought to bear the authority of someone accustomed to the pulpit and to public debate and a theological arsenal that was both more complete than Phil's and better organized. But Phil, ever the Rat, did more than hold his own: Jim was impressed by the traps set by this obscure writer who dressed like a bum and could probably run circles around the entire Council of Bishops. Since they were both fond of contradiction and neither could stand it when they happened to agree about something, they egged each other on in their heresies. In the end, this compulsion for heterodoxy would be of less consequence for Phil than for the bishop, who was actually the more fervent of the two, though the subtler in his thinking.

Pike's obsession at the time was eschatology, particularly the great foment in this branch of theological thinking that the Middle East had seen at the dawn of our era, and he gave Phil what amounted to a course of study in Gnosticism. The Western world, it seems, had come within a hair's breadth of turning out Gnostic rather than Christian, and, to hear Pike tell it, the result was regrettable, as far as knowing the truth was concerned. He gave passionate accounts of the tormented absolutist doctrines that Christian orthodoxy had so successfully managed to silence that many of them are known to us solely through the hostile commentaries of Saint Jerome. Christianity was a religion of dissent to begin with, and the Gnostics were the dissidents within this dissent—the noble losers, the ultimate Punks, a source of perennial fascination to freethinking theologians. How could Phil not fall in love with spiritual masters whose teachings derived from the intuition that something was not right in the world? To them this world was both a prison and an illusion, some demiurge's idea of a cruel joke. Only those who comprehended these dark truths and struggled to remain awake and aware in the face of illusion had any chance of emerging from the shadows in which the demiurge holds us captive and of attaining the true and divine light. Phil realized that he had been a Gnostic all his life without knowing it. He understood Gnosticism as only someone who has inhabited the tomb-world can, yet he also wanted to believe there was a remedy. And that remedy, he thought, the path toward truth and life, could be none other than Jesus Christ.

At this point in the debate, the bishop must have felt like a father who has to explain to his child that there is no Santa Claus. He and Maren had been going to London every two or three months to meet with John Allegro, one of the two British delegates to the international team that had been put together to study and publish the Dead Sea Scrolls. Pike returned from these trips both troubled and exhilarated, a bearer of scandalous truths. According to the latest revelations, he reported with tremulous delight, the Gospels were a fraud and Jesus merely an epigone of an Essenian sect around whom a bunch of clever Jews had managed to construct a colossal scam.

Confronted with these revelations—"scientific discoveries," the bishop assured him—Phil found himself in the position of defender of the faith, a role that both satisfied his love of paradox and accorded with his deepest hopes and beliefs. He responded to his friend's assaults as Mercer himself might have done: even if what Pike was saying was true, he told him, it didn't change a thing. Pike reminded him of the English professor who argues that *Hamlet* wasn't really written by William Shakespeare but by someone *named* Shakespeare. Did that make *Hamlet* any less profound a work of literature? By the same token, Phil explained, if you believe that Christ is the Son of God, that he was resurrected and had defeated death, and then someone comes along and proves to you that he was actually some ecclesiastical subaltern who may not even have existed in the first place, well, did that make the Gospels any less true, metaphysically speaking? Pike was right to seek out the truth, Phil told him, but he should have known that Christ was the truth. Otherwise, all Pike was saying was that he didn't believe in Christ—in other words, that he'd learned nothing.

And indeed, the bishop had to admit that he was no longer sure he believed in the religion he had taken a vow to serve. And this troubled him.

The high point of this period in Phil's life came on mushroom day. Pike had just returned from London with "top secret" news that the Dominicans at the Jerusalem Bible School were hoping to suppress and that even the usually outspoken Allegro was afraid of making public. The members of the sect whose teachings Jesus, or his inventors, had merely popularized had apparently been in the practice of cultivating a certain kind of mushroom in their caves above the Dead Sea and from it had made a kind of bread as well as a broth, which they ate and drank together. Here were the true origins of the Eucharist. But the real bombshell was the news that the mushroom in question was *Amanita muscaria*—a hallucinogen that was the object of a fertility cult stretching way back into antiquity and that was being still used by some Siberian tribes (whose numbers it had helped decimate). Christianity was merely another instance of this cult, and a latecomer at that: the New Testament, which served as a cover for the cult's teachings, designed to placate the civil and religious authorities of the day, was, in effect, a cryptogamic cryptogram.

The bishop complained that from now on when he conducted Holy Communion, it would be with the knowledge that Christianity had been about tripping on psychedelics.

And that Jesus, interrupted Phil, before bursting into laughter, was a drug trafficker. Then he added more soberly that this was something he had long suspected. Yet it didn't diminish in the least his faith in Him.

In February 1966, Pike's twenty-year-old son killed himself with a hunting rifle. There were lots of theories as to why—that he felt overshadowed by his father, or was in love with his father's mistress, or had discovered he was gay, or had had a bad acid trip.

Phil wrote Pike a letter of condolence:

> I have a feeling that in the instant after death everything real will become apparent; all the cards will be turned face-up, the game will be over, and we will see clearly what we have suspected only . . . and unfounded suspicions will be erased. . . . Now it is a mystery to me, a black glass. . . . Behold, Paul says. I tell you a mystery. We shall not all sleep. Or something like that. I believe that; in fact it is virtually all I believe. But even that, unproved, will have to wait for its test, like everything else. But even if I'm wrong and Lucretius is right, I'll be content; I'll have no choice.

But the bishop couldn't wait until the instant after death to discover what was on the other side of those cards and he no longer had confidence in Saint Paul; he needed to find out now, and for himself. Consumed with guilt and ready to do anything to assuage it, he and Maren sought out assorted psychics and spiritualists and, the summer after Jim Junior's death, started telling people that the young man had come back. He had spoken to them and forgiven them, they said, their eyes shining with newfound joy; he wanted them to be happy. Pike, to whom nothing happened that either hadn't come from a book or wouldn't end up in a book, even contracted to write about his experiences with the Other Side. He continued to question the validity of Christianity. *Validity* was the word he used, but Phil found it absurd— it was flabby and fashionable and hardly reflected the battle being fought within his friend's heart. The bishop was counting on Jim Junior to put an end to his doubts, to tell him, with all the authority of a denizen of the Other Side, whether Jesus was merely a preacher hawking the crazy ideas of a band of Middle Eastern dopeheads or truly the Son of God. The whole thing was insanity, Phil told him. It was lunacy to use his son's death the way one might consult a reference work to settle a question of historical fact. But Phil also knew that under the same conditions he would do exactly as Pike was doing, that all his life he, too, had been looking for the Ultimate Reference, and that Pike's quest had nothing to do with historical truth. It was about having faith or losing it—in other words, it was a matter of life and death. For the bishop, losing Christ meant losing everything, this despite the fact that he was already talking, like a business executive coolly weighing the advantages of changing jobs, about leaving the clergy and going into what he called the "private sector."

Pike persuaded Phil and Nancy to join him in a séance with a medium in Santa Barbara whom someone had recommended to him. After some hesitation, Phil agreed to attend and even to take notes that Pike could use for his book. He found it painful to see so brilliant a mind succumb to ideas that were patently silly. Bad money chases out good, he thought: the bishop believed in his son's posthumous manifestations as devoutly as the disciples—or Phil himself—believed in the resurrection of Christ. Who was he to declare Pike's beliefs unfounded or to brush off similar judgments with regard to his own?

Mediums, seers, and parapsychologists in general rely on intuition, cues unconsciously provided by their clients, bits of public information that can sound like revelations when cleverly presented, and of course a good measure of bluff. When they're wrong, they finesse it; when they hit the mark, they've won. Still, anyone who has ever consulted a medium knows that even after one has sifted through all the plausible explanations for his or her clairvoyance, there always remains a residue for which there is no explanation—some small detail, not by itself very significant, that leaves one wondering how the medium knew about it or even managed to deduce it. It's the sort of thing that troubles one but that one then forgets about. That day, through the intervention of the medium, the shade of Jim Junior made reference to a private joke between Phil and Nancy about the owner of a restaurant in Berkeley whom they suspected of being a KGB agent. For weeks afterward, Phil, trying to rationalize how a medium from Santa Barbara could know about a private joke between a couple from San Rafael, figured that maybe the restaurant owner really was a KGB agent—and that the medium was too. Then he forgot all about it. Pike and Maren hadn't even noticed the detail, moved as they were by hearing the spirit of Jim Junior tell them again that he forgave them and wanted them to be happy. But, alas, on the subject of the "validity" of Christianity, the spirit kept silent.

Several weeks later, Maren Hackett, who was suffering from cancer and was worried that Pike was going to leave her, committed suicide, taking a deadly cocktail of Seconal, Amytal, and Dexamyl—pills that she and Pike and Phil were well acquainted with. Phil thought about all the times he had quietly helped himself to some in Jim and Maren's medicine cabinet.

From the beginning of Phil's relationship with Maren, she had been the rock, the embodiment of the strength and hope that Christian virtues can impart to those who practice them. With her death, he wondered whether the wheel had turned once more, whether the favorable cycle had finished and the moment of happiness that he and those around him had so briefly known had come to an end. Darkness was spreading across the passionately carefree sixties. Ever since LSD had become illegal, one heard more and more about bad trips; it was as though Palmer Eldritch himself, taking advantage of the drug's illegality, had set up shop at the corner of Haight and Ashbury, the cradle of hippie culture. The locals marched in the streets, through Golden Gate Park, beating on drums and intoning the ancient sound of "Om" in the hopes of chasing away the bad vibes. All in vain. People were dying now from bad drugs. It was rumored that the Mafia had taken over the drug trade and was peddling all kinds of adulterated wares. People tried to pretend that nothing was happening, but Phil could not. He knew that the worm was in the apple.

His own world, however, had never seemed so stable. Now forty years old, he was heavier, wiser, and more circumspect than ever before. The storms seemed to have receded. The woman he loved was carrying his child. They had moved into a larger house. He was beginning to become known; foreign editions of his works were starting to appear. With the royalties, he bought himself an extravagant gift, the kind of thing that a man who has finally settled down might dream of owning: an enormous lockable, fireproof metal file cabinet into which he could put all the treasures he had been dragging around with him since he and his mother had parted ways: manuscripts, letters, valuable LPs, stamp and comic book collections, and rare issues of science fiction magazines.

The day this monster was delivered—it weighed seven hundred pounds without the drawers and took up an entire wall of his study—Phil felt a twinge of anxiety amid his delight. He knew that once you've bought something like this you never move again, you've dropped anchor. Then he remembered Wagner's *Siegfried*, how Fafner the dragon has to die and lose his hoarded gold, and he found himself consumed with the opposite anxiety, not of acquiring too much but of losing it all. While trying to help the deliverymen with the safe he managed to give himself a hernia, which he interpreted as a sign of divine rebuke. Don't amass wealth, God was telling him. Everything you believe you own will be taken from you.

The *I Ching* had a similarly ominous message for him. *Ming I*, it said: the "darkening of the light."

It was at this moment that Ellison's anthology finally appeared. In the small world of science fiction, nobody talked about anything else. Ellison's hyperbolic introduction, which presented Dick as a dope-smoking genius who wrote his masterpieces while on acid, made him smile, but he had to admit he'd been more than complicit in fostering this myth. Then, acting on an impulse that no writer can resist, Phil reread "Faith of Our Fathers," the story he had contributed.

Set in a totalitarian world inspired by the works of Orwell and Hannah Arendt and by events of recent history, it was one of those Phil Dick specialties. In this world, televisions are equipped with cameras to make sure that people are watching, to allow the authorities to monitor each viewer's attentiveness and susceptibility to indoctrination by the Leader, whose august visage appears daily on the little screen in every living room—just the sort of technology the Nielsen ratings people would have loved to have. Then comes the day when someone, having ingested an illegal substance, sees not the face of the Absolute Benefactor of the People but something else, something horrible—a many-legged nightmare, an avatar of Palmer Eldritch. The man tells himself that what he's seeing must be a hallucination, but he also wonders, Phildickian hero that he is, if his hallucination isn't more real than reality itself. What happens subsequently confirms his suspicion. Having entered into contact with a resistance network, he learns that the drug responsible for his vision is not a hallucinogen but an antihallucinogen. The real hallucinogen is what everyone is taking without realizing it, for it is in the tap water. Under its influence people see the Leader with his handsome features, exuding peace and harmony. Only those who take the antidote, the lucidogen, as it were, see the Leader for what he is—protean in his hideousness, always monstrous in some new and different way. Eventually, the hero meets the Leader face-to-face and realizes that he is God, cruel and capricious, dangerous and terrible. And on that note of disturbing ambiguity the story ends.

"Faith of Our Fathers" is a horrific tale. While writing it, Phil felt a surge of pride. Reading it a year later, after the deaths of Jim Pike Jr. and Maren, he saw it differently. It was still horrific, but in a new and even more distressing way. All his tricks and hobbyhorses were on display: totalitarianism, the *idios kosmos* and the *koinos kosmos*, psychedelic drugs, Ultimate Reality, God. Here was the little world of Philip K. Dick in one neat package. All that was missing were the androids, the simulacra—and for good reason: the story was itself a simulacrum. Had some talented forger wanted to write "in the manner of Dick" or had some computer programmer come up with a software program capable of churning out Dick, the result would have been a story like this one.

Yet he, and not some computer, had written it. And he was real, authentic: Phil Dick and not an android that had taken his place, unbeknownst to everyone. Of that he was sure.

Yet he was also sure that were he an android he would come to the very same conclusion. That was exactly how androids thought. And he knew that the android, having thought that thought, would be struck with fear, if only because that is how he had been programmed.

None of this proved anything one way or the other, except that he, too, Philip K. Dick—or whoever he was—was afraid.

CHAPTER 13

AMONG THE LIVING DEAD

In the spring of 1967, Nancy gave birth to a baby girl whom they baptized with the Wagnerian-sounding name Isolde Freya and only ever called Isa. The baby's birth aggravated the tensions that Nancy's first moves toward independence had already provoked in their marriage. So long as Nancy stayed at home, reading the books that Phil chose for her, listening to the music coming out of his study as she waited patiently for him to emerge, he marveled at how alike their tastes were and let it be known that Nancy was the most empathetic person in the world. All this changed, however, when she found a part-time job and was no longer there all day to cater to him. Surprised and indignant, he couldn't get over this "desertion" or Nancy's own indignation at his reaction. The new baby should have eased the humiliation he felt at not being the family's sole breadwinner, at not being a young wife's entire world. But he proved to be even more jealous of his daughter than he had been of the outside world. He was afraid that Isa would supplant him in Nancy's heart and that Nancy would supplant him in Isa's. Accustomed to treating his young bride as a child, he offered advice culled from his vast pediatric experience, which consisted primarily of having had a twin baby sister who died of hunger, a tragedy he never went a day without mentioning. Nancy breastfed the baby. On the one hand he approved of this, his own mother not having breastfed either him or his sister. Yet he felt excluded by it as well, and, unable to compete with Nancy in this area, he came to regard each feeding as a provocation. He felt superfluous, and so, to even things up, he armed himself with baby bottles and fed Isa himself on the sly, holding her against his chest while telling her over and over that he was her daddy, that he loved her, and that he would never leave her. Isa responded to these double feedings and these anxiety-laden words of comfort by going on a hunger strike that, naturally, mortified her parents. The pediatrician told them the problem was too much tension in the household, not realizing that his commonsense assessment would send the father ricocheting between remorse and resentment. I'm hopelessly paranoid, Phil kept telling himself, and then, ten minutes later, he would be feeling sorry for himself for once again having married a crazy woman.

Phil went through his medicine cabinet and took pills by the handful, hoping to calm his nerves. He also took them to strengthen his resolve, to lift his spirits, and to cope with other people; he took them to fall asleep and to wake up, to work and to relax from his labors. People called him a drug addict, and not without reason, but his substance abuse did have its limits; although he extolled the virtues of LSD, he was terrified of it, and as far as marijuana was concerned, he was strictly a social smoker. He preferred prescription drugs, admiring their precision and the relative predictability of their effects, and he enjoyed all the possible combinations they afforded the connoisseur. In *Do Androids Dream of Electric Sheep?* he had equipped the American home of the future with a "mood organ," a device that hooked up to the user's nervous system and allowed him or her to select a particular mood from a huge catalog of affective states. You could program the device to make you wake up feeling bright and refreshed, ready to take on the world, like a character in a mattress commercial. When you had a fight with your spouse, you could choose between a depressant to calm you down and a stimulant to make you angry enough to win. And if you couldn't decide on a mood or simply didn't feel like dialing, you could select setting number 3, which stimulated your cerebral cortex so as to make you want to choose. Sophisticated users willing to experiment with the machine could design custom-made states of mind like "self-accusatory depression," perhaps to be followed by a salutary dose of "awareness of manifold possibilities."

Phil took pills in much the same way. A few amphetamines transformed him into a dazzling host for an entire evening; with a whole bottle, like the ones he had filched from the bishop's bathroom, he could write a novel in about two weeks, without sleeping. He knew he would pay for these episodes with long bouts of depression and psychotic symptoms—perception problems, memory loss, panic attacks, suicidal thoughts—but with the help of various sedatives and tranquilizers, he could always get over them, at least in theory. He knew that one day, at the bottom of one of these states, he would find Palmer Eldritch lying in wait for him, but that was the price you paid; it was part of the deal. He also knew—or he guessed, for who can know for sure?—that someday he would have to read the small print in the contract. It was too late, however, to back out; he had turned his body into a chemical cocktail shaker and from now on his problem was to find the chemicals that would allow him to face his daily existence, which even on good days called out for some kind of enhancer, plus another fix to manage the side effects.

He needed half a dozen or so doctors to keep his medicine cabinet stocked. Knowing exactly what drugs he wanted and what he had to say to get them, he convincingly described the symptoms that would trigger the appropriate prescription. And like any prescription junkie, he spread his purchases among as many pharmacies as possible, venturing out farther and farther from his neighborhood to get his prescriptions filled. Eventually, he was forced to buy drugs on the street, from dealers who knew perfectly well that, next to heroin junkies, speed freaks were the most dependent of drug addicts and hence the most vulnerable and the easiest to rip off. The uncertain quality of the product his street dealers purveyed played havoc with Phil's vaunted mastery of the art of combining drugs and was responsible, he thought, for the woodenness of his writing, an aspect that had struck him so forcefully when he reread "Faith of Our Fathers" that he now distrusted the whole idea of writing fiction. It was a trap, he felt, set by an invisible enemy so that everyone else might see what was already so tragically obvious to him: that he was washed up, a shadow of his former self, a simulacrum. His bouts of paranoia came more frequently now, and these, too, he attributed to the bad drugs and to the enemies who were selling them to him. That, at least, was how he saw things during his moments of lucidity. A favorite joke of his at the time was the one about the doctor whose patient comes to see him and says, "Doctor, someone is putting something in my food to make me paranoid."

As everyone knows, paranoiacs, too, have enemies, and Phil, at this point in his life, had real troubles. Despite his modest income, he had managed to rack up back taxes, and the IRS came after him hard. For a man who feared authority in any form and was all too susceptible to guilt, the IRS's pursuit seemed to spell catastrophe. It didn't help matters that the audit came in the spring of 1968, not long after the leftist magazine *Ramparts* had published a petition he had signed, along with hundreds of other American writers and publishers, calling on their fellow citizens to refuse to pay the federal income taxes that were funding the war in Vietnam. Coincidence or not, it was enough to awaken familiar terrors: the CIA, the FBI, and J. Edgar Hoover himself were after his scalp, or, even worse, his soul, and they were using the IRS as their cover. The dealers who sold him speed were in cahoots with them as well, he figured, and probably so were his doctors. He was being brainwashed. Soon he would turn into a right-thinking citizen. He would love Big Brother, who now, in his most recent avatar, was none other than his old enemy Richard Nixon. He would hate hippies and freaks and everyone else on the fringes of society. He would no longer believe in God but would put his trust instead in John Birch and Gayelord Hauser. And the most horrible thing of all was that he would think he was happy. He would be well adjusted and mentally balanced, the very opposite of what he was now. Soon neither he nor any of his close friends would have any recollection of the person he now was, since they, too, would have been brainwashed or replaced by androids. Or maybe he himself had *already* been replaced and the android who thought he was Phil Dick had been implanted with these anxieties for the sake of realism, so that he could continue to believe that he was his old self. Meanwhile, convinced that the stories he was writing came from the depths of his soul, he would turn out the books he'd been programmed to write by a state propaganda apparatus that used a veneer of subversiveness to spread hidden messages designed to inflict the masses with a crippling disaffection. Maybe without his realizing it, and without his readers realizing it, his books were spewing out the same subliminal message over and over again: Go ahead, fellas, off the gooks, fry 'em in napalm, rat on your dopehead neighbors. This would certainly explain the disgust he felt at his latest literary efforts. Or maybe his enemies were persecuting him because, merely by following the thread of his own imagination, he had unwittingly discovered and divulged some vital secret that could topple the current administration.

He started rummaging through the pile of paperbacks with their lurid dust jackets—his complete works—trying to find the secret that his hyperlucid ignorance had put him onto. His suspicions ultimately fell on "Faith of Our Fathers," the story in which the government spikes the tap water with hallucinogens to keep its citizens from realizing what horrible monster is ruling over them. He also had his doubts about *The Penultimate Truth*, a novel he had written several years earlier. In that book, human beings live underground, like modern-day Niebelungs, having been made to believe that a chemical war is raging on the planet's surface, and all the while a handful of unscrupulous leaders, experts at creating special effects for television, have the world all to themselves. What proof was there that the images of Vietnam that appeared on the television screen weren't cooked up in a studio with blank bullets, scale models, and ketchup? Who was to say that Vietnam even existed? That *anything* existed outside of this room where he now stood and beheld, in the mirror on the wall, an overweight and prematurely aging man who he knew could only be himself.

———

In *Do Androids Dream of Electric Sheep*, Dick had invented the word *kipple* to designate an entropic state of decomposition and chaos toward which all things naturally tend. Now his own life was becoming kipple. Moreover, what did it mean to say "my life" when he was no longer sure that this life was his to begin with, or even that he was alive?

There was only one thing to do—go back to the typewriter, to the row of letters, QWERTYUIOP, arrayed across the keyboard and start another book—his thirty-second or his thirty-fifth, he couldn't remember. What he did know was that he had to write it to make some money and that if he didn't—if he didn't, what then? He would have to overcome his disgust at his style, which had become so dry he feared the words would shrivel and crumble into dust on the page. His syntax was flat, repetitive, purely logical—the syntax of an android. His vocabulary had grown increasingly abstract, cold, and predictable. There was nothing sensual about it, nothing that might express the material, carnal substance of the world. There was no life in what he wrote; there was nothing but sentences, and not even sentences, only words, and not even words, only letters, which, poured mechanically onto the page, came together more by reflex rather than by design, the way members of a fumigated termite colony, even as they succumb to the gas, might come together and organize themselves into rows and columns, reproducing the figures that their genes have programmed them to form.

Prompted by the instructions of this subcortical program and several tabs of speed, Phil's termites began to clump together, but these agglomerations could not give life to characters; the best they could do was give names to the zombies that were stirring in his brain. Still, it was a start. Now all he needed was a few personality tics to provide them with a semblance of motivation. Phil had developed a theory that the heroic character was entitled to a polysyllabic name, while the perennial depressive loser had to make do with a total of two syllables for his first and last name combined—for example, Phil Dick. So the termites formed Glen Runciter, the boss, and Joe Chip, his hard-luck underling, who is always too broke to cough up the small change he needs to operate his coffee machine or to open his refrigerator or unlatch his front door and is constantly trying to cajole stubborn household robots into working on credit. Phil was pleased with this last bit of business; he could use it shamelessly for the entire length of the book in lieu of real character development. With a few strokes of inspiration like this, he could set the novel on automatic pilot and sit back and watch the termites do their thing. They could be programmed to describe the clothing of every character, even the minor ones, and never lose sight of the fact that the action is supposed to be taking place in 1992, nearly twenty-five years in the future. The resulting wardrobe? Skin-tight trousers woven from synthetic vicuna, saris made of spun spider silk, T-shirts made of Martian jute with a portrait of Bertrand Russell emblazoned on the front. It was just this sort of silliness that turned so many people off to science fiction.

But now what to do with these characters? Write what you know, Aunt Flo had told Phil way back when. If your emotional life has been reduced to a collection of phobias and paranoias, well, draw on them. And that's what he did:

> Defend your privacy. . . . Is a stranger tuning in on you? Are you *really* alone? That for the telepaths . . . and then the queasy worry about precogs. Are your actions being predicted by someone you never met? Someone you would not want to meet or invite into your home? Terminate anxiety; contacting your nearest prudence organization will first tell you if in fact you are the victim of unauthorized intrusions, and then, on your instructions, nullify these intrusions—at moderate cost to you.

Thus runs an ad for Runciter Associates, the company that dominates the very profitable market for paranormal countersurveillance services. Telepaths, precogs, anti-telepaths, anti-precogs. Here Phil had everything he needed to cobble together a plot to exasperate the educated reader. That was his karma, to scrape the dregs from the bottom of what was left of his brain and set his termites marching across the page to come up with this inane plot and hurl themselves at Joe Chip, "first-line electrical type tester." Now there was a profession of the future! In addition to testing telepathic fields and cadging coins from visitors to feed his toaster, Joe Chip has been put in charge of organizing an elite squad of "inertials" and leading them to Luna to do a mop-up job on a certain businessman's factories, which have been infested by "psionics"—miscreants of various paranormal endowments who have lately been spying on and sabotaging the company's operations. Recruitment of Joe Chip's team members, each of them a bit schizophrenic, was always good for a few more pages. Look at *The Seven Samurai*, where practically the whole plot consists of the band's recruitment and the samurai's mission is over in no time: a few blows are exchanged, mostly for form's sake, and then the final credits roll. Dick, on the other hand, after recruiting his sorry band of inertials dutifully sends them to Luna, where, according to plan, force encounters anti-force and all hell breaks loose. He had jotted down some notes on a scrap of paper in handwriting that was increasingly shaky— a bit of plot development in the person of a treacherous dark-eyed girl, the kind of woman he and Joe Chip were always falling for, who has the power to send people back into the past, into a parallel universe from which they cannot escape unless she allows them to. And of course, once back in their "normal" universe, they can never be quite sure it's the same one they left: another house specialty.

Normally, the termites would have pulled this stunt off without too much trouble. After all, they'd carried out similar programs any number of times before. But this time Phil knew that something had gone wrong. The program wasn't working. What point was there in trying to pile up the words, one on top of another, only to have them come crashing to the floor, as his letters were doing now, with a hostile recalcitrance that terrified him. But the letters weren't even hostile anymore, they were inert. Dead. And if he didn't get them moving, his zombies would be stuck on Luna forever, shivering with cold in their faux-vicuna leggings. The termite colony, whose last reflexive movements had given him the illusion that he was getting somewhere, stopped moving. The termites were dead. They say our brain cells start dying from the moment we're born, thousands of them every day. Maybe his were all dead by now. Maybe he was dead.

Snatches of thoughts swam around inside Phil's pill-addled brain like fish in a jar of stagnant water. Dreary aversions, half-formed apprehensions, painful memories. Every now and then one of them would break through to the surface and a jolt of fear would spread through his by now almost completely disconnected nervous system, the way it would in the dentist office's waiting room when he was a kid. The moment the dentist's assistant opened the door, he thought, *This is it. This is what I've been afraid of my whole life.*

Maybe this is how people think when they're dead.

Phil had read an article in a magazine about cryogenics—about how dead bodies, instead of being buried, could be kept on ice until such time as science could bring them back to life. Walt Disney, it was said, had been banking on cryogenics to make him immortal. One could also be frozen just prior to the moment of clinical death and thus supposedly retain a minute trace of cephalic activity that significantly increased one's chance of eventual revival. Sitting in front of his typewriter, his back to the giant filing cabinet stuffed with his treasures, Dick imagined the dark screen of a monitor at the bedside of a frozen body, the silent flicker of the electroencephalogram—its line almost flat, but not quite. To what did those barely perceptible signals from the brain of someone lying preserved in this half-life correspond? Were they dreams, fragments of thought, or images drifting through the darkness? Were they a residue of consciousness, something that, however mistakenly, continued to grasp itself as a self and spin around itself an illusion of space and time? Perhaps from the depth of this coma someone, or rather something that had once been someone, now saw itself in the random form of a science fiction writer whose brain had turned to Jell-O, who was being hounded by the IRS and ground down by entropy, who now sat before a necropolis of letters that refused to take charge of the fate of Joe Chip and his companions. He wasn't asking much: all they had to do was die as well. No one would miss them, and, with all the dangers lurking in the lunar factory where he had sent them, it should have been easy to kill them all off and end

the book on page 80. All he needed was for their host, the factory
owner, to appear, welcome the inertials, and then, without losing his
smile, float up to the ceiling like an enormous balloon.

And for this balloon to turn out to be a self-destructing humanoid
bomb.

And for it to explode.

Curtain.

The smoke clears, and everyone feels about for their legs and arms,
making sure their various body parts are where they are supposed to
be. They can hardly believe they are still alive. The only one who is
seriously wounded is Runciter, their boss. Joe Chip and the others drag
him away and easily make it back to their ship. Too easily, they think.
They put the dying Runciter into a cold-storage room on their ship
and head back to Earth, to the Beloved Brethren Moratorium in
Zurich, where Runciter's wife, Ella, mortally ill, was preserved cryo-
genically a few years before and now lies in a half-life state. Runciter
is immediately frozen and placed in a casket beside hers. Back in the
United States, Joe and his colleagues, now without an assignment, try
in vain to understand what has happened to them—to make some
sense out of that absurd ambush on Luna. They seem to have survived
it, yet oddly that fact almost makes their situation more worrisome.
They feel as if some evil power is toying with them, letting them run
around like decerebrated mice while it watches in amusement as they
try to comprehend their fate. When it has finally tired of this game, it
will simply close its fist around them and deposit their squashed
remains on the treadmill.

As Joe speaks, he takes out a cigarette, but it crumbles into dust
between his fingers as he attempts to light it. "Did it age us?" asks
Wendy, the girl that Joe has fallen in love with. "I feel old. I *am* old;
your package of cigarettes is old; we're all old, as of today, because of
what happened." Later, Joe orders a cup of coffee from a coffee shop
automaton. It tastes like ashes, and a moldy film floats on the surface.
The vidphones won't take their Washington quarters, which have
been out of circulation for forty years, replaced by coins bearing the

likeness of Walt Disney. And soon enough, they discover the body of
Wendy—sweet, warm, and tender Wendy—shriveled, nearly mummi-
fied, crumpled in a heap on the floor of the closet in her hotel room.
Something ghastly is happening and it doesn't make sense. It would be
horrible but at least comprehensible if they could say they were experiencing the aftereffects of the bomb attack on Luna. But if that were
the case, they alone would have suffered those effects, whereas the
world around them seems to have been affected as well. Everything is
rapidly aging, degenerating while at the same time regressing to an
earlier, primal state. Some random process is at work, hurling certain
objects forward toward the final dust that all things eventually
become and others back to the primordial magma, turning some living
creatures into corpses and others into embryos, the two opposite limits of existence. A young woman turns into mummy and a cigarette
crumbles into dust, whereas the telephone book regresses into an outdated version and a television set morphs into a prewar radio set.
Maybe that's it, thinks Joe. This sensation of uncertainty, even about
the general decomposition of the world, is the sign of death nibbling
away at all of them, as though a gigantic laboratory rat, having decided
to avenge the suffering inflicted on his brethren, is enjoying torturing
the little band of men by constantly changing the rules of the game.
There are land mines everywhere, no two of them alike. Step on one
and you grow older, step on another and you regress, step on a third
and maybe nothing will happen to you at all. The elevator you've
walked into, a high-speed, ultramodern affair, can just as easily turn
into a lump of melted metal alloy and thermal plastic as change into a
rickety iron and wood contraption from the previous century—
perhaps operated by a bellboy who looks uncannily like the child that
you once were. Or it might simply start going down without your
being able to stop it—down through more floors than the building
could possibly have, dozens of them, hundreds of them, and just the
thought of the unimaginable horror awaiting you at the bottom makes
you wish that the elevator will continue falling forever.

Is there no refuge? No power greater than the power tormenting
us? Where is the God of Love?

Libera me, Domine!

And then something happens; something appears, or rather someone starts making himself known. Glen Runciter's profile turns up on a coin. Joe picks up a telephone receiver and hears Runciter's voice, distant and staticky; from the deep freeze of his cryogenic casket in the Beloved Brethren Moratorium, Runciter is speaking to him. Joe goes into the lavatory with one of his companions, who is literally dying before his very eyes, and notices some graffiti scrawled over one of the urinals. It's in Runciter's handwriting:

"I'm the one that's alive. You're all dead."

Joe guesses the truth. It was he who died on Luna, he and his companions, and not Runciter. Frozen in a half-life state, their bodies lie in cryogenic caskets. All that remains of their consciousnesses is a dim glimmering, the almost imperceptible undulation of the electroencephalogram. From the outside, there is nothing to see: they appear as though in a deep sleep, a sleep perhaps traversed by inchoate dreams. But in their dreams, in this shapeless nightmare, their lives and perhaps even more than their lives lie in the balance, threatened by a horror beyond words. Glen Runciter has inexplicably understood their situation. He survived the blast on Luna and, now, leaning over their inert bodies, is struggling to reach them, to come to their aid.

Runciter does everything he can to establish some sort of foothold in the shifting world of the half-lifers. Joe, devastated by the death of another member of his team and holed up in a hotel room, turns on the television and chances on an advertisement for a new household product being hyped, with all the enthusiasm of a seasoned professional, by none other than Runciter himself:

"Tired of lazy tastebuds? . . . Has boiled cabbage taken over your world of food? That same old, stale, flat, Monday-morning odor no matter how many dimes you put in your stove? Ubik changes all that; Ubik wakes up food flavor, puts hearty taste back where it belongs, and restores fine food smell." On the screen a brightly colored spray can replaced Glen Runciter. "One invisible puff-puff whisk of economically priced Ubik banishes compulsive obsessive fears that the entire world is turning into clotted milk, worn-out tape recorders and obsolete iron-cage elevators, plus other, further, as-yet-unglimpsed manifestations of decay. You see, world deterioration of this regressive type is a normal experience of many half-lifers. . . . This is particularly true when several memory systems are fused, as in the case of you people. But with today's new, more-powerful-than-ever Ubik, all this is changed!"

And with a TV pitchman's smile, Runciter disappears. Joe sets off in search of this miracle spray, the only remedy against entropy. When he finally manages to find it, it has assumed the form of a bogus patent medicine, circa 1939. A crushing irony: the very substance capable of halting the process of regression has itself fallen victim to it.

This idea, when it came to him, shocked and frightened Phil. The miracle substance that he had pointedly presented in paradoxical terms as an unobtainable mass-market consumer product represented in his mind not merely the pills capable of restoring his mastery over his world but something far more profound—the saving power that snatches us from the gaping jaws of entropy, from the perversity of the demiurge, from death itself.

Phil and his termites had amused themselves by beginning each chapter with an advertising slogan pitching, as Runciter does in the television spot, one of the product's many virtues:

> The best way to ask for beer is to sing out Ubik.
> Instant Ubik has all the fresh flavor of just-brewed drip coffee.
> Ubik drops you back in the thick of things fast.
> If money worries have you in the cellar, go visit the lady at Ubik Savings & Loan.
> New extra-gentle Ubik bra and longline Ubik special bra mean, Lift your arms and be all at once curvier!
> Could it be that I have bad breath, Tom? Well, Ed, if you're worried about that, try today's new Ubik.

But as the novel nears its end, Dick drops the send-up of Madison Avenue and, for the epigraph to the final chapter, renders a pastiche of the first verses of Saint John (and, to some extent, of the first poem of the *Tao Te Ching*):

> I am Ubik. Before the universe was, I am. I made the suns. I made the worlds. I created the lives and the places they inhabit; I move them here, I put them there. They go as I say, and do as I tell them. I am the world and my name is never spoken, the name which no one knows. I am called Ubik, but that is not my name. I am. I shall always be.

The concept of the Eucharist haunted Phil. He took completely to heart such expressions as "whosoever eats of my flesh and drinks of my blood has eternal life." To be able to say that a piece of bread is the body of Christ and have this piece of bread immaterially but incontrovertibly become the body of Christ seemed to him the greatest gift a man could receive, even though it was one that cannot be possessed. This was why it so saddened him when Bishop Pike renounced his ministry to start over in "the private sector." In *The Man in the High Castle*, Phil himself had celebrated—or at least had had his fictional double celebrate—the mystery of the Invisible Kingdom, albeit in a profane and inferior way, by depicting a world different from the one his contemporaries saw and holding this other world out as the true one. And in some mysterious way that neither Phil nor anyone else could prove, he was right.

Phil continued to reproach himself for having committed the sacrilege of describing a negative Eucharist in *The Three Stigmata of Palmer Eldritch*. He felt that in doing so he had empowered the evil demiurge. In the psychic debacle of *Ubik* in which he, along with his characters, was losing his footing, he had just invented the anti-Chew-Z, a positive Eucharist, in other words, the Eucharist itself, though in the form of an aerosol spray. Incorrigible Rat that he was, he could not erect a shelter without having it open directly onto the underground lair of his adversary. Ubik really did exist and offered protection from the forces of death and entropy, but the master of death had the power to subject it to those same forces.

He wrote the last chapters of the book in a panic. The novel had become a wild ride into darkness, strewn with dead bodies and horrible transformations, with Joe Chip constantly trying to get his hands on an unregressed canister of Ubik and to identify the forces that are vying for his life and limbs. "I don't think," he says to himself, "that we have met our enemy face to face, or our friend either."

Phil couldn't decide which face to give this Friend, for whom Runciter was merely the stand-in. One after another, helpful young women pass through the half-lifers' world, offering Ubik and fragile hopes before disappearing in a puff of wind. None of them leave a lasting impression. As for the Adversary, however, Phil knew very well what he looked like, for often in his dreams he had encountered his gaze, cruel and anxious like that of a psychotic rodent. In Ubik, Phil gave him the name Jory. Fifteen years old at the time of his death, Jory lies in a cryogenic casket in the Beloved Brethren Moratorium. Because of his youth, he possesses far greater encephalic energy than Joe and the other half-lifers do and takes advantage of the natural suffusion of their mentalities to devour them, the way a radio transmitter consumes the output of less powerful transmitters operating on neighboring frequencies. Jory shapes the universe within which their consciousnesses move about and does with them as he pleases—torturing them, leading them on, drawing them into the corner of an immense web that he has spun specifically for them. The dead teenager survives and grows stronger and stronger by absorbing what life remains in the dead who surround him.

And he is a twin.

Ubik was an impossible book to finish. Phil generally had terrible problems ending his stories, mainly because he never knew what the real story was. He could not decide whether Ubik or Jory would prevail, and the reason was simply that he didn't know.

The I Ching, wise as ever, refused to give him the kind of answer he wanted. Had he been a conventional Christian, he would have said that in the end the light had to win out. This is what he wanted to believe. But something deep within him believed, almost against his will, in the eternal shadows, in the triumph, not of nothingness, but of living death. If only he could have believed in the triumph of nothing, he would have been reassured, but what he believed in was the triumph of something or someone that *was* nothing, toward which the half of himself that belonged to it since the day he was born drew him in order to devour him.

Having finally reached the requisite number of words at which his program shut down, Phil managed to end his novel by resorting to one of the Rat's old ruses, the one in which the whole story is reframed in such a way as to allow it to close without really concluding. It had become obvious from midway in the novel onward that Joe and the remnants of his team of inertials were stuck in limbo and that Runciter was alive in an "external" world that, however unreal itself, had nevertheless managed to elude not only the capricious dictates of Jory-the-eater-of-human-minds but also the redemptive power of Ubik. And so in the last chapter we find Runciter in one of the visiting rooms at the moratorium, trying to tip the attendant who has just wheeled in Ella Runciter's casket. The attendant looks at the fifty-cent pieces that Runciter has handed him and frowns. "What kind of money is this?" the man asks. Runciter examines the coins and recognizes the profile—it's that of Joe Chip.

In 1968, Stanley Kubrick's *2001: A Space Odyssey* was released. Phil saw the movie, like everyone else, and was particularly struck by the scene in which the astronaut tries to disconnect HAL 9000, which has become a homicidal maniac. The computer's synthetic voice, cold and controlled, grows deeper and deeper, like the voice on a record played at the wrong speed; yet, strangely, it becomes ever more human and pathetic as circuit after circuit is destroyed. HAL, aware of what is happening, first threatens, then pleads. Little by little the enormous electronic brain within which the astronaut is performing his killing work loses contact with its own components. HAL loses the reflexive consciousness that would have allowed it to ace the Turing test, yet what remains is what seems the most human and the farthest beyond the reach of a machine: suffering. Then suffering itself, or perhaps just the ability to express it, disappears, and all that comes out is a babble of incoherent phrases, fragments of ditties and jingles from ravaged memory banks. Then nothing at all.

That is what the books Dick was writing at the end of the 1960s remind one of.

A Maze of Death tells the story of fourteen people living on a hostile planet, bent on one another's destruction. In the last chapter, the reader learns that they are actually passengers aboard a spaceship called *Persus 9*, which, because of a programming error in its computer, is doomed to drift through the universe until the end of time, its passengers shackled together in a common fate until the last one of them dies. To cope with the tedium of their endless voyage—and with one another—they escape, without ever leaving their cots, into artificial, polycephalic universes that the onboard computer programs according to their wishes. The planet on which the novel takes place is merely one of these universes, transposing term for term the facts of the real universe—in other words, those of the drifting ship (which may not even be truly real itself, but only a penultimate reality). The computer appears in the novel in the guise of a monster that replies to questions as a sphinx might, with *I Ching*-like aphorisms, and finally explodes when one of the characters happens to ask it what "Persus 9" means. It is the kind of question Phil himself always wanted to ask, one that would either cause God to explode or make Him reveal Himself, but its role in this novel is difficult to discern; it seems to be merely a tic, an annoying loop in the computer program that Dick's termites are executing. The same goes for the novel's theological armature. Hoping to give an appearance of meaning to the universe it has created for the distraction of it passengers, the ship's onboard computer has used data they provide about their very diverse religious beliefs to create a syncretistic religion, which in reality was the product of long conversations Phil and Bishop Pike had had several months earlier.

Whether by coincidence or Jungian synchronicity, Phil learned of

Pike's death while in the midst of writing this novel of mortal agony. Overwhelmed by grief for his son and for Maren, disappointed by the failure of what he had expected to be his best-selling memoir describing his contacts with the Other Side, the now ex-prelate had joined up with some California businessmen and created the Foundation for Religious Transition, whose goal was to help humanity enter the Age of Aquarius equipped with a religion fit for grown-ups, a universal creed that synthesized the best elements of the various religions that had preceded it. To figure out who would be invited to the party, Pike felt he had to settle that old question about the "validity" of Christianity. He went off to Israel, hoping that, at the wadi of Qumran, where the Essenes had founded their cult, he would learn whether he who was called Jesus could legitimately be considered the Christ, the Lord's Anointed, the Word, and the Son of God, and hence join the "transition" in progress. He was hoping the hallucinogenic mushrooms that perhaps still grew in the caves above the Dead Sea would give him the answer he was seeking. The day after his arrival in Jerusalem in September 1969, he headed out into the Judean desert behind the wheel of a rented Ford Cortina, armed with two bottles of Coca-Cola and a road map that was found a week later spread out on the front passenger seat of the abandoned car. It was several more days before his body was found, in the sand; he had died of starvation and thirst. During the search for him, Pike's brother-in-law prayed to God, Jim Junior, and the famous medium Edgar Cayce for their help. "I think I have never heard a more poignant trinity," noted Joan Didion in an article about the deceased bishop.

Not long before Pike's death, Anthony Boucher had also died, of cancer. Phil hadn't seen Boucher for ten years, but he wept for this kind and charitable man who had been his teacher and had shown that someone could be a science fiction writer, a devout Catholic, a classical music lover, and a righteous person—all at the same time. Soon afterward, Phil's two cats died, Tricky Dick was elected to the White House, and Tim Leary was thrown in prison. From Haight-Ashbury these days one heard only rumors of bad trips and criminality. And when news of the massacre on Cielo Drive of Sharon Tate and her friends hit the papers on August 9, 1969, the world was horrified but somehow not surprised.

That winter an overdose of amphetamines sent Phil to the hospital, where he was diagnosed with serious renal and pancreatic lesions. The moment he got out, however, he was back on speed again. He began another novel, borrowing a title from his current favorite composer, John Dowland, whose airs and compositions for the lute are the ultimate expression of Elizabethan melancholy. At the beginning of *Flow My Tears, the Policeman Said*, someone wakes up to find that he has lost his identity. No one recognizes this man who had been famous only the day before, his identification papers mean nothing, and all trace of his earlier life has completely disappeared. He no longer exists.

At the beginning of the summer of 1970, Phil gave up on the novel. He had foreseen this eventuality a hundred times before, and now it finally had happened; he would never write again—not another word, not a single letter more. The termite colony had died. Broke and without resources, he went on welfare.

By now, Nancy was fed up with his crises, his drugs, and his fears of going crazy. She left him that September, taking Isa with her. The little girl, now three and a half, watched from the rear window while her father ran after the car, his silhouette growing smaller and smaller. Then the car turned the corner and he was gone.

CHAPTER 14

FREAKS

Phil knew that if he was going to avoid killing himself he would have to find a way never to be alone, not even for a minute, and so he filled his house with whatever willing souls he could find. The first two happened to be Nancy's brother and her sister's husband, whom Phil hardly knew. Their wives had recently walked out on them, too, and the trio of brothers-in-law, like characters in a Cassavetes movie, went on a dismal jag. They passed their time getting drunk and stoned while Phil played Wagner on the stereo, and they brought home girls they picked up on the street. Dirty dishes that no one wanted to wash stacked up in the sink, and garbage that no one could be bothered to take out piled up by the back door. They kept telling one another how good it felt to be free, but after several weeks Phil's two houseguests, utterly worn out and frankly frightened of their host, turned tail on this communal existence for a bachelor's life less damaging to their health.

The door was always open at 707 Hacienda Way and the rumor was that you could always find dope at Phil's place. Hard on the heels of the brothers-in-law came everything that San Rafael had to offer in the way of addicts, juvenile delinquents, runaways—in short, a bunch of freaks, to use the word that had replaced *hippies*, which after Wood-stock had come to be regarded as hopelessly co-opted. Since his leav-ing Anne, and with her the world of tidy homes, lawnmowers in the garage, and cordial relations with the local sheriff, the mean age of his social companions had declined considerably. Nancy had been half his age, and her friends weren't much older. Even the Bay Area science fic-tion circle was now mostly made up of a different, younger genera-tion. Bishop Pike, Maren Hackett, and Tony Boucher were gone. At forty-two Phil found himself in a world of kids, a world neatly divided between "freaks" (us) and "straights" (them), and anyone over the age of thirty was one of "them." More because of his chameleonlike ten-dencies than out of some sort of masochism, Phil shared this outlook. He sincerely preferred the company and discourse of these young people to those of his old Berkeley friends of the fifties or even the recently ended sixties—antediluvian years, to hear his new friends tell it. He felt he was on the right side of the barricades, a freak among other freaks, and it didn't take long for them to adopt this strange roly-poly guy, who was both sad and funny at the same time. They called him the Hermit because he hardly ever left the house. You could drop by any hour of the night or day—he never seemed to sleep—and find him there, ready to give you whatever you needed, whether it was attention, drugs, alcohol, music, conversation, or sex, which he pro-posed with sometimes annoying insistence; to the girls, this was the only strike against him.

One day, a new young woman rode into his life, on the back of a Harley-Davidson driven by a guy covered in tattoos. "Donna," like almost everyone else who appears in this chapter, has been extrapo-lated from a character in *A Scanner Darkly*, Dick's novel that draws more heavily than any other on this otherwise sketchily documented period in his life. The real Donna had another name—as did others I write of here—which she has asked not to be used in print. Donna had black hair, dark eyes, and a black leather jacket, and she treated everyone in the house with an aggressive distrust. She got into a fight with the tattooed guy, who rode off without her. Not having anywhere else to go, she accepted Phil's hospitality.

That first evening, he played her his favorite piece of music, "Flow My Tears." Never one to pander to the common herd, he refused to hide his culture and erudition from his audience, and in fact when his guests were in the right mood, they enjoyed listening to him tell about third-century Egyptian monks who ate grasshoppers or spin out his eccentric theories about God. They liked it when he played them those really strange records from his incredible collection.

Some years later, a veteran of Hacienda Way recalled those days as twisted and dangerous but confessed that if she had to choose some-one to spend eternity with, it would have been Phil. Of course it seemed to them all that everything would last forever, that they would always be there, listening to music, smoking dope, letting the good times roll.

They were always stoned, and inevitably there would be clashes. A hash smoker zoned out on one of the dilapidated sofas would have a hard time following the conversation of the guy sitting next to him, who had crammed himself full of amphetamines. Everyone seemed to be living in his or her own movie, simultaneously audience, actor, scriptwriter, and director, and the various separate films were just not playing at the same speed. Nevertheless, everyone was convinced that their movies were incomparably richer, more spontaneous, and more magical than the depressing collective black-and-white documentary the straights had to settle for. And sometimes the private films that the members of the little group were spinning out for themselves man-aged to be in synch—not completely, of course, but long enough for a few images to match up with each other. Everyone would get the feel-ing of having just seen, understood, and thought the same weird thing at the same moment as everyone else, and they would burst out laugh-ing, each of them knowing exactly why. Someone might return from the bathroom at the end of the hallway and say something like, You know, if you think about it, a hallway is a really weird kind of room, and add that the architect who came up with the idea of a hallway must have been totally stoned at the time. Then everyone would laugh, both because the comment was right on the mark—if you think about it, hallways *are* weird—and because it showed how stoned the guy was who made the comment. And what about waiting rooms, someone else, trying to raise the stakes, would say, laughing until the tears ran. Can you believe that there are really things called "waiting rooms"?

One time, everybody piled into the car and went to the drive-in to see three of the *Planet of the Apes* films. Stoned, Phil entertained his companions by coming up with five more sequels—all the way to number 8, *Son of the Return to Planet of the Apes*, in which the audience learns that all of history's great figures—Julius Caesar, Shakespeare, Lincoln, Napoleon—were actually apes. He started miming the parts, scratching his armpits and yelping wildly. His audience spilled the popcorn they were laughing so hard.

After the drive-in they went to a self-service car wash and drove through the tunnel of spinning brushes and cascading foam. It was like driving through an earthquake. As soon as the machine stopped, they put in more coins and drove through again. Everyone agreed this was better than a movie, especially since Phil, still in great form, continued his monologue, shouting over the noise. He told them the business about apes impersonating historical figures reminded him that there were not only imposters in the world but also fake imposters. He'd seen one on TV. The guy had passed himself off as a surgeon on the medical staff of Johns Hopkins University Hospital, a Harvard physicist, a Nobel Prize–winning Finnish novelist, and the ousted president of Argentina, who had a movie star for a wife.

Someone asked if he had ever got caught.

Phil said he hadn't. Remember, he told his listeners, this guy was a fake. He hadn't done any of those things. He was pushing a broom at Disneyland when one day he read a magazine article about a famous imposter. He said to himself, What the hell, I can pass myself off for all those guys, too, if I want. Then he thought about it some more and asked himself why he should go to all the trouble. All he had to do was *pretend* to be an imposter. He made a bundle at it, as much as the real imposter. And now there were guys pretending to be the imposter's imposter.

Another time, someone got the idea of painting all the windows in Phil's house black, so that they couldn't tell if it was day or night. It didn't much matter anyway, since they never opened the blinds. Someone else suggested painting all the record labels black, so that you'd never know what record you were putting on. Phil was against the idea.

Another time, one of the straights who lived next door asked if someone could come over and kill a giant insect that had gotten into her kitchen. When the insect was dead, she said, "If I had known that it was harmless, I would have killed it myself." For a long time, the phrase served as a catchword, epitomizing the whole straight mentality in all its heinousness. All anyone had to do was start the sentence and everyone else would guffaw, pleased that—whatever their problems— at least *they* weren't like that.

Another time, someone brought over some books by Carlos Castaneda, and they made the rounds. Of all the teachings of the Yaqui sorcerer, the one that particularly stuck was the one that said that everyone needed to find his or her place. Not just in the world but in a room, a place that was right for him, that was *his* place. For several weeks, it became a ritual, then a joke, to find your place. Whoever was sitting in the best easy chair could defend his claim by announcing that he'd found his place. Coming from a straight, the phrase would have summed up all the possessive pettiness of his world, but if the right person spoke it in just the right tone of voice, the claim was unassailable.

Another time, the idea of getting involved in drug smuggling came up. As everyone was stoned, the discussion soon went off the rails. One of the housemates complained that when you were asked if you had anything to declare in customs, you couldn't just say, "Yeah, man, I've got a little dope." So someone should take a giant block of hash, he said, and carve it to look like a human being. Then they could hook it up with a windup motor and a little tape recorder and stick it ahead of them in the customs line. And just when they were about to go through customs they would turn it on. When the customs guy asked the dummy if it had anything to declare, it would say, "No, I don't," and keep on going until it reached the other side of the border.

Someone suggested using a solar battery instead of a motor. That way the dummy could go on working for years:

"What's the use of that? It'd finally reach either the Pacific or the Atlantic. In fact, it'd walk off the edge of the Earth, like—"

"Imagine an Eskimo village, and a six-foot-high block of hash worth about—how much would that be worth?"

"About a billion dollars."

"More. Two billion."

"These Eskimos are chewing hides and carving bone spears, and this block of hash worth two billion dollars comes walking through the snow saying over and over, 'No, I don't.'"

"They'd wonder what it meant by that."

"They'd be puzzled forever. There'd be legends."

"Can you imagine telling your grandkids, 'I saw with my own eyes the six-foot-high block of hash appear out of the blinding fog and walk past, that way, worth two billion dollars, saying, "No, I don't."' His grandchildren would have him committed."

"No, see, legends build. After a few centuries they'd be saying, 'In my forefathers' time one day a ninety-foot-high block of extremely good quality Afghanistan hash worth eight trillion dollars came at us dripping fire and screaming, "Die, Eskimo dogs!" and we fought and fought with it, using our spears, and finally killed it.'"

"The kids wouldn't believe that either."

This was more or less how conversations went at 707 Hacienda Way, and the days flew by. *Bela jai*, Phil would say, meaning "time flies" in Bengali. And everyone would laugh and say, *Bela jai*.

———

Another time, Donna told him not to believe a word she told him because she lied all the time. He explained that she was not the first to say that, then told her about the Liar's Paradox, in which Epimenides, a Cretan, asserts that all Cretans are liars. Thus, Phil told her, he couldn't believe her, which is to say, he continued to believe what she told him.

Another time, she told him that she couldn't sleep with him because she needed to be careful with her vagina; she planned to cross the Canadian border with a pound of coke hidden inside it. And anyway, she didn't like anyone touching her.

Because Phil seemed so dejected at hearing this, she decided to give him a supercharged hit, sucking deeply off a joint and then, with her mouth full of smoke, blowing it into his mouth. Apart from the fact you could get twice as stoned this way, he loved feeling Donna's lips against his and the sensation of warm smoke leaving her mouth and entering his. It would remain one of his most erotic memories.

Another time, a man, whom Phil called Barris in his novel, told him that he could get them all the cocaine they wanted for eighty-four cents a gram. That was about what it cost those days for a large can of Solarcaine. When Barris got back home he turned the kitchen into a small chemistry lab to isolate the crystals of cocaine in the can. He pointed to the label with the list of ingredients. "Benzocaine, one gram." There are only a few people, he told Phil, who know that's the commercial name for coke. Obviously, he went on, if they said on the label there was cocaine in this stuff, everyone would be rushing to do what he was doing. Standing around the sink, they began to imagine dump trucks backing into the factory in Cleveland, where the stuff was made, unloading tons and tons of pure, uncut cocaine, which was then mixed with oil and all kinds of other junk, after which it came out the other end in bright yellow cans of Solarcaine that would find their way onto drugstore shelves everywhere. What they ought to do, someone said, was to buy a dump truck and stop fooling around with piddling quantities the way Barris was doing. They figured they could make off with seven or eight hundred pounds in one fell swoop, maybe a lot more. How much does a dump truck hold, anyway?

They spent the afternoon pondering the question. Meanwhile Barris's experiment in the makeshift chemical lab was a complete fiasco. Only the next day did one of them point out how unlikely it was that anyone would sell for eighty-four cents a product that contained a gram of coke worth a hundred dollars.

Another time, Paul Williams, who wrote for *Rolling Stone*, came to visit Phil, whose books he admired. He had met him in 1968 through the cartoonist Art Spiegelman, and they had spent a hilarious evening together. Phil wasn't the first drug-ravaged writer Williams had seen, precocious veteran that he was of the counterculture, but he was nevertheless taken aback at the change in Phil, who now presided as resident guru over a tribe of perpetually stoned young people. He couldn't help thinking that before the events of Cielo Drive, Charles Manson and his family must have made a similar impression on people.

Another time, a girl who had lived with them for a week went into a coma during a bad acid trip. Terrified, Phil rushed her to the hospital, where her condition was diagnosed as general vasoconstriction—half of the blood vessels in her brain were blocked, probably irreversibly. The doctor in charge didn't even bother to ask what had happened; he saw cases like this every day. The girl survived, but with permanent brain damage.

Another girl, some days later, locked herself in a closet and, when she finally came out, tried to hack her arm off with an axe. She didn't entirely succeed. She too had to be taken away.

————————

Another time, Phil forgot the combination to the fireproof file cabinet
in his office. He had been careful not to write it down anywhere,
because theft was common in this world of drug users he now lived in.
Any object of any value whatsoever had been stolen originally, the reasoning went; that was how you knew its value to begin with. Phil had
kept some possessions from his former life and was quite attached to
them. He thought they would be secure in the locked safe. Now that
he had forgotten the combination, he consoled himself with the idea
that they were safer than ever.

But these memory lapses worried him. Somebody had to remember their pitiful, miserable little lives, their shared moments of joy, like
the day they went to see *Planet of the Apes* and then kept running the
car through the car wash. These moments shouldn't be forgotten.
Some trace of them had to be preserved for better days when there
might be people to understand them.

Another time, a girl they knew had a run-in with a lover, who was also
her heroin dealer. He had concealed two small packets of powder in
the handle of the girl's clothes iron, then made an anonymous call to
the police. The girl found the heroin and injected it immediately—her
arms looked like pincushions—so that when the police arrived they
couldn't find any sign of it. The dealer was furious and beat her up.
During the days that followed she worried that he might try to kill
her. She confided in Phil, who decided to hire hit men to protect her
and, if they had to, to knock the guy off. Two large black guys showed
up at the door and introduced themselves to her, and for days they
wouldn't leave her side. She wondered whether they were putting
her on, or whether Phil was putting them on, or whether they were
putting Phil on, pocketing what he gave them for a job that, when
push came to shove, they would never carry out. On the other hand,
who knew? The girl never found out whether the guys really were hired
killers or just a couple of clowns. She soon left to live in another city.

Another time, the person he called Jerry in his book started shaking his head to get the lice out of his hair. He didn't actually have lice but it was no use telling him that. He spent hours in the shower, and when he came out he still kept finding the nonexistent lice. Soon they were invading his entire body, even from the inside. Their bites were driving him crazy. He bought cans of every insecticide he could find and sprayed them all over the house, nearly asphyxiating everyone. He spent days in the shower, screaming. Finally they had to call for help. The emergency psychiatric workers came and led him away, still screaming. He committed suicide several months later.

Over the course of the year, Phil visited at least a dozen of his closest friends at the psychiatric hospital. You had to say at least this about him: he didn't drop people, even when there was nothing more anyone could do for them. He himself was hospitalized three times, following bouts of depression or panic attacks. The doctors told him he was in fairly good shape, especially for someone who was putting away a thousand tablets of Methedrine a week and forty milligrams of Stelazine a day—not to mention the various little fixes of this or that drug that he could never turn down.

Another time, someone told him about the death of a mutual friend. The person who came with the bad news didn't say, "Gloria killed herself," but instead, "Gloria killed herself *today*."

As though it had been bound to happen, the only question being when.

Another time, he felt the steering on his car starting to drift, and he nearly drove off the road. It wasn't the first time something like this had happened. Nothing bad had ever come of these minor incidents, but he knew that the most effective kind of sabotage consists of creating damage whose criminal origins are impossible to establish. Connecting a bomb to the starter would give away the game. But little accidents spread out over time, seemingly attributable to normal wear and tear, are another story. The victim doesn't know how to respond. He starts to doubt himself. My car is fucking up? This sort of thing just happens, he tells himself; I must be getting paranoid. That's what his friends think too—that it's all in his head—and their reaction is the most devastating of all.

Another time, sitting down to drink a cup of coffee someone had made for him, Phil couldn't let go of the idea of how easily it could have been laced with a potent strain of acid that would set an unstoppable film rolling in his head, a film that would last his entire life. If someone really had it in for him—and in the world of dopeheads he inhabited someone surely did—they could certainly manage. Or when he was asleep, they could shoot him up with a cocktail of heroin laced with strychnine, not quite enough to kill him, but almost. The result would be the same: he'd be just barely clinging to life while the horror film played endlessly inside his head. He would end up bouncing off the walls of a psychiatric hospital, trying to shake off the head lice and wondering why he could no longer bring a fork all the way up to his mouth.

Every dealer must have had this fear, and every narc as well. The border between dealers and narcs was fuzzy. Everyone knew that in neighborhoods like the one Phil and his friends were living in, the cops wore beards and dressed like freaks and drove around in dilapidated VW microbuses covered with psychedelic paintings. Everyone knew that narcs sometimes tried to pass themselves off as dealers and sold hash, even horse; dealing served as a perfect cover and had the additional advantage of giving them a little side income. Everyone knew that some of those narcs took drugs and not only became wealthy dealers but addicts themselves—without ever quitting the police force. Everyone knew that dealers could also become narcs and start informing on their associates and clients—either because they had a score to settle or because they thought the narcs were about to nab them. Everyone knew all this, but it didn't help to see things clearly. Cops, dealers, users—they all changed roles depending on the circumstances and depending on what role others were playing. There was no way out.

Another time, Phil became convinced that Donna was a narc. He confronted her. She replied that she understood why he would think that. In their world it was the kind of thing that was entirely possible.

Another time, returning home from the movies, they were sure the police, or someone, had raided the house while they were gone. Maybe one of the people who hung out with them had tipped the intruders off. Whatever the case, someone had been there, and the proof was in the care with which all evidence of entry had been wiped away. They could see, as if in a film, the police pulling the drawers out of the dressers and looking for drugs taped to the bottoms or unscrewing the bases of lamps, expecting an avalanche of pills to come tumbling out, or sticking their noses into the toilet bowls looking for little packets that could be flushed down in an emergency. But what was even scarier was the idea that the narcs hadn't come to the house looking for dope but to plant it there, so that they could bust them whenever they wanted. It could be anywhere—in the telephone, behind the wall sockets, under the floorboards. They went through the house with a fine-tooth comb. That they never found anything didn't put their minds at ease.

Another time, Phil convinced himself that the house was under twenty-four-hour surveillance. He knew that the phone was tapped, and even if it wasn't, basic prudence dictated that one act as though it were. No one ever used the phone to score dope, and when they used a pay phone they resorted to codes, such as dividing the quantity they wanted to buy by ten, the idea being that the narcs would never bother with such small amounts. Phil was also convinced that tiny cameras and microphones had been installed throughout the house.

He wondered how the cops did it. Did some guy specially assigned to 707 Hacienda Way really spend his entire day in front of a bank of TV monitors, watching everything that was going on in every room of the house? Listening to all those endless, pointless, circular, stoned conversations? Watching all those miles and miles of film of people flipping out on drugs? Obviously the guy had to fast-forward though all that. But wouldn't he risk missing the critical moment when a deal went down or that important piece of information he'd been waiting for, the one all the surveillance had been set up for to begin with? He must worry about that constantly. It was, Phil decided, a hellish job.

On the other hand, he would have loved to have been in the narc's place. That way, he could be sure who his enemies were and know what was going on in his house while he was out and what was happening in one room while he was in another. When a tree falls in the forest and no one is there to hear it, does it make any noise? He wondered what Donna was like when he wasn't there to observe her. What did she say about him behind his back? Whom was she sleeping with? Was she really stuffing coke into her vagina? And what about his cat? He imagined it opening up a pillowcase looking for valuables, stealing anything it could out of sheer malice, lighting up his joints, making long-distance calls to drive up his phone bills, walking on the ceiling. And what about himself, for that matter? If the cameras had been filming him day in, day out, wouldn't he be surprised to see what they had caught? When he awoke in the middle of the night and thought he was getting up to pee, what was he really doing? If you don't recognize your own voice the first time you hear a recording of it, the same must be true of seeing yourself on film. You think you're a big fat guy with a beard but what you see is some puny little guy with glasses. No, he knew he would recognize himself, by his clothes or simply by process of elimination. If it lived here and it wasn't Donna, or Barris, or a dog, or a cat, then it had to be him.

In theory, at least.

CHAPTER 15

FLOW MY TEARS

One evening on returning home, he opened the front door and flipped the light switch, which was located on the wall to his left. What he saw made him drop his box of groceries. Papers and broken objects lay strewn across the floor. The stereo was gone. The windowpanes were blown out of their frames, the gigantic steel-plated fireproof file cabinet had been ripped apart by explosives, and the whole house had been turned upside down. His first reaction was gratitude: now he knew he wasn't paranoid.

For the past two weeks or so, he had been waiting for something like this to happen. He had had a series of mishaps with his car and had been getting threatening phone calls, one of which, having woken Donna up late at night, sent her into hysterics. She kept saying, over and over again, that they were going to be attacked. It didn't take much doing to get Phil to share her fear. He went out and bought a pistol and began to prowl around the house, gun in hand, peering outside through the lowered window blinds and pausing in the shadows. He hounded his friends, describing the danger he was in, and he even called the police to ask for protection. The cops told him to get lost, and as for his friends, they were used to it. Everyone knew that Phil

lived in a perpetual state of crisis, that he liked to re-create in his life
the atmosphere of his books, in which the main characters were
always convinced they were being persecuted by unseen enemies and
the job of the hero's friend was to tell him he was dreaming it all up, that
it was all in his head. Phil's friends, knowing what he expected of them,
were happy to play their part. Besides, in his books the hero, against all
evidence, always turned out to be right, and now reality had consented
to play along as well. Phil Dick's world had turned Phildickian.

He phoned the police in a state of near euphoria, feeling a little like
the boy who has cried wolf once too often and now, in the pit of the
animal's stomach, both worries that no one will come save him and
revels in the prospect that his death will lay an enormous guilt trip on
everyone. The police hung up on him. It was just that nutcase, the guy
from that drug hangout on Hacienda Way who'd been pestering them
for the past couple of weeks. They had grown tired of his antics.

Two police detectives eventually did stop by, grudgingly, and surveyed the damage. As they were about to leave, one of them asked Phil
why on earth he had done all this. Someone else might have
responded indignantly, but Phil began to tremble, out of both anger
and fear, and in a voice that had suddenly jumped an octave in pitch,
protested that he wasn't even insured. The next day, when he went to
the police station with a list of things that were missing or damaged,
the officers wouldn't take the information; no one had reported any
break-ins in his neighborhood, they told him. Then one policeman
took him aside and, in half-paternalistic, half-threatening tones, said
that San Rafael could do without troublemakers like him and that it
might be better for everyone concerned if he left town before something worse happened.

Dick had lost his stereo system, all the mementos he'd been keeping
in his safe, and whatever remained of his sense of security; at the same
time, he had gained something, and not just the satisfaction of having
his paranoia confirmed: he had been given a new subject for endless
speculation. For the next three years, until life finally gave him a bigger

bone to gnaw on, he turned the break-in of November 17, 1971, over and over in his mind. Who had done it? And why?

He dismissed out of hand the possibility that he had been the victim of a "normal" crime, that neighborhood hoodlums or maybe one of the countless hangers-on who had passed through his house over the course of the year had done it. The fact that explosives had been used seemed to rule out these small fry—particularly since, according to a mysterious unnamed source, the explosive was of a rare variety, available only to the military. The motive therefore couldn't have been plain old greed. Someone either had wanted to spook him or had been looking for something.

By one of those meaningless coincidences that Phil would have thought highly significant, a mind-blowing example of Jungian synchronicity, my own house was burglarized just as I was beginning to write this chapter. I learned from the police who came to inspect the crime scene that nearly everyone who has ever been the victim of a break-in has the impression that his closets and drawers haven't been rifled through randomly and feels certain that the burglar was seeking something specific. According to the police I spoke to, people wrack their brains to come up with some logical explanation for the burglar's having made off with this or that piece of worthless junk while passing over more valuable objects, whereas in fact the reason is usually haste, ignorance, or both.

This benign manifestation of the need for meaning that drives all of us played havoc with Phil's psyche; he figured that for someone to have gone to the trouble to blow up his file cabinet, it must have contained—or someone must have thought it contained—something either very valuable or very compromising. But what? Once again, he imagined that, in one of his stories, he had somehow stumbled on a dangerous truth, and his thoughts immediately turned to *A Maze of Death*, his most recent novel. In the preface to that book, he had mentioned his theological discussions with the late Bishop Pike, who in his own book, about his contacts with the Other Side, had thanked Phil and Nancy for their help and support. This acknowledgment had touched him deeply at the time, but now he wondered whether Pike hadn't inadvertently placed him in grave danger. Pike's views had caused a scandal. Quite possibly, some religious fanatics, members of some fundamentalist sect, had suspected Pike's friend Phil Dick of continuing to promote the former bishop's heresies or, in any case, of possessing documents that might allow someone else to do so. Perhaps they contained revelations about Jesus Christ's involvement in drug trafficking.

Another possibility seemed even more far-fetched. It involved *Flow My Tears, the Policeman Said*, the novel Phil had given up working on when Nancy left him, which had to do in part with a new drug that inhibited the neural centers governing spatial-temporal continuity and sent the user headlong into a universe in which he couldn't find his bearings. No one had read the unfinished manuscript, which was supposed to be locked up in a safe in his agent's office, but he suddenly remembered that one evening he had discussed the novel with a suspicious-looking guy who had been staying at his house for a few days. The guy had tried to convince him that the CIA was investigating just this kind of phenomenon, conducting experiments with an LSD derivative code-named Mell-O Jell-O. Not long afterward—and right before the break-in—another guy, as shady as the first, had paid a visit, claiming he was with a government health agency and was looking into the spread of a virus that had originated in Vietnam. The symptoms he described were exactly like those the first guy had said were caused by Mell-O Jell-O: you got home and thought you had come to the wrong address because you didn't recognize anything or anyone, and what was even worse, no one recognized you, or at least that's what you believed.

This was precisely what happened in his novel: Jason Taverner, the world-famous television variety-show host, wakes up one morning in a strange room and discovers that he has lost his identity. No one has ever heard of his show, which thirty million people had watched the evening before. No one recognizes his face, which had appeared on the cover of *Time* magazine that very week. His mistress, his agent, and his secretary have no idea who he is and refuse to see him or speak with him. He has no identification papers; there's no trace of his existence

anywhere, neither in police records nor in the memories of his contemporaries.

The first time Phil heard about Mell-O Jell-O, about a year after he
had abandoned the novel, he had only half believed the story. Sure, it
was a troubling idea, but not all that different from the ravings of various dopers he'd heard over the years. The coincidence would have
been more telling had his visitor told him about the CIA experiments
before he had described the plot of his novel rather than after. But the
break-in, and in particular the military-grade explosive the burglars
had used, eroded his skepticism. It now seemed to him quite plausible
that an elite force working for the military-industrial complex had
been rummaging through his papers to find out whether he knew
more than he had let on in conversation. They had been looking for
the manuscript, and they hadn't found it. These government spooks
wouldn't stop there; they would go after his literary agent. Phil would
have to call him to find out whether his safe had just been blown up
with plastic explosives too, or whether he had perhaps just hired a
new secretary or received enticing offers from people claiming to be
publishers and interested in buying Phil's manuscript. Then he had
second thoughts. Such a call would only arouse suspicions. He also
worried that his agent would say, "Come on, Phil, don't you remember? Just last week you asked me to send the manuscript back."

He would have liked to reread the manuscript to get a better sense
of the story's subversive potential, for it wasn't only about the mind-
bending drug. The real subject was the parallel universe the drug sends
Jason Taverner into—a universe in which an all-powerful police force
holds a totalitarian society in its iron grip. In and of itself the story
didn't amount to much; science fiction was full of these Orwellian sce-
narios that no censor in the free world would think of bothering with.
But that was just it: his novel was explicitly about the supposedly free
world. It took place in America and in the early drafts referred to the
country's president by his real name—Richard Milhous Nixon. Phil
knew that if he wanted his book published, he would have to change
that name, and he had even settled on his choice: Nixon would
become Police General Felix Buckman.

Phil had a theory about the ex–vice president and former senator from California, the crook with the famous five o'clock shadow whose rise to power had seemed to coincide with Phil's own plunge into the depths, and he argued for it with as much conviction and every bit as entertainingly as he did his theory about the connection between Philip Morris, which manufactured Marlboro cigarettes, and the Ku Klux Klan. According to Phil, the white and red pattern on the Marlboro box formed three Ks, one on the front of the box, another on the back, and a third on the bottom panel. As for Nixon, Phil would remind his listeners of the adage *Cui prodest scelus, is fecit*—The one who derives advantage from the crime is the one most likely to have committed it. Who stood to benefit most from the assassinations of JFK, RFK, and Martin Luther King Jr. and the attempt against George Wallace if not some second-rate politician, crafty and ugly like Richard III, someone who, like Stalin, would have no qualms about eliminating anyone who stood between him and his ultimate objective? Nixon had come to power using the same methods and tactics as Stalin's. He had his own informants everywhere, and the intelligence agencies were behind him. The Soviets were supporting him, too, because he served their interests—because, in fact, he was one of their own.

By this point in the demonstration, Phil's audience was usually howling with laughter. So Nixon was really a Commie—this was vintage Phil. But he persisted: one only had to stop and think about what he was saying to realize how plausible it all was. Nixon had been in the pay of the Communist Party from the very beginning and, relying on the reputation as a hard-line political conservative that he had acquired during the McCarthy years, he had slowly been turning this land of freedom into a crypto-colony of the Soviet Union. American citizens were under organized surveillance, but whereas *Homo sovieticus* knew he lived in a prison, the average American had no idea of his true condition. The Nixonian dictatorship was approaching the ideal that the Nazis had not had time to realize and that the Russians, who followed in their footsteps, had totally fumbled, handicapped as they were by their atavistic barbarism.

Phil had read Solzhenitsyn, or at least he had read articles about him when he won the Nobel Prize. Though Phil admired him, he couldn't help thinking that, all things considered, the Russian had an easy job of it. At least people believed him; it was impossible for a reasonable person not to believe him. But if you were an American Solzhenitsyn who spoke the truth about what your own country had become and denounced Nixon's crimes the way your Russian counterpart denounced Stalin's, no one would bother locking you away in a nuthouse trying to convince others you were crazy; people would already have come to that conclusion on their own, and your message would go unheard. Phil had believed that in describing a totalitarian America in *Flow My Tears*, he had merely been extrapolating, but the more he thought about it, the more he came to regard the novel as his own *Gulag Archipelago:* it was the work of a prophet exposing an invisible and inadmissible reality. And as for those in the know, the criminals running the state—well, they harbored no illusions. They had set their IRS lackeys after him, were hounding him with threatening phone calls, and had broken into his house; they would not hesitate to eliminate him if they had to.

Like Solzhenitsyn, Phil lived henceforth in a state of fear. His enemies had struck and they would surely strike again. His friends, who no longer felt the Hermit's house was the safe hangout it had once been, took off, along with certain other individuals who, as far as he could tell, seemed troubled by a guilty conscience. As for the police, they treated him more like a criminal than a victim. They might come to arrest him at any moment. If he wasn't executed on the spot, he would end up in a concentration camp in Alaska.

While sorting through what remained of his manuscripts and papers in the empty, music-less house—where the least little noise made him jump—he came across an invitation to a science fiction convention that was taking place in Vancouver in February. Normally he would have shunned that sort of thing, but during these dark weeks the idea of going to a new place, being an honored guest, and having all his expenses paid gave him something to look forward to. He would have to give a speech, which would serve, he imagined, as a kind of last will and testament. He might go down, but he wouldn't go down before telling the world, loud and clear, what he thought, just as Solzhenitsyn had done in Stockholm.

He sat down at his typewriter for the first time in a year and a half. Either out of loyalty or because she didn't have anywhere else to go, Donna still dropped by. She even let him talk her into coming with him to Canada. She would stand by his side, representing the hope of America, its rebellious youth, whose praises he was going to sing at the convention.

In the police state that he saw the United States becoming, only the freaks could be counted on to put up any resistance. When push came to shove, the political opposition would side with the fascist enemy, as it always did, or would allow itself to be manipulated. People over thirty, imbued with a sense of their own importance, ultimately wanted nothing more than to love Big Brother and were more than willing to trade their fragile and fallible humanity for the programmed certainties of that model citizen of the totalitarian system: the android. If there was any hope left for freedom, it lay with the young and their anarchic, defiant spirit. "Go ahead," he would tell them. "Cheat, lie, evade, fake it, be elsewhere, forge documents, build improved electronic gadgets in your garage that'll outwit the gadgets used by the authorities. If the television screen is going to watch you, rewire it late at night when you're permitted to turn it off—rewire it in such a way that the police flunky monitoring the transmission from your living room mirrors back *his* living room at *his* house. When you sign a confession under duress, forge the name of one of the political spies who's infiltrated your model airplane club. Pay your fines in counterfeit money or rubber checks or stolen credit cards. Give a false address. Arrive at the courthouse in a stolen car. Tell the judge that if he sentences you, you will substitute aspirin tablets for his daughter's birth control pills. Or put His Honor on a mailing list for pornographic magazines. Or, if all else fails, threaten him with your using his telephone credit card number to make unnecessary long distance calls to cities on other planets."

The plan was for Donna to sit in the audience and for Phil to turn to her at the end of his speech and ask her to stand. This ambassador of youthful rebellion, in leather jacket and boots, her black hair falling into her eyes, would then cross the auditorium at the University of British Columbia and join him on the stage. She would kiss him on the mouth, in front of everyone, and hand him a joint, which he would light up as the audience applauded. This little scenario made up somewhat for the pain of all those nights she refused to sleep with him.

On the day they were supposed to leave, Donna didn't show up. She had sold the ticket he had bought her and disappeared. Phil went alone; in his suitcase were a change of clothes or two, a Bible, and his speech, which now, given Donna's betrayal, seemed absurd to him.

To those of us who have become Good Citizens, firm believers in democracy and the democratic process who blush at the very thought of having ever called the police fascist pigs and our elected leaders dictators, the speech seems absurd as well. Yet nothing in it could have surprised the audience who heard Phil speak that February afternoon, for they had been listening to American radicals say similar sorts of things every day. That same year, Timothy Leary had called for people to fight "the current period of robotization," maintaining that "to shoot a genocidal robot policeman in the defense of life is a sacred act." Phil thus got the kind of applause a member of the board of supervisors might get at the county fair by proclaiming the local cows to be the best in the world and castigating the bureaucrats in Washington who wanted to put an end to farm subsidies. Nonetheless, the warm reception Phil received, predictable though it may have been, was enough to lift his mood. He was interviewed, photographed, taken out on the town—which he found quite lovely—and introduced to a number of young female admirers, whom he found even lovelier. He was taken out dancing at a nightclub. He wasn't left alone for a single moment. Donna, the break-in, the fascist menace all faded away: in Vancouver he had found a safe harbor and a new circle of friends who greeted with a mixture of incredulity and enthusiasm his decision, which he announced the very first evening, to make a new life in Canada. To celebrate the news they all got drunk. Everyone gave him their addresses and phone numbers and told him that he was welcome to come stay with them anytime. Phil was the kind of person who took seriously even the most casual, pro forma invitation. Once the convention had ended and his hotel room was no longer covered, he was taken in by a young couple, a journalist and his wife, Susan, who told him that she loved his novels. For the first few days his wild stories and sense of humor completely captivated the couple. He had them in tears of laughter by utterly mystifying a young Jehovah's Witness who had made the mistake of ringing their doorbell while Phil Dick was at home and would probably remember for the rest of his days the big bearded guy with sparkling eyes who held forth on entropy, the laws of thermodynamics, and the mystery of transubstantiation. But as the couple's apartment had only two rooms, the presence of the big man camping out on their living room sofa quickly become awkward. Susan, still a student, was studying hard at home while her husband went to work at his newspaper. Phil thought that she would be delighted to have some company. Not quite as intent on finding a place to live as he had led them to believe, he would go see an apartment only if she agreed to come along. Those were the only times he left the house. The rest of the time he went in and out of the living room, read the Bible, listened to music, and every five minutes knocked at Susan's door to ask whether the music was too loud or whether she wanted some coffee or whether whatever it was she was studying was interesting. In a plaintive voice he sang to her the Dowland air that had become his theme song:

Flow, my tears, fall from your springs.
Exiled forever, let me mourn . . .

Though at first touched and flattered to be courted so floridly, she didn't like it when he began to put down her husband. Rebuffed, Phil turned aggressive, suspicious, and manipulative. He answered their phone when they were out and complained about them to their friends. Susan and her husband had a hard time getting rid of him, yet years later, when they spoke to a biographer about their experience with Phil Dick, they did all they could to describe the man, whom they continued to admire, in the best possible light. "Phil lived at a higher level of intensity than anyone I had ever met," said the husband in all earnestness. "He insisted that you be a participant in his world, rather than merely tolerate its existence. I didn't want to."

Nor did any of the various dark-haired girls who, caught up in the excitement of meeting him, had made him promise he would call them if he stayed on in town or came back to visit. When Phil followed up, many of them seemed surprised and embarrassed, as if since the convention they had heard unpleasant things about him (his suspicions fell on Susan, of course). Some didn't even remember who he was, or pretended not to remember. It was as though they had all read *Flow My Tears, the Policeman Said.*

Once again, something had gone dreadfully wrong. He had thought he had finally gathered the momentum he needed to start his life over—*nel mezzo del cammin*—and instead he found himself all alone, a stranger in a strange land. At best, no one cared about him, and at worst . . . at worst, he had been lured away, far from home, and had only to wait for his enemies to come finish him off. The cop at the San Rafael precinct house had told him to go hang himself somewhere else, and he had gone off to do just that. A few days before he left for Vancouver, when he still thought they would be leaving together, he had remarked to Donna how strange it was that he was finally doing what a cop had told him to do, that he had finally been brought to his knees. What if at the last minute he decided not to leave, he had asked Donna. What if he foiled their plans? Donna, who knew him so well, had said something that had struck him even at the time. If he didn't go to Vancouver, she told him, someone else would go and give the speech, and from then on that someone else would be Philip K. Dick in his place. Maybe that was what was happening. Maybe he wasn't himself but some government agent, an android assigned to play his role. During the convention he had played the role so well that he suspected nothing: he had been implanted with a false memory and believed that he was Phil Dick, subversive writer, amateur theologian, unrepentant skirt chaser. And then he had decided to stay on in Vancouver. Had that decision been programmed in as well? Or when he made it had he introduced a glitch into the program, wrecking the plans of those who had been trying for weeks to get their hands on him, either to liquidate him or to steer him back to the android workshop to find out what had gone wrong? In the official version of the universe, he had left Vancouver according to plan. It was hardly surprising that the world was acting as though he wasn't there. By having ventured into a segment of reality in which he was the only occupant, he had turned into a ghost.

Were I writing a novel, I would have no qualms about extrapolating at this point and would feel free to describe in detail the next two weeks in Dick's life. These two weeks constitute a black hole in my subject's biography, and I don't think one can be a novelist and not dream of building a nest in a hole like that—of following Agatha Christie to wherever it was she went when she mysteriously disappeared for eleven days in 1926, or Robespierre to Ermenonville, where he withdrew on the eve of the Thermidor, or Christ into the desert. A powerful novelistic magic informs those places that lack witnesses. And I feel there is a profound though generally unremarked inequality between those who can avail themselves of this luxury of being able to live for a week or six months unseen by anyone but absolute strangers—which is tantamount to not being seen at all—and those whom the constraints and obligations of their lives force to remain permanently under the gaze of those who know them.

Glenn Gould used to say that for each of us there is an optimum ratio of time spent alone to time spent in the company of others. The problem was, he said, that most people didn't realize this. He himself felt he needed whole days to cleanse his soul for each hour spent in society. Dick was the opposite; he was mortally afraid of being alone. His ideal was to be able to shut himself up in a room when he felt like it, while in the next room a woman sat up and waited for him. That is why, although it is dangerous to conjecture as to what was going on inside his head, the biographer of Philip K. Dick has little trouble accounting for the facts of his subject's life, where he was on what day and with whom. Five wives and dozens of friends are there to provide testimony. Hence the great mystery of these two weeks in Vancouver. In a less exposed life than Dick's they would go unremarked.

Just as any number of people have had their homes broken into, so any number of people have spent a few days by themselves in a strange city. It is very likely—though it cannot be known with any certainty—that Dick had been the victim of an ordinary burglary, not much different from the dozens reported every day of the year to suburban police stations everywhere; it is also likely that during the month of March 1972 he wandered aimlessly around Vancouver, watched television in hotel rooms, took pills by the handful, made hundreds of telephone calls to girls who told him to get lost. But there are no witnesses to any of this, not even Dick himself; once they had passed, or even as they were slipping by, those two weeks in Vancouver vanished from his memory.

On March 23, he found himself again. Like Jason Taverner in *Flow My Tears, the Policeman Said*, he was lying on a bed in a fleabag hotel room. He phoned Susan, the journalist's wife, to tell her that he was going to "turn out the lights." She hung up on him, apparently not having understood the allusion to Dowland's "Flow, My Tears":

Down, vain lights,
shine you no more . . .

But he assumed that she knew exactly what he was talking about and that her hanging up on him meant "Drop dead." At which he took seven hundred grams of potassium bromide and went to sleep. Emerging from his stupor a little later, he saw a number written in ink on the palm of his left hand, a number that at some point his right hand must have scrawled. Somehow he managed to dial the number, which connected him to emergency assistance.

Phil spent the next several days in the hospital. He was out of danger

soon enough, but the question was, what to do with him now? He
swore to his doctors that he had nowhere to go, that he was a drug
addict and would try to kill himself again the minute they let him out.
Weren't there any detox centers in Canada? Of course there were, he
was assured. There was X-Kalay. But be warned, they told him, it was not
a spa: they took you off drugs cold turkey, they gave you no medications to help you through withdrawal, and they kept you under constant surveillance. He told them that that was exactly what he needed.

Yes, but X-Kalay only treats heroin addicts.

No problem, he replied. I'm a heroin addict.

The doctors must have looked somewhat skeptically at the girth of
this patient who seemed to bear the ravages of every drug in the world
except heroin. Nevertheless, as the facts attest, Phil must have had
great influence over his doctors: he weighed 240 pounds and, after an
interview with experienced personnel who were not prone to levity,
was admitted to X-Kalay, a clinic devoted exclusively to the treatment
of heroin addicts.

Apart from the fact that one passes through its doors of one's own
accord—in Phil's case, at his own insistence—checking into a detox
center like X-Kalay is not so very different from being incarcerated.
You exchange your civilian clothes for coveralls and cloth slippers,
your first and last name for a single first name that is not your own and
is assigned to you randomly; you're asked not to talk either about your
past or about anything else having to do with life outside the center;
you're stripped of your will. Everything you do from then on is closely
monitored and structured.

Paradoxically, yet like many others who have been in a similar position, Phil felt an enormous sense of relief on being admitted to the
center, which resembled nothing so much as the concentration camp
he had been sure he would one day be sent to. Normally so jealous of
his freedom, he could think of no place he would rather be than here.
All his decisions were made for him—when to get up, when to go to
bed, when to start his chores, when to relax. He felt liberated. The
man who had never tired of complaining about the police surveillance
he was sure he was the target of had just learned the hard way about

the void you fall into when no one pays any attention to you at all. Without anyone to witness his existence, he had ceased to exist. He had suspected this might happen, those last few months at Hacienda Way, when he was afraid—and in reality hoped—that the police were filming him. Even if he never saw the footage, even if no one would ever see it, there was still comfort in knowing—or even just suspecting—that it existed somewhere, that buried beneath boxes and files of both useless and vital material deep down in the bowels of some state or federal building was evidence of everything that he had done, minute by minute, for all those days and nights that he could no longer recall. Granted, such documentary evidence could only show him the movements and the words produced by the human machine named Phil Dick. What it could not capture was his thoughts. Still, he would have given practically anything to find out whether or not he had signed such and such a check that, going over his bank statements, he couldn't remember signing, or whether or not he had been crude to well-meaning people who had called him and later berated him for his behavior. It wasn't he, Phil had tried to tell them, but some junkie living in the house at the time who had answered the phone, thinking he'd be a wise guy and pass himself off as Phil Dick. He could tell, however, that no one believed him, and even he did not quite believe himself. Of course, the high point of the film would be the break-in, perpetrated by Nixon's police, he believed, despite the fact that not only the police but also some of the aforementioned well-meaning people thought he had done it himself—to get rid of papers that the IRS had been demanding to see, or to get attention, or simply because he was crazy. Who had really done it, Nixon or he? Assuming that (a) the film existed and (b) the government hadn't tampered with the images, those reels and nothing else would establish the truth. He prayed for the day when he would be allowed to see them for himself.

Patients at X-Kalay weren't filmed, but they were also never left alone. They slept in common dormitories, showered in groups, and, when they used the toilet, they had to leave the door open.

Those toilets were his entire world that first week. No other task, it was felt, was so aptly suited to the needs and capabilities of newcomers to the center. When he arrived, he was one of two newcomers, and there were three bathrooms, one on each floor. As the counselors had told them in handing each of them his bucket, mop, and broom: It's not what you do that's important; the important thing is that you do it well, so that you can be proud of your work. A compliant Phil cleaned the toilets with the care of an art restorer. Without losing himself in the work, he managed to apply himself wholeheartedly to his task and stretch it out to fill the allotted time. After spending an hour or two working on the same toilet bowl, he would stop, judge the job finished, and go on to the next toilet. Such behavior bespoke a mental balance not widely seen at X-Kalay. The other newcomer, for example, could never finish a single chore. Given the job of waxing the floor, he would start out doing as he had been shown but after a few minutes would run up against some invisible obstacle and have to start over. He would start again and the same thing would happen at exactly the same spot. He could spend the whole day doing the same thing, again and again and again. Phil thought of helping him, but to what end? He could certainly finish waxing the floor for the guy, but what he couldn't do was thaw the vitrified lump of slag to which years of heroin had reduced the man's brain. His hands, eyes, and tongue all seemed to function, but the person using them had disappeared. All that remained was an automaton, a reflex-action machine that repeated over and over the last instructions it had been given—"Keep trying, keep trying." People tend to think that parrots understand nothing of what is said to them, which is why Jerry, a former tenant at Hacienda Way, had thought it funny to teach his bird the sentence "I don't understand what they've made me say." But the normally obedient parrot never could, or perhaps never wanted to, repeat those particular words. Phil's workmate, too, departed from the repetitive program to which his psychic life had been reduced when he looked up at Phil with empty eyes and, instead of repeating the last thing he had been told, complained piteously, "Why can't I do it?"

This blew Phil away. It was like one of those heartwarming scenes from films like *The Miracle Worker*, when the parents realize that their child can hear or that the quadriplegic can walk. But as Phil was trying to think of something to say back, the man began repeating this new phrase, "Why can't I do it?" and Phil began to wonder if unthinkingly, maybe in his sleep, he had spoken those words in the man's presence. In any case, what was he supposed to tell him? That the reason he couldn't wax the floor was because his brain was fried? Flushing the toilet would have expressed that thought more eloquently.

For someone who hadn't yet reached the point where a stint in detox was wasted effort, the treatment at X-Kalay had its virtues, not the least of them that of utterly crushing any romantic notion a person might still have about drugs. The hopeless cases served as examples to the others, who bonded in a common, hysterical hatred of these walking testimonies to what their own drug dependency had nearly done to them too. Many of those who had managed to kick their habit but were afraid of facing the world outside X-Kalay stayed on as counselors, forming the bulk of the clinic staff. Undoubtedly, they thought they were punishing the sin and not the sinner, yet they were notoriously brutal.

Hatred of drugs ruled this new world in which Phil found himself, just as the obsession with getting drugs had ruled the world in which he had been living since Nancy's departure. Chameleonlike as ever, he immediately adopted the new value system and proved himself its most eloquent champion during group therapy sessions. Everyone was supposed to say whatever came into their heads, and the conversation usually consisted of dreary exchanges of insults. Phil didn't seem to mind being called a butt-fucked piece of shit or asswipe cocksucker any more than the next person, but he was far less tolerant of jibes having to do with his sister. This was duly noted by the others, and the jibes increased: "So, did you fuck her, or what?" But he scored a signal victory when, in reply to some idiot who wouldn't stop badgering him, he said, "No problem. I'll just come back on Thursday." The retort made everyone laugh, at least everyone who could still follow a conversation or remember what someone else had been saying a minute before. Phil was alluding to a story that one of them had just finished telling, about a guy he knew who had gone to visit an old friend of his named Leon. The guy got to his friend's house and asked the people there if he could see Leon. "I'm very sorry to have to tell you this," one of them told him, "but Leon is dead." "No problem," he replied. "I'll just come back on Thursday."

After that, whenever someone at X-Kalay didn't understand what he had been told, or didn't want to answer, or couldn't find the roll of toilet paper he had been sent to fetch, he would deal with it by saying, "No problem. I'll come back on Thursday." Authorship of this ritualistic reply was implicitly attributed to Phil. When, at the end of that week, the participants in the group therapy were drawing up a list recognizing everyone's contributions to the sessions, as they did every week, he was credited with having brought some humor to their therapy. According to one of the doctors, Phil had maintained his ability to see the funny side of things, despite his piteous personal condition. Everyone applauded him, and he acknowledged the accolade, repeating, like a parrot, "No problem. I'll just come back on Thursday."

CHAPTER 16

THE SOUL'S WINTER

At the end of two weeks, it was decided that he had cleaned enough toilets, and, one of the governing principles of X-Kalay being that every patient should be asked to do what he did best, Phil found himself sitting behind a typewriter, working at what could be called public relations. He prepared reports on the center's goings-on, compiled press clippings having to do with drug problems, wrote letters soliciting donations from potential benefactors. In his spare moments, he worked out a theory about the clinic—that it harbored a clandestine heroin laboratory. The very hand that distributed the poison was offering the antidote, the goal being to create a new kind of individual—docile, alienated, the android-citizen of the future—whom the organization would enslave, first by getting him hooked on drugs and then, in a far subtler manner, by saving him from them, by teaching him to hate drugs and love the master who alone could protect him from them. He, Phil, had become a cog in the machine, a wonderful vantage point, he thought, from which to observe the organization.

Dressed in his white coveralls, he prowled the corridors with a nonchalant air, opening every door he came on in the hope of finding the way into the secret lab. His suspicions didn't prevent him, however, from expressing a sincerely felt warmth and gratitude to every member of the staff he happened to pass in the hallway. For the first time in his life, he felt useful; he had found a family. If they really wanted him to, he would spend the rest of his life at X-Kalay, doing all he could for those poor lost bastards—his brothers and comrades.

To the respectable friends he still had in the States (whom he knew from before his days at Hacienda Way) he wrote enthusiastic letters explaining the program of redemption through service to others. Their recipients found them disconcerting, arriving as they did a mere month after the desperate pleas for help he had written during the darkest days of his Canadian disillusionment, not long after his triumphant announcement that he was going to settle in Vancouver. Several replies to his various letters eventually found their way to X-Kalay. In one, the novelist Ursula K. Le Guin deplored the fact that he had nowhere to go but firmly refused his request to move in with her. While staying with the young couple in Vancouver whose lives he had managed to poison within a matter of weeks, Phil had written to Le Guin, whom he had never actually met, detailing his woes and offering his services as a houseguest or perhaps a model roommate and doing his best to dispel the rumors that he suspected were flying around about his being a paranoiac whom no one could stand to live with. Other requests for shelter, addressed in pathetic terms to people whom he had met only once or twice but whose names he happened to have in his address book, remained unanswered. In fact, he had forgotten he had written to most of these people in the first place. Thus his surprise when he got a letter from a Willis McNelly, a professor at California State University in Fullerton and a passionate fan of science fiction who had unsuccessfully tried to get Phil to come talk to his students. He was sorry to learn that his favorite writer was homesick, he wrote, but he was delighted—also a little surprised—that Phil would think to turn to him for help. The academic community of Cal State Fullerton and the town's small circle of science fiction fans would welcome Phil with open arms; maybe he would even do their library the honor of donating to it what remained of his manuscripts after the break-in. And in any case, two students—two female students, Phil noted—who were admirers of his work and to whom the professor had read Phil's letter had offered their hospitality.

This new prospect cast his current plans—to devote his life to washing the feet of the sick while penning antidrug screeds in the rain-sodden city of Vancouver—in a new and suddenly less appealing light. A month of withdrawal and daily domestic chores had put him more or less back on his feet. The day he received McNelly's letter, he took his coveralls to the laundry, asked for his own clothes back, signed a discharge form, and caught a plane for Los Angeles, promising to be back on Thursday.

The Phil Dick who got off the plane looked like someone who had fallen from a train and walked along the tracks all the way to the station. He was a man who had lost his momentum, and if anything drove him, it was a vague and residual instinct for survival; he was, to put it simply, at the end of his rope. At least that's how he looked to his welcoming committee of three: the two young—but, sadly, not very pretty—women who had been moved by his plight and a kind-faced young man named Timothy Powers who wanted to write science fiction.

Phil hadn't checked any baggage; a small weathered suitcase, held shut with string, a trench coat draped over his arm, and a Bible seemed to be his only possessions. To relieve the awkwardness produced by this somewhat sad first impression, Powers joked about how much better it always was to travel light. In a loud voice, Phil launched into a speech about the break-in, about how they'd taken everything he had. From the window of the car, he watched the miles of freeway stretch out through the endless suburbs south of Los Angeles. When they came to a sign indicating they were entering Orange County, Nixon's old home turf and a symbol from his Berkeley days of almost preternatural political villainy, he laughed. He didn't know at the time that he would be spending the ten remaining years of his life there.

During the first weeks in Fullerton he let himself be treated like a shell-shocked soldier come home from the front. When left alone, he was overcome by panic attacks. If a car happened to drive by too slowly, he became suspicious; he studied every radio antenna, trying to figure out which ones were transmitting rather than receiving signals; he threw the *I Ching* to learn whether among his new friends there wasn't some agent of the powers that were plotting his demise. Luckily he was rarely left alone. People rallied around him. As often happens with writers who have stopped writing, his reputation had grown and he had become what was not quite yet called a cult writer. Thanks to Professor McNelly, he had been welcomed by a circle of would-be priests of the cult, who couldn't get over their good fortune at being able to rub shoulders with the author of *The Man in the High Castle*. Much like on Hacienda Way, Phil was surrounded once again by people decades younger than himself, but apart from their youth, these kids had nothing in common with the freaks from San Rafael. Their drug use was confined to the occasional shared joint, which they smoked just for the fun of it or to get into the music they liked listening to. The conversations were relaxed yet stimulating. People were always dropping in on one another, preparing impromptu dinners consisting mainly of gigantic salads of whatever they happened to have on hand. Everyone was broke, but their poverty had nothing in common with the sordid, squalid impoverishment of his old doper friends. They lived the friendly, trusting bohemian life of students and aspiring artists who held part-time jobs to get by. It might have been the atmosphere of Berkeley, of his youth, had he not been so unsociable back then. The collective existence that most people experience in late adolescence, spending their time in the constant presence of a group of friends, was something Phil hadn't known until he was older, and the experience had turned into a nightmare. How sweet it was to discover at the age of forty-four a peaceful, sunny version of that life, consisting of trips to the used-record store, evenings at the movies, rides in the car.

To really get back on his feet Phil needed a wife. The young men and women around him paired up easily yet without promiscuity. He was the only one on his own. Almost immediately on his arrival he had made the acquaintance of a girl named Linda, whose babylike cheeks reminded him of his new idol, Linda Ronstadt, whom he bombarded with fan letters he sent to her in care of her record company. Officially he was "dating" Linda, but only in the most literal sense, which is to say, they went out to movies together or had long conversations late into the night; she drove him everywhere, since he still didn't have a car, which in Los Angeles, then as now, was a serious handicap.

Linda, only twenty-one at the time, was flattered by the interest of this brilliant and cultivated writer whom everyone around her admired and who was old enough to be her father. It was clear he had lived through some tough times. Despite his paunch, he probably wouldn't have had much trouble getting her into bed had he played on her impression of him as someone-who-had-lived. But here is how he went about trying to seduce her:

One evening he was having dinner with Harlan Ellison and another science fiction writer and he brought her along: it was an evening of grown-ups, and she was thrilled to be asked to join them. Before going into the restaurant, Phil handed her a letter and told her solemnly that his life depended on her reply. Then he ignored her for the rest of the evening as he talked shop with his two colleagues—a surefire way of embarrassing a girl who was already shy and insecure. Linda ran to the bathroom and burst into tears. Then she opened the envelope Phil had given her and began to read. The letter, which was very long, stunned her. He loved her, he wanted to live with her, he wanted to marry her. If she refused him, he would die, the world around him would come apart, just as it does in *Ubik* (being surrounded by admirers, he had gotten into the habit of making allusions to his own works that assumed everyone was familiar with them). Yes, to him, she was like Ubik—the way, the truth, life. Did she want him to live or to die? More broadly speaking, was she on the side of life or death? " 'See,' said the Eternal, 'I have set before you this day life and good, death and evil. Choose.' "

Choose, Linda.

She went back to the table utterly alarmed. No one paid any attention to her. But as soon as they were in the car, Phil looked at her seriously from behind his gray beard and said, "So?" Linda stammered. He concluded that this meant no and instantly began to mock her. How could she have been stupid enough to take his letter seriously? She had once told him that she had never been proposed to and so now someone had gone and broken the ice. It was a joke, get it?

The drive home was grim. She dropped him off at his place without saying a word. Yet, despite this, they continued to see each other. He acted as if nothing had happened and, picking up where he had left off, continued to court her in his adolescent, insecure way, arrogantly one day and pleadingly the next. To Linda it was as if this grown man were acting out some monstrous comedy. Not knowing what he was saying about her behind her back, she began noticing she was becoming the central story of their little Fullerton family. Impressionable and bewildered, she started to believe she was somehow at fault, telling herself that *she* was the immature one when Phil sent her postcards like the one showing an arrow-pierced heart bearing their initials to which he had glued the definition of *masturbation,* cut out of the dictionary. Not only did he persuade her to go with him to marriage counseling—when they hadn't even slept together—but he succeeded in placing on her shoulders all responsibility for what was wrong with their life as a "couple," to say nothing of the harm she was doing to him specifically. He had to be in love to put up with her anxieties and go with her to therapy, he who had never in his life had anything to do with psychiatrists. (When, years later, Linda learned that he had been going to a psychiatrist since the age of fourteen and that even many of his admirers considered him a lunatic, she felt enormously relieved; she hadn't been crazy after all.)

Linda's ordeal came to an end when one evening Phil met Tessa Busby, who consented to sleep with him. She moved into his apartment the next day. Her agreeableness convinced Phil that she was in the pay of his enemies. Knowing the kind of woman he liked, they had chosen well: Tessa had long dark hair and a petite, graceful, supple body, which she kept in shape with kung fu. She wanted to be a writer. She was eighteen. He had never met anyone with such marvelous empathy.

For want of a literary outlet, his passion for theorizing focused on

two subjects: the break-in, about which he came up with a new explanation every day, and his love life, in which, according to him, two opposite tendencies collided, the first driving him into the arms of castrating,
tyrannizing women like Anne and the second inclining him toward
fragile, dark-haired young girls. How sad, he told himself and everyone
around him, that most of his sweet, dark-haired innocents turned out,
like Nancy or, more recently, like Linda, to be castrating, tyrannical,
and schizoid as well. But this time it was the real thing—even the *I
Ching* had said so. He had broken the pattern. After all his years of
wandering he had reached safe harbor and had found in Tessa the
dark-haired girl in whom, after so many counterfeits, he had almost
stopped believing: warm and human, capable of loving a man just as
he is without wanting to change him. He loved watching her in her
leotard as she went through her martial arts exercises, her movements
slow and precise, her breathing quiet, regular, and calm. He loved
going shopping with her, watching television with her, listening to
music with her. He loved to read to her chapters from *Don Quixote*,
which Tim Powers had given them. He loved it when she brought him
his food in bed on those days when he just didn't feel like getting up.
He hated it when she was apart from him for even a minute.

By autumn, Tessa was pregnant. To have something to dedicate to
her, and also to earn a little money, he got hold of the manuscript of
Flow My Tears and decided to finish it. As he was no longer taking
amphetamines, he didn't write as quickly as before and the job took
him several months. During that time the government's investigation
into a break-in that had taken place the previous summer in Washington, D.C., took an unexpected turn.

In the beginning, the Watergate break-in had seemed a nonevent—
just another of those dirty tricks that political parties are nearly always
playing on each other during election years—and if the burglars who
were apprehended in the offices of the Democratic National Committee had connections with CREEP—the Committee to Reelect the
President—that fact didn't prevent Nixon from winning reelection in
November. The whole story disgusted Phil, who turned the TV off
every time politics came up. His interest returned early the following

year, when the trial of the seven Watergate burglars—the "plumbers," as the *Washington Post* had dubbed them—started. Along with everyone else in the country, Phil watched the televised proceedings of the Ervin Committee, which every day brought new revelations—government wire-tapping, illegal searches, secret slush funds, FBI-backed operations against those whom Vice President Spiro Agnew called "political thugs," and the machinations of the CIA on U.S. soil. According to a growing consensus, since the end of the 1960s the civil liberties guaranteed by the finest Constitution in the world were under siege.

With each new Watergate revelation, Phil's prestige among his friends in Fullerton increased measurably. He had known what was going on. People had made fun of him, called him paranoid, and smiled indulgently when, for the umpteenth time, he blamed the Hacienda Way break-in on agencies so secret that no one had ever even heard of them. But now everyone was talking about those very same agencies; in fact, people seemed to be talking about nothing else. There was no getting around it: Phil had been right all along.

To everyone's surprise, his satisfaction seemed somehow muted. It may have vexed Don Quixote that people kept seeing windmills when he knew they were knights in armor, but imagine his unhappiness if all of a sudden they became convinced that he was right. Phil had never liked it when people changed their mind in a discussion with him and came over to his side. He would take a new position immediately. The more his friends celebrated his prescience, the more evasive and mysterious he became, as if he considered them even blinder than they had been before, now that they believed the scales had fallen from their eyes. When they asked him eagerly about his new novel, figuring he was cooking up some new literary Molotov cocktail to throw at Nixon, he shrugged his shoulders and said all that was ancient history. He was writing about more pressing matters.

In the spring of 1973, he got down to what he believed would be his greatest work, the distillation of his experiences in that world of treachery and mental derangement into which he had sunk after Nancy left him. The books that he had written earlier about drugs now struck him as naive. When he wrote those books, he hadn't known the drug milieu. And now that he was out of it, he could offer his testimony.

He started to write *A Scanner, Darkly* in a frame of mind comparable to that in which Dostoevsky had written *The Possessed*, drawing the lessons from the terrorist utopia that had landed him in prison after a terrifying mock execution. The book would be dedicated to Donna and to his friends at Hacienda Way and X-Kalay, some of them dead by now, the rest having become either vegetables or paralyzed lumps of eternal terror. After years spent playing at being a subversive drug addict and trying to go one better than Timothy Leary, he now looked at all drugs with a perspective so altered that he actually was planning on adding Richard Kleindienst, Nixon's attorney general, to the long list of his new book's dedicatees, in recognition of Kleindienst's fight against drug traffickers. The idea repelled his friends, for whom Kleindienst was anathema, and in the end Phil was content to send Kleindienst, who had been forced to resign from his position along with Dean, Haldeman, and Ehrlichman, letters of support, which, if they ever arrived, probably baffled their recipient.

He worked at night while Tessa slept. Everything he had lived through in those days of confusion and helplessness came back to him: the endless conversations, the camaraderie, the distrust, the jokes that went nowhere or turned sour, the giggle fits, the leering smiles, the stupid cackling, the spaced-out looks, the throes of terror, the afternoons spent looking for a joint that was sitting right in front of you, the fear of the police, the memory lapses, the feeling of living within an endless film loop, with those worrisome little alterations each time the film passes through the projector, slight changes here and there that you can vaguely sense but can't quite put your finger on. He listened to the stereo through headphones, playing Linda Ronstadt and Dowland's *Lacrimae* over and over again. He didn't miss the amphetamines, as he feared he might. But sometimes, at dawn, Tessa would find him sitting motionless at his table, his eyes open, fixed in a frozen stare and filled with tears.

He knew his novel would have to be science fiction if he wanted to sell it. The material being so obviously realistic, this constraint weighed on him, but it also led him to an inspired solution.

Bob Arctor, his hero, a drug addict living in a squalid dump of an apartment he shares with most of the other characters in the novel, is also "Fred," a member of the Orange County narcotics squad. It's hard to tell whether he's a policeman who has been taken over by his cover or a freak turned informer, but so common are cases like his that the department, to protect its narcotics officers from the agents of the drug cartels that have infiltrated its ranks, has found a way to obscure their identity and make them anonymous by means of an invention called the "scramble suit." This skinlike membrane, which covers a policeman during his contacts with his superiors, is connected to a computer in whose memory are stored millions upon millions of physical characteristics. As the computer runs through its data banks it constantly reprograms eye color, hair color, the shape of the nose and the teeth and the lips and so forth—each morphological trait—in such a way that the membrane assumes a new configuration every microsecond. The same goes for the policeman's voice. All this makes it impossible to describe, identify, or capture on film or tape anyone wearing the suit, and thus turns him into the perfect Everyman.

The novel's plot starts to come together when, not knowing who Fred really is, his superiors order him to tail Bob Arctor—in other words, to investigate himself. Fred dutifully plants cameras and listening devices in his own house and sets about monitoring everything that goes on there twenty-four hours a day, seven days a week. This was Phil's dream, of course, but it wasn't his dream alone: on July 16, 1973, in one of the most astounding revelations of the Watergate scandal, a White House aide revealed that for years the president, using voice-activated recorders, had been taping all his conversations without his interlocutors being aware of it. America was appalled, but not Phil, in whom the revelation, which came as no surprise, produced a sudden surge of sympathy for his old enemy. What public opinion regarded as technological blackmail appeared to Phil an indication of an insecurity that he himself knew only too well. In his view, Nixon was not as interested in keeping a record of what his visitors were saying as in keeping track of what he himself had said. He was spying on himself as much as on others. Did he sometimes listen to the tapes, Phil wondered, or was it enough for Nixon merely to know that they existed? Did he tape himself while he was listening to them, like Bob Arctor, who, every two or three days, dons his scramble suit and sits in front of the bank of screens that show him everything that has been and is going on in his own home? The problem for Arctor is that there are twenty-four hours of film to look at each day, and even if he could stay awake for all twenty-four hours it wouldn't do any good, since he is the true subject of the film and thus spends a good part of the time on the monitor rather than sitting in front of it. Arctor believes he has found a way around this dilemma by forgoing exhaustiveness and merely sampling the tape, the way one might fast-forward or rewind a video while looking for a particular scene—glancing quickly at what's passing by. Merely by listening to a couple of minutes out of every three hours, one can usually follow a conversation between two people who are high on drugs and not miss anything important; such conversations rarely go anywhere. Police wiretaps in totalitarian societies work on the same principle: you record everyone and, since you don't have enough personnel—you can't recruit everyone, after all—you listen here and there and hope to get lucky. But that isn't enough for Arctor. What happens, he wonders, if the crucial information resides in one of those parts of the tape that he's passed over? Doubt gnaws at him, especially as the information is not about just anyone but about him, someone who has started to pique his curiosity more and more.

What does Bob Arctor do, wonders Fred, when he's alone and thinks no one is watching him? Might he not be, as some suspect, a bigger link in the drug chain than he seems?

What does the president do? Richard Nixon must have wondered. Does he really work for Moscow? Did he order the Watergate break-in? Was he the one who erased the tape that proves he did? Is there a second tape in which he can be heard erasing the first?

What was Philip K. Dick doing, wondered Philip K. Dick, when someone was breaking into his house in San Rafael?

————

The more he thought about it, the more plausible it seemed that the police were actually onto something when they asked him why he had broken into his own house. He had no memory of having done so, but he also knew that that proved nothing. When his friends, who at first had shared the police's suspicion, ultimately rejected the idea, they were so unanimous in dismissing it that he himself dragged it out of the rubbish heap and wouldn't let go of it. Without the film or any hope of getting access to it, he resigned himself to the fact that he would never know the truth about the incident. Above all, he asked himself what the ability to arrive at such a sober conclusion suggested about his mental state. Had he taken a step closer to lunacy or, on the contrary, finally achieved enough lucidity to realize how crazy he had been?

Although he knew it proved nothing, he had to admit that he did feel more lucid than before. Now that the whole country seemed to have embraced its paranoia, he divested himself of his own, like a snob who renounces some personal preference that has suddenly become too popular. Reducing his paranoia to the status of a symptom, he tried to reconstruct its underlying causes. Just as he believed that— thanks to Tessa—he had gotten to the bottom of his disastrous love life, he believed he had discovered what had been governing his intellectual and psychological life.

For as long as he could remember, he had rejected the idea that what happened to him was the product of chance, a random dance of electrons, the luck of the draw. He believed that everything had meaning and he was constantly examining his life accordingly. But it is all too easy to slip from believing that there is significance concealed behind everything in one's life to believing that there is some intention or design behind it as well and to wondering whose design it is. This feeling, which everyone experiences to varying degrees of embarrassment, finds its fullest expression in two modes of thinking, the first being religious faith, the second paranoia. Having been on intimate terms with both, Phil came to doubt more and more that there was any real difference between them.

He had burned his fingers once too often and no longer wanted to believe that reality concealed anything at all behind it, that it was like a tapestry of which, even as we pull the needle back and forth through the fabric, we see only one side but will one day know its other side too. He had listened to Saint Paul and Winnie-the-Pooh for too long: "We look through a glass darkly, but one day we shall see and be seen face to face. . . . in that echanted place on the top of the forest, a little boy and his bear will always be playing." The time had come to heed the wisdom of Lucretius: "We will never know because we will no longer be"; there will be no one to see face to face in the light, and what we now believe we see darkly in a mirror is but our own reflection, distorted by the fear of death and by the fear of having suffered for nothing. Even though in modern, agnostic societies, this materialism passes for the official expression of good sense, Phil knew that few people really believed it, since it was anathema to their desires. Despite everything, we want to believe, we want meaning. Learning where this could lead had cost him. Now it was his duty to warn others.

When someone now came to interview him, he would trot out his new theory about reality, which held that all theories about reality are futile, false, and purely symptomatic. Reality is as dense and simple and stupid as a stone—nothing more. There's no false bottom to it. People need to observe the repetitions that occur in it and from them deduce rules that govern their everyday lives, but they must stop there and face the fact that most events happen by chance. With the same vehemence that former Stalinists and defrocked priests denounce their respective churches, he provided a thousand examples of the errors into which people are led by their desire to find meaning where there is none. A girl he knew who was studying the Bible came away from her readings with the conviction that Jesus Christ lived in the center of the earth in a glass coffin that protected him from wizards. Even Phil himself, under the influence of the remarkable Bishop Pike, had come to believe in things hardly less extravagant than that. But he had found his way back, just as he had found his way back from the hell of drugs, and he could now bear witness and alert others to the dangers of trying to find meaning in life. He used to talk, half seriously and half in jest, about leading a group of recovered meaning-seekers, something along the lines of Alcoholics Anonymous. At least he would know what he was talking about, he argued, unlike the guys who give antidrug speeches without ever having taken drugs or known their pleasures.

He had himself known the thrill that truth-seekers feel when they come to believe, for the umpteenth time, that ultimate revelation is finally at hand; he sometimes still felt that thrill, and this made his warnings even more important. Though not cured, he knew he was afflicted. He had regular relapses. Every year he grew increasingly nervous as November 17 approached, and with it another anniversary of the break-in; he spent that day barricaded in his apartment with Tessa. The terror he felt was real but didn't cloud his judgment; it was an anxiety attack, nothing more. From behind closed blinds, he watched himself sweat bullets, just as Fred the narcotics cop watched Bob Arctor. Comparing himself with his unlucky hero, he refined the diagnosis: split personality.

Like certain other very sick people, Phil had a lucid understanding of his disease, and henceforth he drew a clear distinction between (a) writing that organizations like X-Kalay were actually secret drug laboratories or that Nixon was a Communist, (b) believing it, and (c) believing that it was true. He thought that it was possible to write such nonsense, inasmuch as he was a science fiction writer and writing science fiction was all about coming up with hypotheses of precisely this kind, but that it was reprehensible to believe it. Above all, he understood that he could believe something without its being true, because he wasn't only a science fiction writer but also a confirmed paranoiac who tended to confuse the real world with the worlds he created in his books. Phil was proud to be so lucid and was determined to stay that way, but, like anyone else who has survived a nearly fatal vice, he found life rather grim without it.

The final chapter of *Don Quixote* gives us the knight sadly cured of his illusions and dying from the cure. On his deathbed, Quixote gives speeches that are as moving as they are reasonable, as he praises Sancho Panza for his good sense and denounces chivalric novels. It is one of the saddest chapters in all literature.

Toward the end of 1973, Phil's life in Fullerton resembled this last chapter in many ways. He wasn't dying. He had a new wife, and a new baby boy whom they named Christopher. He was surrounded by new friends. He had started to write again. The events of the times were confirming long-held intuitions. Unmistakable signs of literary recognition were beginning to appear. But he had also stopped mistaking windmills for knights, and when he did mistake them he knew that he was wrong. He saw himself as a Don Quixote of the mind; his adventures had been no less exemplary, but now they were finished and their lessons drawn. He had reached the final chapter and, without either haste or drama, and while savoring the small pleasures of invalid life, was waiting only for that final moment when he could write the words *The End*.

CHAPTER 17

THE EMPIRE NEVER ENDED

On February 20, 1974, Phil moaned in pain as he paced around the small apartment that he shared with Tessa and baby Christopher in Fullerton. He had just had a wisdom tooth pulled, and, the effects of the sodium pentathol having worn off during the night, his world had become a bottomless chasm of unspeakable pain. He knew, rationally, that the throbbing in his jaw would soon subside, but that thought didn't help; all he wanted was to not be there, to not exist until the pain had stopped, assuming it ever would.

Tessa called the dentist, who prescribed painkillers. Since Tessa's leaving the patient's side for a single minute was out of the question, the dentist phoned the prescription into the pharmacy, asking them to deliver the medication as quickly as possible.

Half an hour later, the doorbell rang. Phil, a damp tea bag clenched in his teeth, opened the door and found a young woman with thick black hair, dressed in a white uniform. From a delicate gold chain around her neck hung a gold pendant in the shape of a fish. Mesmerized by the ornament, Phil simply stood there, unable to speak.

"Eight dollars and forty-two cents," the young woman said, probably for the second time, as she continued to hold out the bag with the medication.

Phil pulled a ten-dollar bill out of his wallet.

"What—is that necklace?"

"An ancient sign," the girl said, raising her hand to the golden fish. "Used by the early Christians."

Holding the bag of medication, Phil stood frozen on the doorstep, studying the fish that gleamed softly in the shadows of the entryway. He had forgotten the throbbing in his jaw, forgotten what this young woman was doing there and what he was doing there himself. Tessa came out of the bedroom, where she had been drying her hair, and took in the scene; following the path of her husband's gaze, she assumed it was the young woman's breasts that had inspired the ecstasy she read on his face. At this point, the girl finally gave Phil his change and left. Tessa closed the door, making some kind of crack that later she couldn't remember and that Phil himself never heard, so no one has any way of knowing what line of dialogue should go at this particular place in this biography.

In *The Man in the High Castle*, when the Japanese businessman contemplates a piece of jewelry in harmony with the Tao, the veil of appearances lifts from before his eyes and for the first time he sees the world as it really is. It was only sometime later that Phil drew the parallels between his experience that day and what had happened to Mr. Tagomi, a character in a novel he had written twelve years earlier. But he knew that what had just happened on his doorstep was something he had been waiting for his whole life.

The moment of truth. Debriefing. Anamnesis.

It had finally come.

He knew who he was, where he was, and where he had always been.

The golden fish hanging around the neck of a delivery girl from a pharmacy was the code that had been there forever, waiting to deactivate the amnesia module that had been implanted in his brain and launch the program that would lead him back to reality.

He was ready.

THE EMPIRE NEVER ENDED.

When this phrase, strange yet also familiar, sprang into his mind, he understood its truth. The young woman was a secret Christian, and so was he. She had come to let him know this, bringing with her a sign to unlock his memories.

But why all the secrecy, the equivocal announcement, the tentative approach?

To foil the surveillance of the Romans.

But what Romans? This was Orange County, California, and the year was 1974.

No.

No, we only believe—or, to be exact, *most of us* only believe—that we are living in 1974 in the democratic United States of America, just as Ragle Gumm believed that he was living in 1950, just as Mr. Tagomi believed he was living in a world in which Japan had won the war, just as Joe Chip and his companions believed they were alive and Glen Runciter wasn't. They are waging the battle for truth, and you, Philip K. Dick, have just joined their ranks.

You have become part of the invisible troops of the Awakened, those who can see beyond the hologram foisted on the unsuspecting masses for whom the highways, the electric sockets, and the Howard Johnson restaurants have the compact, placid density of reality; now you, too, can make out the iron bars of the enormous prison in which the Empire holds its slaves. You may not have known it, but you have always been one of them, and today you have joined up with the secret resistance, the bearers of light who walk among the shadows.

Do you feel it? Something has been set into motion deep within you, at the core of your being. Your internal clock has been reset with the correct time and date.

We are in the year AD 70.

But that you now know this, that you now know the truth shouldn't surprise you. Deep down you have always known it.

The Savior came and then He left. But soon He will return. He promised to do so—and before this generation was finished. You'll see. Do you doubt the words of the Savior? No, you are like us and with us. You are awaiting His return. Despite the persecutions, you are preparing for it with gladness and joy.

He who has been graced with this knowledge must not run from his responsibilities. He must not shield himself from the truth with rationalizations—telling himself that what he has seen is a hallucination, an allegory, a past-life experience. No, he has seen the truth, literal and unmediated, the only truth. Rome is here, now. The average American sees nothing, but Rome is the underlying reality of the world in which he lives. The Empire never ended. It has merely hidden itself from the eyes of its subjects. It has spun a fantasy universe, like a film projected onto a prison wall, a shameless fiction that the inmates take for a factual documentary depicting nineteen centuries of history and the world in which those years have culminated. But while the movie plays, the war goes on. Those who refuse to watch the film and to believe that it is real are hounded mercilessly. They aren't permitted to leave the room, they are massacred in the restrooms. Some, out of caution, play along with the charade; they sit facing the movie screen, their eyes closed and their minds alert. They follow their own path; they serve a different king. They bear neither shields nor weapons; their only possessions are their robes, their sandals, and sometimes around their necks or on their wrists the golden fish by which they recognize one another. They form a secret society bound together by hope and by danger, a society that communicates in code, through cryptic signs scratched in the dust.

Praise the Lord, we have found you. You are back among us.

During the nights that followed, Phil dreamed a great deal and understood that his dreams were intended to complete his initiation. In most of them, opened books appeared before him. Had he been able to read these books and remember what he read, he would have found the answer to all the questions he was now asking. Unfortunately, however, the pages flipped by too quickly, as though before the moving lens of a photocopier. And they seemed to have been written in a foreign alphabet. He woke from these dreams frustrated yet convinced that the information he was supposed to glean had nonetheless been imprinted on his brain, without his knowledge. Perhaps it was supposed to be hidden from his consciousness as a safety measure.

———

How to put it? An aura drifted down and hummed around him, like a living, intelligent form of life, surrounding familiar objects and energizing them. His mind, the apartment he shared with Tessa and Christopher, their entire little world seemed like a nearly dead battery that someone had suddenly charged up.

He looked at Tessa, curled up into a ball on the couch like a tiny animal, sipping her coffee from a Snoopy mug. He looked at Chris, crawling along the carpet in his pajamas. He looked at the cats. Apparently, no one suspected anything.

He would have to teach his wife certain codes, the basic precautions, without revealing the whole truth to her. Luckily, he was a pro at that. What most people considered his paranoia was a blessing in disguise, the very condition on which his initiation depended. For so long he had been afraid of everything—the IRS, narcs, the police, the FBI—and all that time he had been right, and wrong only these last few months when he had tried to let go of his fears. They had sharpened his senses, had given him the reflexes of someone gone underground.

He was also known for saying strange things. People sometimes couldn't tell whether he was joking or being serious, whether he believed what he was saying or was trying out on his listener some new crackpot theory that had just occurred to him and would soon be replaced by some other crackpot theory. It was widely understood that a conversation with Philip K. Dick did not follow the normal rules and that nothing he said should come as a surprise. This tacit protocol gave him substantial maneuvering room in which he could do and say what he wanted without being taken for a complete lunatic. Still, the risk was there, and he would have to proceed with extreme caution.

He sent Tessa to buy some votive candles for a little altar he was setting up on a shelf in their bedroom, complete with a primitive painting of the Virgin appearing before Saint Philip, in front of which the candles would burn continuously.

While Tessa was off at the supermarket, Christopher, who had awoken from his nap, started to cry. Phil went into the kitchen to make some cocoa for him, and when he returned to the bedroom the baby reached for the bottle. Phil gave it to him. Without knowing why, he had also picked up a piece of bread that had been lying on the kitchen table. Suddenly he understood why. He started to go back to get some water, then changed his mind. If the Romans were somehow watching all this, the connection between the bread and the water would surely alert them. Everything would have to look as if it were happening naturally, so that anyone who didn't actually know what was happening would see nothing other than a father playing with his son. He gave a tiny piece of bread to Christopher, using the opportunity to take back the bottle, whose nippled top he gently unscrewed, just enough so that a little bit of the chocolate milk spilled on the child's head. Quickly Phil traced the sign of the cross with the milk on Christopher's forehead, whispering, in Greek, "In the name of the Father, and of the Son, and of the Holy Ghost." Then he gave the bottle back to the child, and, while Christopher drank from it, he hugged him and said in his ear his secret Christian name: Paul. The whole ceremony had not taken more than a few moments, and an unapprised observer would have had no idea what he had just witnessed. Phil had carried out all the gestures from instinct, with authority and precision, impelled by a force that was infinitely greater than him yet concerned with the well-being of both father and son.

The hostilities began the night of Christopher's baptism, on the easy-listening station to which, for several days now, Phil had gotten into the habit of leaving his radio tuned all night long. He kept it on at a low volume, and the sound reassured him, allowed him to remember where he was when he woke with a start and couldn't get his bearings. Thus they slept, Phil, Tessa, and Christopher, protected by the Virgin of Saint Philip, surrounded by scented candles and by the smooth sounds of Carly Simon, Olivia Newton-John, and—Phil's favorite singer—Linda Ronstadt.

Sometime around three in the morning, Tessa was woken from

sleep by a sudden commotion. Phil was sitting bolt upright in the bed, rocking back and forth, his hands over his ears. In a quavering voice, he kept repeating, "*Libera me Domine!*" Tessa, scared out of her wits, didn't dare move, but he suddenly became aware of her presence and yelled at her to turn it off. She didn't have time to figure out that "it" referred to the radio. Phil had already scrambled to the foot of the bed and pulled the plug, then run with the radio into the kitchen. When he came back, he was trembling.

He explained that he had been woken by Linda Ronstadt singing "You're No Good," a song off her latest album, one that normally Phil was very fond of. But this time his name had somehow become part of the lyrics, like a kind of interference. It was to him, Phil, that Ronstadt was viciously repeating, "You're no good, you're no good, you're no good, baby, you're no good," finishing the refrain with the words "Die, die, die." Ronstadt, or the anti-Christian terrorists who were using Ronstadt, wanted him dead.

Tessa calmed him as best she could. They went back to sleep. A little later the unplugged radio switched back on. This time, instead of Ronstadt, there came a slow, deep, echoing voice—doubtless synthesized—that, playing on his name, kept repeating childish and menacing obscenities against a background of bubble-gum rock. These were interspersed with death threats, or rather veiled incitements to suicide that terrified him with their persuasive power.

He finally mustered the courage to go into the kitchen, but the voice stopped, only to pick up again the moment he returned to the bedroom. Awoken again, not knowing what else to do, Tessa listened in vain for the voice. In the end Phil threw the radio into the sink, filled the sink with water, and put wax in his ears.

The next morning it occurred to him that he was not supposed to have consciously heard what he heard. His enemies had broadcast the program to condition his mind while he slept. He had once received an advertisement in the mail for foreign language instructional cassette tapes that you listened to on a speaker placed under your pillow while you slept. By waking up while they were trying to imprint their incitements to suicide on his cerebral circuits, he had fouled up their plans.

But for how long? And how many times, without being aware of it, had he been exposed to these lethal sound waves?

It was as though his brain, having been reactivated by the appearance of the golden fish, had become a radio receiver, picking up several frequencies simultaneously that bombarded him with contradictory information. The trick now was to separate the channels, determine the source of the broadcasts and the intentions behind them.

It was not going to be a pretty fight.

If his brain was going to have to be a radio receiver, he might as well try to control it as best he could. In a popular science magazine to which he and Tessa subscribed he had read that a person could improve the communication between the two hemispheres of the brain by taking massive doses of vitamins. Phil decided to overlook the fact that the treatment had been tested only on young schizophrenics. Three times a day he ingested several handfuls of pills, which kept him from sleeping and set off dazzling displays of phoshenes beneath his closed eyelids. His thoughts raced through his brain, like reptiles darting through a dark corridor. Spots of color floated in the shadows of the bedroom. When he managed to fall asleep, toward daybreak or in the afternoon, he was visited with strange dreams, most of them seeming to have something to do with the Greco-Roman world. He was locked in a cage in the middle of the Coliseum and giant lizards were tearing at the door. He saw a black and gold vase sitting on a three-legged table, and a voice told him the year was 842 BC. The voice spoke Greek but he understood it. When he woke up he wondered what had happened in the year 842 before Jesus Christ. According to his *Encyclopedia Britannica*, that was the Mycenaean era. He scoured his brain for some explanation as to why everything was pointing to this date, eight centuries before the apostolic era toward which all the other signs were pointing.

One night when he was moping about in the kitchen, casting side-long glances at the radio that Tessa had rescued from the sink, he realized that he'd made a mistake in his vitamin dosages. The vitamin C pills he had been taking contained five hundred milligrams, five times more than he had thought. This meant that for the past eight days he had been taking seven more grams a day than he should have been taking—not even counting the other vitamins. He went back to bed feeling a bit worried. The votive candles flickered on the shelf before the painting of the Virgin and Saint Philip. Everyone else—Tessa, Christopher, Pinky the cat—was asleep. The only sounds were their breathing, the hum of the refrigerator, and the distant but constant rumbling of cars hurtling down the freeway.

Suddenly floating patches of color started to climb up the wall. Quickly, and then quicker still, as if propelled by centrifugal force toward some enormous, consuming beyond. They were moving toward the edge of the universe, Phil thought, and that idea terrified him. Lying perfectly still on his bed, he was entering a corridor of light that extended endlessly before him. He was in it now, falling, plunging at the speed of light. It was like the end of *2001: A Space Odyssey*, when the astronaut leaves the solar system.

Then the colors produced forms with defined contours that linked together, permutating and transforming at dazzling speed. They seemed like abstract paintings. It was if he had looked at a hundred works by Paul Klee in a matter of seconds. Then came the Kandinskys and the Picassos, of various periods. This went on for hours. Thousands upon thousands of paintings by these artists—many more than they could ever have painted during their lifetimes, even had they lived several centuries. Each one passed by in a flash, one following another in rapid succession but lingering long enough to leave an impression of its sovereign perfection on his mind. Phil was no aesthete and always maintained that he had no visual sense. For the first time, the violent and ineffable beauty of forms was revealed to him. He would have loved to have been able to enjoy the spectacle unreservedly, without thinking about what he was seeing, but that was precisely what he had never been able to permit himself to do: there was no room in him for pure enjoyment, only for meaning, and already he was trying to figure out what these visions meant. He would have liked to have had a camera attached to his retina so that he could preserve a trace of this mar-velous art collection and have it authenticated. Seeing wasn't enough; he needed to know where this visual feast came from and what it meant. It had to mean something; it couldn't simply be gratuitous, a random event. Someone was sending him telepathic messages, mes-sages that had been transformed into brilliant colors and displayed like abstract paintings, messages whose nature he couldn't grasp.

Later, Christopher cried out, and Tessa shuffled grumpily into the kitchen to prepare his bottle. Phil remained in bed, bathed in the last remnants of the nocturnal orgy; the patches of color were slowing down and fading in intensity, then, gradually, they disappeared. He arose, certain that he had been transformed.

The transformation did not have much effect on his taste for conjec-ture, which had free rein in the days that followed.

It kept coming down to the same question: had these messages that he had been receiving originated within himself or had they come from some outside agency?

From a materialist perspective that saw the mind and body as inex-tricably linked, the answer was readily at hand. Nonetheless, he reread carefully the article about the vitamin regimen he had been following, studied the labels on the bottles, and leafed through the medical dic-tionary that, as a lifelong hypochondriac, he always had at his side. From this research emerged a theory brilliant in its scientific verisimil-itude: the acidity of the vitamins had dramatically lowered the level of gamma-aminobutyric acid in his brain. At adequate levels, this substance, also known as GABA fluid, inhibits the firing of certain neural circuits, the very ones that make people see parades of pink elephants or won-drous displays of Klee or Kandinsky paintings hurling past their reti-nas. GABA fluid is the opposite of LSD; when there is not enough of it, the phantasmagoria begins. He found this hypothesis satisfying enough, much like a motorist who, when his car begins to make strange noises, tells himself reassuringly that "it must be the spark plugs."

At the same time, however, he kept up a parallel line of inquiry,

sending Tessa to the library to check out books on Klee and Kandinsky
for him. He discovered that the Hermitage in Leningrad had a large
number of their canvasses in its collections. This information brought
back a memory. Years before, someone had told him about experiments the Soviets were doing on telepathic communication. Could it
be that he was the object of such an experiment—in which the Soviets had decided to film the abstract works in the museum and trans-
mit the montage at enormous velocity halfway around the world to
bombard the neural circuits of a resident of Fullerton, California?

Perhaps they had, but then the question was why. Why choose Phil
Dick rather than some other Southern Californian? And why choose
abstract paintings—was the choice random, because they had to test
the transmission with some message or other and these paintings happened to be at hand, or was there some significance to the paintings?

As for the first question, he asked it only as a matter of form, for he
had no doubt that he had indeed been targeted specifically. He was certainly aware of his tendency to find it suspicious, or at any rate mean-
ingful, that a vacuum cleaner salesman would ring his doorbell on the
same day as a Jehovah's Witness; he would have very much liked to
doubt his own logic, but facts were facts, and the principle of parsimony
that underlies all scientific explanation precluded his imagining that
there was no relationship between his being contacted by secret Christians fighting against the Empire, then by Soviet telepaths, all within a
matter of three weeks. He just had to figure out the connection.

Did the Russian scientists working on this program belong to the
confederacy of the golden fish? It seemed more logical to imagine
them working for the Empire, of which the Soviet Union was the most
obvious, though not the most sophisticated, avatar. But what about
the dissidents? Maybe dissident scientists were risking their lives trying to contact him. Maybe, but maybe not. Perhaps the real truth was
that Soviet scientists—not dissidents but, on the contrary, loyal ser-
vants of the Empire—had somehow happened upon the message the
fish worshipers were trying to send him and now they were doing
what they could to disrupt it. When he lived on Hacienda Way, one of
the freaks—a kid who had since died—used to call out random num-

bers in a loud voice whenever someone started to make a telephone call, so that it was impossible for the person to remember the number he was trying to dial. If that was what the Russians were up to, then the whole point of the message was to overload the frequency and therefore the message had to be completely random. But he didn't want to jump to conclusions too quickly. The fact that the message confused him didn't prove it was not the real one that his invisible friends wanted to reach him. For there was a strong possibility that this message wasn't intended for his conscious mind but was aimed directly at some deeper and safer subcortical region of his brain. And, despite this reasoning, nothing could shake his certainty of having begun to amass a data bank that, unbeknownst to his conscious mind, was starting to affect his nervous system and cause it to change profoundly. To his benefit, perhaps, or at any rate to hasten the triumph of the light.

In the days that followed, Phil's dreams became even more intense. He felt as if he were in an accelerated learning program, though without knowing what the crash course was trying to teach him. Yet now and again, and to his great displeasure, he found he could identify the language—Russian. Page after page, hundreds at a time, technical manuals printed in Cyrillic letters filed past his eyes.

That was when he remembered Lem's article.

Several months earlier, someone had sent him the German translation of an article that had first appeared in a Polish magazine under the name of Stanislas Lem, reputed to be the greatest science fiction writer of the socialist bloc: his work had been translated into dozens of languages; and the great Tarkovski had based his film *Solaris*—the Soviet answer to Kubrick's *2001*—on Lem's novel of that title. And now, this important writer had apparently gone to the trouble to write a long analysis of American science fiction, the gist of which was this: it was one vast wasteland, with the exception of Philip K. Dick.

Inasmuch as Lem's indictment of American science fiction was based on high cultural arguments, his estimation of Dick was surprising since only with great difficulty could one cast him in the role of belletrist among the philistines. And, indeed, Lem didn't try to do so; on the contrary, he underscored Dick's bad taste, his pedestrian style, his limping plots. Yet in spite of all this, Lem believed, the gulf between Dick and his contemporaries was no less great than the one separating the Dostoevsky of *Crime and Punishment* from the writers of pulp crime fiction. For all his naïveté, Dick managed to express a truly visionary perspective on the modern world, and nowhere was this more apparent than in *Ubik.*

Phil had been flattered by Lem's praise, but it troubled him as well. He himself had never thought of *Ubik* as one of his better works. He remembered the novel far less vividly than he did that terrible period of his life when he was working on it, when his home and brain were falling apart. And here, within the space of several months, a number of Europeans were discovering in this thrown-together novel profoundly mysterious dimensions. One of his French editors, Patrice Duvic, had come to visit him that fall and announced with solemnity that he considered *Ubik* one of the five most important books ever written.

Phil assumed Duvic meant one of the five best *science fiction novels* ever written. But Duvic said no, he meant one of the five most important books in human history. Phil never asked why, or what the other four books were. Duvic had spoken with such conviction that Phil didn't know what to think.

He had started to correspond with Lem, who was planning to publish *Ubik* in Poland. These plans went awry when it emerged that under Polish law, authors could only collect royalties in Poland, not abroad. Lem had suggested that this restriction offered an incentive for Phil to do a little traveling. Perhaps he might like to attend an upcoming literary conference in Warsaw, where a pile of zlotys awaited him. Unpredictable as ever, Phil dug in his heels. He wrote furious letters to his agent, his publisher, and particularly Lem, whom he at first accused of wanting to make off with the royalties by counting on his never showing up to claim them and then of trying to use the money as bait to lure him to Poland, which he would never be allowed to leave. This latter hypothesis offered richer possibilities than ordinary embezzlement, and Phil spent the winter exploring its tortuous implications—on his own, since Lem had stopped answering his letters.

To all appearances, the Eastern Bloc intelligence agencies were trying to determine how subversive his work was. They had started to decode it—witness the article by Lem, who probably wasn't even an individual but most likely a collective writing under that name. They saw Dick as a potential Solzhenitsyn, perhaps even more dangerous because he threatened to expose the secret Sovietization of America—to say nothing of the secret of life after death—to what remained of the free world. Weren't people beginning to speak of him as a writer of Nobel Prize caliber? Duvic had passed on a comment to that effect that had been made on a late-night cultural program on French television, and from it Phil had surmised that a group of French intellectuals was lobbying the Swedish jury on his behalf; he was already wondering what he would do when Nixon's apparatchiks refused to allow his now illustrious adversary to go to Stockholm to pick up his prize.

Before it could come to that, his enemies in the East were looking for a way to disarm the ticking time bomb. They were making overtures to him; they were floating trial balloons his way. And who knew? Perhaps Duvic was involved as well, though maybe unwittingly. Clearly these French intellectuals—who were all Marxists anyway and read Phil's work as a critique of capitalism—were being used by the KGB to influence public opinion in the West in furtherance of their aims. Duvic was a pawn they had put into play so as to draw Phil out into the open. That's where Lem came in; the groundwork had been laid, and his job was to soften Phil up and get him to Poland. Phil wondered what would have happened to him in Warsaw had he taken the bait. He could just imagine it: the lecture, the banquet that night, the toasts to his success, and then the next morning, when he would wake up with a hangover in a room with stark white walls, surrounded by guys in white coats holding syringes. "This won't take long, *Gospodin* Dick, and you won't feel a thing. You'll even be able to give your lecture this evening." And that evening he would find himself before an even larger crowd than before, because the foreign press corps would have been invited, and he would hear himself tell them that he had decided to stay in Poland, land of freedom.

Luckily he had thwarted their designs and, at least for now, managed to escape their brainwashing. He had a good laugh thinking of all the heads that were probably rolling within the ranks of the Lem collective, but then it occurred to him that perhaps his enemies had failed on purpose and weren't trying to get him after all, at least not yet.

He felt the uneasiness of the chess player who realizes his opponent is about to mount a devastating assault but who can't tell where it will come from. Lem's efforts to get him out of the country, the pages of Cyrillic characters, the dream visions of paintings from the Hermitage—it all heralded the return of the diabolical Russian theme in the symphony of his life. He waited.

The shot was fired on March 20, though it was on March 18 that he first had an inkling of the impending disaster, when Tessa signed for a registered letter. In labored English, the author of the letter proclaimed himself an admirer of Dick's work and wanted an autograph or, if possible, a signed photograph. It was a classic fan letter of the sort he felt he never received enough of, particularly from women, but this one came from Tallinn, Estonia.

In all his life no one had ever written him from Estonia. He opened his atlas and was not surprised to find that Tallinn was located near Leningrad and not far from Warsaw. The net was beginning to close around him.

Suddenly words came out of his mouth, as if on their own and without premeditation: "Today is Monday," he told Tessa. "On Wednesday, another letter will come. It is highly dangerous."

He refused to provide further explanation and didn't get out of bed for two days.

On the morning of the twentieth, he sent Tessa out to get the mail. She returned looking anxious and solemn and handed him the seven letters that had arrived that day. Phil glanced at the envelopes without opening them. Six were easily recognizable: ads and bills for the most part, letters whose senders he recognized by their return address or the familiar handwriting. The seventh had no return address. The post-mark indicated it had been mailed from New York.

"That's the one," he told her, his voice constricted in fear.

He asked Tessa to open the envelope and to describe the contents without showing it to him. It was a single sheet of paper on which two book reviews had been photocopied, both from the *Daily World*, a left-leaning New York newspaper. The articles praised a certain Soviet writer living in the United States for her lucid depiction of capitalist decadence. The words *decline* and *death* had been underlined in red pen on the photocopy. Tessa said that the name and address of the novelist were on the back of the page. Everything seemed to indicate that the photocopy had been sent by the novelist herself.

Phil kept his eyes shut as he listened to Tessa. If he chose to, he could explain away the situation. It was thoroughly banal: a Soviet writer, aware of his reputation among leftist intellectuals, had sent him a photocopy of a couple of articles praising her talents because she admired his novels and wanted to bring her own work to his attention. But he knew better. Ever since the registered letter from Estonia had arrived, a voice inside him had been telling him that a supreme test—an ordeal in the literal sense—awaited him. How he handled it would determine his entire destiny.

" 'See,' said the Eternal, 'I have set before you this day life and good, death and evil. Choose.' "

Now it was his turn. He considered every move he might make and calculated every possible consequence, all the way to checkmate. If only he knew who his enemy was. Obviously it was the Russians, but that was precisely the problem: it was too obvious. Did they really think that, having turned down the enticing offers from Lem and his clique, he would fall for such a clumsy ploy? Then maybe the letter had come from the secret Christians, who, in the purest spiritual tradition, had strewn his initiatory path with temptations to see whether he would resist them. Same problem. He wasn't tempted in the slightest to get in touch with the Soviet novelist. In fact, everything having to do with the Soviet Union terrified him, and those who were subjecting him to this test would have known that about him. The test must therefore have some other meaning. It was not simply a matter of replying to the letter and thereby failing the test or of not replying and thereby passing it. Suddenly he understood: the way he would fail the test was not by replying to the letter but by *not* replying. That was the trap. Whoever had sent him the letter had expected him to burn it, bury his head under his pillow, try to put it out of his mind. So that's just what he *wouldn't* do. Did that mean he would reply? No, he wouldn't do that either.

Two hours after the letter arrived he phoned the FBI.

CHAPTER 18

THE TYRANT'S FALL

The police are used to nutcases—people who come to the station house to confess to crimes they haven't committed or who claim to have seen flying saucers or to have stumbled across a plot against the president of the United States. The problem is that every now and then one of these wild declarations contains a kernel of truth. And so when someone claiming to be a world-famous science fiction writer whom the French are talking about as a contender for the Nobel Prize, someone who almost had one of his books made into a movie by John Lennon ("Yeah, John Lennon of the Beatles"), who had been given the book by Timothy Leary ("Not that I approve of Leary, by the way. Quite the contrary. I've even written a book in which I come down hard on drugs; it hasn't come out yet, but I plan to dedicate it to Richard Kleindienst. That should tell you my position, which, I should add, has unfortunately been misunderstood, thanks largely to an irresponsible article by Harlan Ellison in which he claims I wrote my books on LSD, which is patently untrue")—and when this guy, who can't start a sentence without letting loose a torrent of parentheticals within parentheticals, finally tells you after twenty minutes of preamble that he received a letter from a reader in Estonia and two days later—

just as he predicted—a photocopy of some articles that appeared in a newspaper that may not be exactly Communist but is definitely pinko and that this photocopy is clearly from the KGB, and then, just to make sure you believe him, launches into a complicated story about frozen royalties in Poland that are part of a plot to lure him behind the Iron Curtain and then brainwash him, well, what can you do except listen patiently, tell him you'll look into it, and then finally, when the guy asks you what he should do, start by calling him by his first name. "Phil," you say, "you've already done a lot. You've done the right thing here. Don't tell anyone else about this. We'll take it from here."

Said with a proper tone of authority, in a serious and confiding voice, phrases such as these will generally bring the conversation to a close. But don't kid yourself: you can fool him for the time being, but nine times out of ten your average nutcase will figure out that he's been had, and he won't take it lying down.

As soon as he hung up, Phil wrote a letter recapping the phone conversation—if what he had said was a little disorganized, well, he apologized for that—and sent it off along with the relevant exhibits: his correspondence with Lem, Lem's article, the letter from the Estonian fan, and the photocopied reviews from the *Daily World*. The letter to the FBI, the first of fourteen he would write over the next four months, was the only one to which he received a reply. "Your interest in writing as you did is indeed appreciated and the material will receive appropriate attention," wrote William A. Sullivan, director of the FBI's Los Angeles office.

Naturally, Phil took this communication as a request for him to gather more material. In fact, nothing could have been easier, for the material was coming in hard and fast and from every direction; he was swimming in it. Not all of it, of course, would interest William A. Sullivan, whom Phil suspected of being indifferent to matters of theological importance, just as George Smith and George Scruggs had been. But having sent the threatening photocopy from the *Daily World*, he felt he couldn't hide from the FBI agent what he had suddenly understood the following night.

Guessing the danger contained in the letter from the Soviet novelist—a danger for him alone, because for each of us there's a magic word out there, a secret phrase with the power to either kill us or save us—he had been careful to have Tessa describe the contents without reading it to him. And since he had forwarded it to the FBI that very evening, just after the phone call, the ominous document had spent only a few hours under his roof. But while stuffing it into an envelope on his way out the door to mail it off, he couldn't help stealing a glance at the lethal page. A few words struck his retina. They had hit their mark.

He tried to forget them but he couldn't; he shouldn't have seen them in the first place. Now they danced before his eyes:

Antonetti   Olivetti   Dodd Mead Reinhardt   Holt

They were proper nouns, probably the names of authors or publishing houses. They meant nothing to him personally, yet someone wanted him to see those words.

That night, the letters moved under his eyelids, broke apart, then came together again, like dancers changing partners. When dawn broke, only one couple remained:

Olive Holt

Olive Holt. Of course. The babysitter he had in Berkeley many years before, who used to talk endlessly about the Soviet Union, where people lived so happily.

How many years had it been since he had given any thought to her, or even remembered her name?

Forty years ago, the name had been imprinted on his neural circuits so that, when the time came, it could give the Communists access to his brain, the way a traitor who has snuck his way into a besieged city will open the gates from the inside and deliver it to the enemy. The name Olive Holt played the same role for the Commies as the golden fish had for the Christians—and that fish that had stirred inside him fifteen years earlier, while he was writing *The Man in the High Castle*, had probably been implanted in him even earlier than that, in his earliest childhood. Thank God the fish had emerged before his babysitter's name had. The anamnesis had worked for the benefit of the Christians rather than for the Empire.

It would be best not to mention the fish and the underground Christians to William A. Sullivan. But he did tell Sullivan about Olive Holt. A week later, he also told him about the group of Canadian and French Marxists who were planning to visit him. What should he do about these visitors? Let them come so as not to fuel their suspicions? Bolt the door and not answer the phone? Go away on a trip? His panic-stricken letters to Sullivan went unanswered, and the man was always out of the office when Phil phoned. He would have to handle things on his own. This was probably another test—they weren't going to hold his hand this time. At first he tried to get out of town, but, exactly as he had predicted, the car refused to start. Sabotage. So he did an about-face and spent the afternoon with the Marxists. The next day he wrote Sullivan about how his visitors, microphones in hand, had tried to pump him for information but how he had refused to confirm any of their interpretations of his novels and managed to avoid all their traps. Not bad for an amateur.

I'm sorry to say that nothing of what I've been relating is invented. The one-sided correspondence with Sullivan exists; it was published not long ago in the first volume of Dick's collected correspondence. Paul Williams, the editor, compiled the letters from carbon copies that Dick kept. Williams admits that he considered destroying them, to protect the memory of his friend and the feelings of some of his correspondents.

As for the latter, their versions of the facts appear before each letter in the collection, and it is clear that Stanislas Lem and Peter Fitting—one of the "Marxist group" that came to visit Dick—refer to what most of us would consider reality. The fearsome Marxist group, for example, consisted of a rock musician, his wife, and an academic who had written a book on science fiction that contained a preface by Jean-François

Lyotard—in other words, typical representatives of the circles from which, during the 1960s, Dick's foreign fans emerged: dyed-in-the-wool hippies, Marcuso-Reichian leftists, scruffy but harmless individuals whom Phil felt it was his obligation to report on to the FBI.

It is the nature of a conversion experience to turn a person inside out like a glove. He no longer thinks what he used to think or acts as he used to act, and often, ironically, especially if the transformation is religious, he thinks and acts in ways that would once have repelled him. Yet he is enraptured by these changes, whose very idea would have been odious to the man whose being he has cast off. They attest to the authenticity of his experience, to the fact that another self has emerged within. To prove his disdain for who he once was, he will embrace the caricature of who he now is. The skeptical, arrogant intellectual who becomes a Catholic will adopt the more popular, not to say sentimental, forms of his new faith—the little devotions, the miracle-working medallions, the inspirational writings, the kitschy art. That is what it means to repent—to go against one's natural inclinations.

Rebel, punk, the enemy of authority in all of its forms, Phil would never on his own have thought of calling the FBI and asking for their protection, let alone informing for them. If, several weeks before the photocopy from the *Daily World* arrived, someone had told him he would be doing precisely that, he would have scoffed. A Berkeleyite does not truck with the cops—or if he does, it proves only one thing: he isn't himself. He's been replaced, or some outside force is controlling him, or someone else is acting in his stead.

Exactly, Phil thought bitterly. That's exactly what's happened to me.

And the best part of it is that I'm overjoyed. And that I'm positive I'm right to be overjoyed.

Here are two examples of conversion.

Saul, a devout young Jew and an enthusiastic persecutor of the new Christian sect, underwent a strange experience on the road to Damascus, the upshot of which was that he turned into the Apostle Paul and began repeating, with the contagious fervor for which he is known, "I no longer live, but Christ lives in me."

The hero of Orwell's *1984* gradually finds the courage to battle the tyranny of Big Brother. But he is arrested, tortured, brainwashed, so that by the end of the novel not only does he profess genuine allegiance to Big Brother, he actually "loves" him.

There are several key differences between these two stories, both of which are about the ravishment of a human consciousness. However, one is about torture, the other about illumination. And whereas both Orwell and his readers find the hero of *1984* magnificently lucid before his arrest and tragically deranged afterward, the author of Acts of the Apostles and doubtless most of his readers share the certainty that his conversion is an improvement. What is troubling is that the religious convert and the brainwashing victim are driven by the same sense of certainty: now that they love Christ or Big Brother, they walk the path of truth; previously, they erred. And the proof of it all is that before their transformations, their greatest fear was that what has happened to them might happen—yet see what a blessing it has turned out to be! This rupture makes communication between the convert and those around him about as difficult as that between Dracula and Van Helsing: people are afraid of being bitten by the living dead because they know that once contaminated by the vampire's bite they'll be glad they were. And what's most frightening, for those who haven't yet been bitten, is that they know that if it happens, all that will remain of the self they once were is the part that delights in no longer being oneself. Before, one was afraid; afterward, one is no longer there, someone else has triumphed.

For Phil, calling the FBI was an act of self-deliverance. In psychological terms it was what the fugitive feels when, exhausted from his years on the run, he finally turns himself in and experiences an incongruous sense of serenity. Probably for his own psychological reasons, Phil preferred to explain what he had done in spiritual terms—as a surrendering up of his old, tired, fearful, and anxious self in favor of an infinitely wiser entity using him to take steps for his own good that he himself could never have taken on his own. When his enemies, whoever they were, had tried to trap him with the photocopy from the *Daily World*, this entity had shown him the one way of responding to their ruse that he could never have imagined and therefore the only way that would actually work: calling the police. He won on all counts, however you looked at it. If the FBI, whatever its failures, was still up to its mission, then it was only normal for him to seek their protection from the Communists who were harassing him. He was knocking on the right door and expiating the sins of his leftist past in the process. But if, on the other hand, the FBI had secretly become the repressive tool of some crypto-Communist leader, the best way of escaping this wolf in sheep's clothing was to throw himself into its jaws: by feigning innocence, he might beat the enemy at his own game, forcing him to act according to his official role as the defender of democracy. And last but not least, it was also possible that, with the final days of Nixon and his gang in sight, the forces of light and the forces of darkness were battling each other within the bureau itself; in that case, he had chosen well. Obviously, he would have preferred to know which side William A. Sullivan was on and whether he read Phil's reports with sympathy or rage; but the entity that had now taken over Phil's being had evidently decided not to share with him what it knew of these matters. It guided him without explaining why it did what it did or where it was leading him. Phil simply had to follow.

During the spring of 1974, having gotten Phil to recognize the folly of his left-leaning ways, this entity, whatever it was, began to clean house, throwing itself at the job with the same sort of energy with which a new bride might set about ridding her husband of his bachelor habits. It made him trim his beard and cut the little hairs that protruded from his nostrils with special scissors he had never known about but nevertheless bought at the drugstore, as though he had been trimming his nose hairs all his life. It made him buy new clothes. It went through his medicine cabinet, throwing out what it knew—and now he knew—was harmful to his health. It discovered that wine, being acidic, upset his stomach, and from one day to the next he began drinking beer, which he used to hate but now found thoroughly enjoyable. It straightened out his problems with the IRS. It read over his contracts and his royalty statements and found irregularities. It got him to fire his agent, an act that seemed to him a very adult thing to do and that he boasted to his friends about. He ultimately relented and he returned to his agent, who wrangled a contract for his next book that was better than any deal Dick had signed before. Phil returned home from these battles the conquering hero, mightily pleased with his exploits.

Lastly, it saved the life of his son, Christopher

For several days the little boy had seemed in pain. His pediatrician had said there was nothing wrong with him, but he continued to whine and fuss. One morning, Phil was in his easy chair, his eyes closed, listening to "Strawberry Fields." When he heard the line that began "Living is easy with eyes closed," a beam of pink light flashed across his eyes. He knew at that instant that he had just received a transmission of some vital information, and he got up and went into the baby's room, where Tessa was changing Chris's diaper. In the toneless voice that, as he had now begun to recognize, came out of him from time to time, he informed Tessa that Christopher had a birth defect. When Tessa replied that the doctor had said there was nothing wrong, Phil told her that the boy had a strangulated right inguinal hernia, that it had already descended into his scrotal sac, and that the membrane had given way. The boy needed an operation immediately.

He insisted Tessa drive the baby to the emergency room at the Fullerton hospital. Chris was examined by a Dr. Zahn, which in German means "tooth"; given the circumstances of his illumination earlier in the year, Phil thought this was a good omen. Dr. Zahn confirmed Phil's diagnosis. The child's health was in danger and he would have to be operated on that same evening. Afterward, Christopher never fussed again.

Dumbfounded, Tessa questioned her husband long and hard about the incident. For the first time, a concrete fact had emerged to lend some substance to the bizarre statements that had been coming out of him for the past few months. But Phil never stood by his positions unless someone disagreed with him, and when Tessa and their friends professed true astonishment at his revelations, he immediately became evasive. His explanations varied: one day he would say that he'd learned about Christopher's condition from the Beatles, and another day he would swear that he'd heard the child murmur, "*Eli, Eli, lama sabachthani.*" Nevertheless, what he told Tessa was that sometime between March and August 1974 a benevolent entity had entered his mind and inspired him to change his life. He explained the process in terms familiar to anyone who uses a computer. A password—the fish—had opened up his cerebral circuits to this entity, which had then installed a program in his brain. The program had been running ever since. It had collected the data—the events great and small in the life of Philip K. Dick—and dutifully processed them. To keep its host informed so that he could act effectively, it burrowed like a computer worm into all his normal perceptual channels and data banks, and where necessary, into the less normal ones as well: lyrics of songs he had been listening to, letters of text from books, road signs, cereal boxes, and fortune cookies. Often the information came to him in his dreams, but as he slept little at night and often catnapped during the day, the lines between waking, sleeping, and dreaming were not clearly marked. As the message mattered more to him than did the medium, he saw little difference between a sentence he saw in a dream and one he read while awake. He suspected that the books or bound galleys that he was given to read in his dreams really existed somewhere. Quite prosaically, he saw the dreams as time-savers, sparing him trips to the library. Sometimes it happened that what he learned in his dreams whetted his appetite for more information, and on those occasions he would go to the library to continue his investigations.

For several weeks in a row a book appeared to him in his dream visions, and he became convinced that it held the answers to all his questions. The text went whipping by his eyes too quickly for him to know what it contained, but the bibliographic clues grew clearer and clearer from one dream to the next. The book was a hardcover volume with a blue jacket and contained no fewer than seven hundred pages. The copyright dated from 1966 or perhaps 1968—he wasn't sure which. The title ended with the word *Grove,* and it had another word that could have been *Budding.* Several times he saw the pages surrounded by flames and decided that it must be a particularly sacred text. Perhaps the text that is mentioned in the Book of Daniel.

He looked in libraries and bookstores, and one day he found the book. He was sure it was the right one. Blue, thick, published in 1968 under the title *The Shadow of Blooming Grove.*

He opened the book, persuaded that his quest was at an end. The secrets of the world would now be revealed to him.

It turned out to be a biography of Warren G. Harding.

Someone else might have concluded that the whole thing was ridiculous, or at least that this was the wrong book. But Phil concluded that it proved one of two things: either all the secrets of the world truly were to be found in a biography of Warren G. Harding (probably in some subliminal form and without the author's awareness) or the entity feeding him information was gently making fun of him. Whichever the case, his method reminded him of something—or rather of someone.

Glen Runciter.

Glen Runciter who, in *Ubik,* stayed in communication with his employees lost in the labyrinth of half-life, guiding them and trying to make them understand, through recourse to trivial-seeming means, what had happened to them. He left them graffiti on bathroom walls: ALL OF YOU ARE DEAD. I AM ALIVE. Advertising leaflets, slogans that skywriters, puffing out smoke behind them, displayed in the air, the codes contained in the design of cigarette packs—all these told them what to do if they wanted to survive. Runciter even appeared on television, where he demonstrated the efficacy of Ubik spray, the only weapon effective against entropy.

Phil began to understand what book his recurring dream was heading toward—not the biography of Warren G. Harding but the novel that the entity, having analyzed his mental processes, knew the biography of Warren G. Harding would eventually make him think of. He was now beginning to understand what people like Stanislas Lem and Patrice Duvic were trying to say. The sacred book, the book surrounded by flames, the book that revealed all the secrets of the universe, was *Ubik*.

It didn't seem so odd now to think that he had written one of the five most important books in history, a book, like the Bible or *Bardo Thodol*, to which men would have to turn to learn the secret of their condition. *Ubik* described that condition in literal terms.

He was careful from then on to distinguish *Ubik* the book from Ubik the entity in the book that helps people battle against entropy. He now understood that if *Ubik* the book was so accurate in its description of Ubik the entity, it was because Ubik the entity had through its intermediary written *Ubik* the book. The book was nothing other than a message that the entity had sent to mankind, in order to reveal itself to them. It was perfectly logical that this revelation would have chosen to communicate through an SF novel by an unknown scribbler: it completed the panoply of advertising slogans, television spots, and bathroom graffiti. Figure and ground, message and medium coincided perfectly.

Since the month of February 1974, when the entity had first made direct contact with him, Phil had secretly given it a code name—Valis. An acronym, it stood for "vast, active, living, and intelligent system." To Phil's mind, the name had the advantage of being purely descriptive and without religious association. It could have been the name of a computer program. Several years earlier, he had given the entity the code name of Ubik—that which is everywhere. And, more or less consciously, in composing the slogans that had served as epigraphs for the chapters of his bardo novel, he had suggested that this was also his name for what Saint John, in the the first chapter of his Gospel, calls Logos—the Word.

In essence Phil meant God, though he was loath to use that name, which he found somehow unclean: sullied and tarnished, compromised by the narrow religious frameworks into which it had been forced. Like the Jewish mystics, Phil believed that there were various names for God which got it more or less right and that at the bottom of this sack of names was the true name of God, the one that God alone knew, this knowledge being perhaps the ultimate attribute of His divinity. And as he certainly didn't know that name, and no one else did either, Phil figured he might as well use a purely conventional term. "Valis" did the trick.

Besides, Phil reminded himself, it wasn't such a conventional term as all that, because it had sprung into his mind and Valis itself suffused his mind with its knowledge. Unknowable and unnamable, the entity revealed itself to him under this name that he believed, as he had with Ubik, he had merely imagined.

But there was someone in his life whom he still had to identify—an intermediary whose presence he could only sense, a Runciter. Runciter was not Ubik but simply an ordinary man trying to find his way into our sick consciousness. He is an awakener, a kind of salesman, hawking Ubik's spray of concentrated Logos however he can. In a way, Phil believed he was playing the same role with his readers. But someone was playing it with him; someone, acting on behalf of Ubik and Valis, was giving him messages to guide him. Like Joe Chip, he thought he recognized a familiar tone within this haze of confused and contradictory signals.

As always when he posited a new hypothesis, Phil was amazed at how easily all the facts fell into place. Ever since he had contacted the FBI and routed the Soviets, he had stopped dreaming in Russian and his dreams had begun coming to him more and more in classical Greek. He had only ever known one person who understood ancient Greek, and that was Bishop Pike. Pike, moreover, was well versed in the ancient world and the religions that were the focus of Phil's daily and nightly reveries; he had a fondness for reference books and intellectual scavenger hunts, and, as Phil now recalled, had spent his final years exploring the possibilities of communication between the dead and the living. And finally, Pike used to trim his nose hairs with those special little scissors; Phil had come across them while looking in Pike's bathroom for amphetamines he could steal.

All these clues pointed to the dead bishop as the most serious candidate for the dual role of tutor and spiritual squatter. There were others, whose prospects rose and fell along with the various intuitions that came to Phil through his dreams, readings, and free associations. With the help of his *Encyclopedia Britannica*, he delved back into the depths of time and found himself drawn to any number of possibilities—the Sibyl of Cumae, Zoroaster, Empedocles, Basilides the Gnostic, and the pharaoh Akhenaton. But of all these spirits who had taken up temporary residence in his mind, the one to whom he became closest was a certain Thomas, who stayed on for three months.

Thomas was the only exception to the penchant for A-list religious figures that generally characterized Phil's ever-changing roster of possible spirtual godfathers. Thomas was an unknown, born of Phil's observation that since March 1974 he had been harboring within him the thoughts, worldview, and even words of a thoroughly Hellenized first-century cleric. The type of Greek he spoke, which Phil had finally been able to identify by showing samples of it he had transcribed from his dreams to a professor from Cal State Fullerton, wasn't classical, literary Greek, the only kind that Pike knew; it was Koine Greek, a kind of pidgin spoken throughout the Near East during the time of the apostles. In other words, Thomas's Greek wasn't the language of Plato but that of Saint Paul. Thomas had not personally known Christ, any more than Paul had; he belonged to the second generation of Christians, who suffered the most brutal persecutions. But like all his brethren, he explained to Phil, he knew the secret of the Resurrection. The promise of eternal life that Jesus had made to his small flock was not some sort of joke. It was real and involved the ingestion of a holy food, the famous mushrooms of which John Allegro and, after him, Pike had made so much and of which the Christian host was but a symbol that paled by comparison with the real thing. Each morsel of this food of life, like each puff of spray from a can of Ubik, contained in its entirety information of which the material world was merely the hypostasis (Dick loved this word, which Bishop Pike had taught him).

Realizing that his death was approaching, Thomas had eaten of the mushroom and carefully inscribed somewhere in his brain the sign of the fish, which would permit him when he was resurrected to learn when the time was right who he really was.

Everything went as planned, except that Thomas, who had believed like everyone else at the time that the Second Coming was close at hand, expected to wait perhaps twenty years for his revival, whereas two thousand years had passed. Why? Because after the fall of Jerusalem in AD 70, the Romans had seized all the sacred mushrooms and destroyed them, just as they destroyed all the objects of any cult they didn't understand, the result being that this living information, the only rational element in our irrational world, had disappeared, swept into the darkness by the Empire and its minions. Yet not completely: a few specimens of the mushroom had been hidden in a jar in a cave along the shores of the Dead Sea. There they rested for nearly two millennia while illusion and barbarity governed the earth. Real time remained suspended until 1947, when archeologists uncovered the site at Qumran and set the Spirit free. Pike had guessed rightly that here was the place to search for ultimate truth, but he had come too late—hence his tragic death. The Spirit—Ubik, Valis—had left its hiding place, and it had already been at work for several years, moving about freely wherever it wished—for example, into the conscious and unconscious mind of a teenage kid in California who would have been surprised to hear that in reality his name was Thomas and that, like everyone else around him, he was living sometime around AD 70. Little by little, without his knowing it, the Spirit had instructed this teenage kid. He had instilled doubts in him and had secretly lifted before his eyes the curtain of appearances. The kid had grown up and started to write science fiction novels through which the Spirit made himself known to men and revealed to them their condition. Yet for all his obscurity, the Empire never took its eyes off him. Its agents could tell from certain allusions in his novels that his wisdom was growing, and they knew that one day he might prove dangerous to them. He suffered persecution. Then, one day, the hour had arrived. He was shown the fish, and the anamnesis had begun.

Since that day, Thomas lived in the body of the man he thought he had been for forty-five years. That man was still there, and once several reforms had been instituted, their cohabitation proved rather pleasant. It was like one of those cars that driving schools use, with two steering wheels. Thomas completed Phil's education, taught him Greek, as well as the tricks of a seasoned veteran who knew all the traps the Empire would set—it was Thomas who had made him contact the police in order to foil their plans. That had been a stroke of true genius. In return, Phil guided Thomas through a world whose real nature this gentle being knew but whose false, phenomenal appearance he often failed to grasp. That was Thomas's most touching trait, those small mistakes he sometimes made, reminding you he was a stranger to this world. Occasionally, when he was playing the part of Phil, he stumbled—and Phil would have to whisper into Thomas's ear what he had to do or say. Phil could now explain the oddities of his behavior that, before he knew of Thomas's existence, he attributed to the hypertension for which he had been briefly hospitalized that spring. At that time, he couldn't remember the names of his cats or whether they were male or female; breaking a lifelong routine, he reset the margins on his typewriter; he couldn't recall which knob controlled which function in his car and, like Ragle Gumm and his light cord, kept looking for a vent switch that didn't exist. One day, Tessa was stunned to find Phil standing in front of the refrigerator, grumbling, "There's no more beer, and I was sure there was one left"; then, a few minutes later, he slapped himself on the forehead and said, "But wait, I don't even drink beer," and then finally, "But this isn't my refrigerator!" All of this, which had worried him at first, he now ascribed to Thomas's little confusions. When he asked Thomas, the truth emerged. All in all, they had a great time together, the two of them.

What pleased Thomas the most about this world of illusions in which the Empire held mankind captive was television. He spent days sitting in front of it. Of course, those were the days the fall of the Empire was being broadcast live and direct from Washington, D.C., and the prisoners, whether or not they understood their condition, followed the whole soap opera with close attention. Would Nixon turn over to

Judge Sirica the tapes on which he discussed Watergate? First no, then finally yes—but only after he'd erased substantial parts of them. Would the House of Representatives dare to impeach the president? Yes—for obstructing justice, destroying evidence, suborning witnesses, using the CIA to protect himself from scandal, violating the constitutional rights of his fellow citizens, installing electronic surveillance, and even tax evasion.

That last detail in particular delighted Phil. Sitting on the couch, a can of beer in hand, he cheered on the news with the enthusiasm of a sports fan. Thomas, sitting at his right, behaved more like a coach watching his team win. He commented expertly on what was happening, calling the plays before they unfolded. Under Thomas's influence, Phil understood that a mysterious but direct connection linked his own spiritual life to the defeat of the anti-Christ now occupying the White House. During the month of February, after a lifetime of failed efforts, he had finally broken through—he now had access to the truth. He understood that despite what everyone's abused senses were telling them, the Empire had never ended, but that Parousia, the Second Coming, was close at hand. As promised, it would come before the end of the first century. His anamnesis had been the symbol and the door through which Spirit would return to destory the simulacrum, bring down the walls of the prison, and drive out the demiurge who in the Acts of the Apostles was called Simon Magus, in his own books Palmer Eldritch or Police General Felix Buckman or Ferris F. Fremont, and in the world of illusions that was America in 1974, Richard M. Nixon. The Spirit was making use of him, Philip K. Dick, alias Thomas, to make the world real once again.

When Nixon resigned on August 8, Phil turned to Thomas to say, "So we've won." But Thomas didn't reply. He was gone, and Phil, alone inside his own brain, was saddened by his departure. After several days he accepted the loss, for he understood that Thomas had accomplished what he had come to do and that now it was up to him, Phil, to find a way to explain, both to himself and to the world, what had happened.

CHAPTER 19

HORSELOVER FAT

After Thomas left him, Phil tried to write a book about his experience. He had recently been asked to add to a collection of novels attributed to imaginary writers, like Nabokov's Sebastian Knight and Kurt Vonnegut's Kilgore Trout, and thought that such an approach was perfect for his subject. He would take up the pen under the name of Hawthorne Abendsen, the renowned author of *The Grasshopper Lies Heavy*.

Whenever Phil reread one of his own novels, he was inevitably stunned by the prophetic nature of his writing. In 1960, he had imagined that someone could gain access to reality merely by chancing to gaze on a piece of jewelry and that a novel that to all appearances seemed to be describing an imaginary world could mysteriously yet irrefutably reveal a truth that lay hidden from human eyes. And when, as he was writing the final pages of that book, the *I Ching* assured him everything he thought he was imagining was actually true, he inserted the oracle's pronouncement into his text without understanding what it meant. Now, fourteen years later, he understood. He was Hawthorne Abendsen. It was only logical that Hawthorne Abendsen should now come back and say, "Yes, all that was true," and convince the world that it was so.

A sequel to *The Man in the High Castle* seemed a natural to Phil. Since it was his best-known book, the only one to have won a prize, there was perhaps money to be made in continuing the story. The novel would open with Abendsen having reached the end of his rope—sick and penniless, abandoned by his wife and children, beset by burglars, and persecuted by the cryptototalitarian regime against which he had been speaking out for all those years, to no avail. He was a voice crying out in the wilderness, but he cried out no longer. He was lying low. And then . . .

And then what?

And then everything got complicated and the novel broke down. Phil Dick soon discovered an enormous difference between *The Man in the High Castle* and its long-awaited sequel. In 1970, he had been fabricating, or at least that is what he thought he had been doing. He had been free to invent, or so he believed. This time, he had to tell the truth. He couldn't get it wrong.

And so he started taking notes to tease it out, and once he started, he never stopped. He set aside the novel and put away his hand-me-down typewriter, and night after night, delving deep into the pages of his trusty *Encyclopedia Britannica*, his headphones blasting John Dowland and Olivia Newton-John into his ears, he did what God had placed him on this earth to do: he spun hypotheses.

When I say that he never stopped, I mean it literally. The note-taking would occupy him for the eight years he had left to live. Some of these writings he later destroyed, but around eight thousand pages remain. No one has read them all; he himself never did. Nor did Lawrence Sutin, his scrupulous biographer, who admits to having resorted to a sort of random sampling technique to cull the material and come up with the selection of excerpts that eventually saw publication. The excerpts give a good sense of the restless themes that haunted Dick throughout these years, but unavoidably they truncate the long and breathless runs of text, often fifty or sixty pages long, that he produced in the course of those sleepless nights that ended only when utter exhaustion forced him to put down his pen.

He called these notes his "Exegesis." In theological terminology the word has a precise meaning, of which he of course was well aware. It refers to a work of doctrinal interpretation of a sacred text. And a sacred text (allowing that such a thing exists in the first place) is a text recognized as having a divine origin, inspired if not actually dictated by the Holy Spirit—the looser definition allowing for some slight margin of initiative, and therefore of error, on the part of the human redactor. A sacred text therefore, this one qualification aside, speaks the truth, and it does so in each and every one of its parts. Catholics hold such a text to be "infallible," in something of the same way that the Jewish mystic operates on the radical premise—an utter certainty as far as he is concerned—that nothing in the Torah is there by chance: for the Cabalist, each word opens a door to He who is.

Bishop Pike was fond of saying that nothing holds greater fascination for those interested in the sciptural religions than the study of the formation of their canons, which is to say, the process by which their texts came to be declared sacred. When, how, and by whom was the Pentateuch written? When, how, and by whom were the Gospels of Mark, Matthew, Luke, and John granted canonical status while other texts were declared apocryphal, banished to the margins where the James Pikes of every age have found their greatest inspiration.

Phil attributed a divine origin to the bursts of information that had been shooting into his brain ever since February 1974. God, whom he coyly called Valis, spoke to him as He had spoken to Moses, Mohammed, and a few others whom He had chosen to receive His Word. He was once again seeking a writer to transcribe His message, this time in a modern form that He believed would best suit His latest revelation. That form was science fiction. Phil couldn't quite understand God's utter confidence in his professional capacities. He was more than willing to transcribe—but what? What canonical corpus would his Exegesis explicate?

The possibilities were endless: there were of course the books that appeared in his dreams, the words he retained from them and the information he managed to remember—concerning his son's hernia, for example. There were his own books as well and the new discoveries he made in rereading them. And then there were those sudden, blinding flashes of certainty: of having lived in AD 70, of having run the anti-Christ out of the White House. But other certainties, no less blinding, had immediately followed, and only by carefully and tediously stitching all of them together—much the way he used to cobble together a novel by combining plot lines from two earlier short stories—could he reconcile them with one another. Now that Thomas was gone, his world had become confused again. Without that gentle soul to hold the threads together, the tapestry of truth he had revealed was unraveling. Left to his own devices, Phil couldn't understand why the world, which, after his own anamnesis and Nixon's fall, had been brought once again into line with the divine plan, hadn't changed more visibly. He tried to reassure himself with the thought that the changes that had taken place might be every bit as radical as they were subtle and that it was the mission of his Exegesis to tame and harness them. His vocation perhaps demanded that he grope his way amid the uncertainties, guided only by intermittent illumination, that he feel, even as he labored for the greater glory of God, he was on the wrong track, an unworthy servant unequal to the task that He had set before him. When the moment came, the Holy Spirit would sort everything out and dictate to him the revelation that would convert all humanity. All he had to do in the meantime was write everything down—all his doubts and all his conjectures. The corpus on which he would write his commentary would be everything he was living through now and had lived through in the past, everything he dreamed, everything that went through his head: in other words, all the information received and processed by the program called Philip K. Dick.

Wary of speaking about what had happened to him, he confided in no one but Tessa and a woman with whom he was exchanging letters—she was writing a thesis on him—but had never met. Otherwise he made only vague allusions, humorous quips he could easily take back.

In the fall of 1974, his young admirer Paul Williams, who had made a name for himself as a journalist with *Rolling Stone*, proposed to the magazine's editor doing a long profile of Dick, presenting him as a guiding light of the American counterculture. Having got the go-ahead, Williams headed down from San Francisco to Fullerton for a marathon interview, his undisguised goal to make its subject a famous man. Aware of the stakes, Phil, who had toyed with the idea of coming out of the closet as a mystic visionary, realized that to do so might alienate the very public he at last had a chance to reach. Socially maladroit though he was, he always understood what his interviewers expected of him, and knowing that Williams wanted the eccentric rebel, not the religious visionary, he was careful not to show his hand. And Williams, for his part, with his journalistic instincts, knew that no one would be interested in a didactic article about Dick's books; far better to give a sense of the strange workings of his mind. It didn't matter what particular topic they talked about. The break-in of 1971? That would do just fine. The victim of the break-in would inspire readers to rush out and get ahold of the writer's novels. And that is precisely what happened. With Williams egging him on, Dick improvised a startling four-day-long monologue that resembled nothing so much as that famous cube the Hungarian architect Reno Rubik had just invented—dozens of configurations, from the nearly plausible to the purely lunatic, were tried out, rejected, tried out again, and combined with others. Knowing that the average *Rolling Stone* reader was predisposed to believe any story about the White House plumbers, Dick obligingly elaborated his theory that the Nixon gang was behind the break-in on Hacienda Way, and then, like a demented trial lawyer who decides to switch sides as soon as he senses he has swayed the jury, he found arguments to shoot that theory down. Those whom he accused, exculpated, then reindicted included, by turns, the John Birch Society, the Black Panthers, a sect of religious fanatics who objected to the writings of Bishop Pike, the next-door neighbors, local dopers, the police, extraterrestrials, and last but not least, himself. For nearly three years, he had obsessed over the question of who was responsible, but in the six months immediately preceding the interview other, more pressing, more cosmically important matters had entered the picture: perhaps he thought he might have some fun applying the investigative methods he had since developed for his Exegesis to what he now

regarded as the relatively trivial matter of the break-in. Williams left
Fullerton delighted, convinced that he had the makings of a truly
mind-blowing article. By coincidence, the issue in which his interview
with Dick appeared also contained one of the decade's great journalistic scoops—Patty Hearst's confession; everyone in America bought
the magazine that week and, when they came to the end of the Hearst
article and flipped the page, they discovered the writer who had managed to turn his burglarized bungalow into the epicenter of the universe's every mystery. From one day to the next, Dick became if not a
celebrity then at least "that guy, you know, that nut *Rolling Stone* had
an article about," and everyone knew who you meant.

When Williams got back to San Francisco, he had thought he might
round out the interview by conducting his own investigation. He went
to the San Rafael police station, looked at their records, spoke to various police officers, and discovered exactly what he had expected he
would discover: nothing. Dick in all likelihood was the victim of a
completely ordinary burglary, the kind that happens in Marin County,
California, a little over twenty-five times a day, on average.

Williams, who had decided to emphasize his subject's feverish
imagination and would have been embarrassed to discover that he had
been speaking the truth, was reassured by this nondiscovery. Phil,
however, remained unconvinced. Without excluding the possibility of
a garden-variety break-in, he remarked that if that wasn't what it was,
then the plumbers, or the John Birch Society, or the extraterrestrials,
or whoever was behind it would have made damn sure it at least
looked like one. Similarly, he professed not to be surprised when,
thanks to the Freedom of Information Act, he finally got his hands on
his FBI file, expecting to find it stuffed with twenty years' worth of
reports, and found that it contained only one document—the letter
that, in the early 1950s, even before he had met George Smith and
George Scruggs, he had written to the Soviet physicist Alexander
Topchev, in the hopes of learning more about supposed flaws in
Einstein's special theory of relativity. The presence of this single doc-

ument, and not a particularly compromising one at that, proved one thing and one thing only: that the FBI had purged its files before opening them up to the public; the law that was supposed to put an end to Nixon's police state was a red herring.

As comforting as he found this explanation, Phil still had to face the possibility that the file on his encounter with God might contain exactly the same thing as the police files on the break-in or his FBI files—in other words, nothing. Well, actually, either nothing or what comes down to the same thing—the product of an imagination that, depending on your inclination, you can see as either marvelously fertile or pathetically deranged.

Within him was a man inspired by God, who had chosen him to carry His word to late-twentieth-century America. But there was another man in him as well, a man who never tired of denouncing the illusions that the other man, the Inspired One, was all too willing to succumb to. Night after night, these two selves fought over the Exegesis—one of them as the lord of the castle, defending his position, the other as its assailant, laying siege to the former's arguments. Because he didn't know which of these two selves to side with, Phil was unable to find the words to convey what had happened to him in a way that others would understand. Still, he nursed the hope that he could end this solipsistic standoff by letting the two voices battling within him each have their say. Within the space of a few weeks in 1976, he wrote a novel called *Valisystem A*, which no publisher was interested in (it was published in 1985 under the title *Radio Free Albemuth*). It revolves around a Berkeley record salesman named Nicholas Brady and his old friend the science fiction writer Philip K. Dick. Nick's life has it all—the infected wisdom tooth, the golden fish, the phosphenes that form themselves into paintings from the Hermitage, the photocopied article, the foul-mouthed radio ("Nick is a prick, Nick is a dick"), the baby son with the strangulated hernia. As for Phil, he plays the part of friend and confidant, skeptical yet sympathetic. He plays this role in later works as well, whereas the Nicholas Brady character becomes

Horselover Fat, an alter ago whose name is an English translation of the Greco-Teutonic Philip Dick (in German, *dick* means "fat," while *Philip* in Greek means "lover of horses").

Horselover Fat, then, is a madman who has seen God, and Phil Dick is his rational friend. Fat glosses his visions in the Exegesis, while Phil discusses Fat's Exegesis in drafts for his novels. Fat sees himself as a new Isaiah; Phil sees him as a paranoid schizophrenic. Phil considers himself lucid; as for Fat, if the whole world thinks he's crazy, that's just fine by him. He insists that nevertheless the truth is on his side, whereupon Phil shakes his head in dismay—and then everything starts all over again, the carousel turning round and round and round and round . . . till the end of time.

Scrupulously evenhanded, Fats assembles all the arguments proving he has gone crazy and all those proving he has fallen into the hands of the living God. Even this effort at impartiality cuts both ways. One day he takes it as an encouraging sign of mental health, since crazy people generally think they are completely sane. But the next day, he panics, for he remembers having heard somewhere that one of the first symptoms of insanity is the fear of going crazy.

Phil matches Fat's roster of the various spiritual squatters who may have taken up residence inside his brain with a list of his own, cataloging the possible causes of his alter ego's psychological decline. Excessive distress and anxiety could have led him to withdraw into himself, like one of the autistic characters that appear in so many of his books. Or maybe the culprit is too much dope. For twenty years he has treated his body like a cocktail shaker for assorted chemical substances, and now he is being handed the bill, along with a fortune cookie rolled up inside of which is none other than the divine presence Himself. Harlan Ellison has a crude formula to describe this sort of trajectory: "Took drugs. Saw God. BFD [Big Fucking Deal]."

Phil couldn't decide whether to take comfort in or be depressed by the fact that his adventure was so commonplace. The drugs he had taken during the 1960s, he was convinced, formed a chemical soup in which his brain now stewed. All of California, in fact, was crawling with freaks like him who nursed their cherished acid flashbacks while mumbling their favorite mantras over and over.

Acid flashback—it was the all-purpose explanation. After the federal government outlawed LSD-25 in 1967 and public opinion turned sharply against it, the conservative press began to treat this relatively rare phenomenon as though it were a sword of Damocles hanging over the head of everyone who had ever taken acid, casting it as a threat every bit as fearsome as, some fifteen years later, the human immunodeficiency virus, with its long incubation period, would turn out to be. No one who had ever taken acid could be sure he could close the book on that experience. Horrific stories were told of people who, succumbing to peer pressure, had taken LSD in their student years and later, having become junior executives at IBM or General Motors, would suddenly and without warning, right in the middle of a business meeting, find themselves tripping out of their minds, with telephone cords morphing into snakes and their friendly coworkers into malevolent robots. Once in a while, it was said, some poor guy whose drug experimentation of years before finally caught up with him would take a hatchet and try to massacre everyone around him. In the seventies, whenever a particularly gruesome murder occurred "acid flashback" would be the first explanation the police would trot out before the press. Phil was not impervious to this line of reasoning and for a while looked to his 1964 acid trip, his one and only experience with the drug, as the possible source of his divine obsession. At the time, he had thought the *Dies Irae*, the Day of Wrath, had arrived, and for eight hours he had sobbed and pleaded and prayed in Latin. And now they were playing the sequel for him, a film that would last not eight hours but eight more years. Thanks, Sandoz.

Sad as it was, this explanation seemed the most cogent to him, except for one small detail, which Fat pointed out: who had ever heard of acid's being able to make someone speak Latin who didn't know it already? Who had ever heard of anyone having flashbacks in dialects of ancient Greek? Of course, anyone high enough on acid or deep enough asleep can *believe* he is speaking Greek, or Latin, or Sanskrit—or Martian, for that matter. But in 1964 Ray Nelson, his friend and sometime collaborator, really had heard him blubbering on in Latin, a fact that pushed the origin of the problem ten years further back without doing anything to actually resolve it—of course, Nelson was on acid himself at the time. If prayers came out of Dick's mouth back then, now it was words that came into his mind, words that he didn't understand when they appeared in his dreams but that he transcribed phonetically on awakening. He discovered they were Koine Greek. You can be as skeptical as you want about all this, Fat told Phil, but then explain this to me: how does a guy living in California in 1974 suddenly start thinking in the language in which Saint Paul wrote his Epistles?

And more generally, Fat insisted, how do you explain the presence in our brains of information that doesn't belong there? It's too easy just to blame drugs or to say that "an encounter with God is to mental illness what death is to cancer: the logical outcome of a deteriorating illness process." The real question is whether my experience in February 1974 was a theophany, "a self-disclosure by the divine." If God exists, so does theophany. "Moses did not create the burning bush; Elijah, on Mount Horeb, did not generate the low murmuring voice." I realize, Fat said, that distinguishing true theophany from hallucination—a far more common occurrence—is a delicate matter. But I would like to propose a basis for judgment: if the voice—let's say a voice *is* involved—communicates information to its subject, information that the subject didn't and couldn't otherwise know, then I'd say the phenomenon on our hands is real and not fake.

Agreed?

Phil was willing to agree, but with reservations. For one thing, he thought that Fat was somewhat overstating the extent of his ignorance. One night as they sparred over the Exegesis, he caught Fat marveling at being able, in his dreams, to understand German, a language he spoke fluently. He suspected that Fat, who was never very good at keeping track of what happened when, would often reverse the sequence of events: for example, after spending a few hours paging through his *Encyclopedia Britannica* and finally locating some vital piece of information, he might then doze off, dream about the precious piece of information he had just discovered, and wake up having completely forgotten everything he had been doing before. He would go back to the encyclopedia, find that same piece of information, and express astonishment at the amazing coincidence. Instead of seeing the hand of God at work in these various coincidences and puzzling abilities, Phil suggested, Fat might want to look inside himself, at all the stuff buried in his unconscious. Three decades of psychoanalysis—Jungian, it's true—couldn't rid Fat of his magical, primitive conceptions of the nature of dreams. Refusing to see them as a brown-bag meeting where the only lunch you get to eat is the one you've brought with you, he kept looking for messages in them, messages from outside himself. Hence occurrences like the one with the delivery girl with a golden fish around her neck: after she had gone and he took the painkillers she had brought him, he dozed off and saw the number 842 in flaming letters. The minute he woke up, he set about trying to find out what might have happened in the year 842 BC, imagining who he might have been in pre-Mycenaean days—all this instead of remembering the price of the medication the girl had delivered. She had even had to repeat it: eight dollars and forty-two cents.

You got me there, Fat admitted. Now explain the Greek.

Here Phil appealed to the notion of a collective unconscious, phylogenic memories. He realized this tactic was tricky, moving the argument from the strictly rational terrain on which he had wanted to confine it. Still, playing the Jungian card was perhaps the only way he had left to keep God out of the picture.

Okay then, replied Fat, with that thin smile that always accompanied his most crushing argument, what about Chris's hernia? Did the collective unconscious warn me about that?

Phil scratched his head. He couldn't deny the facts or that he found the whole thing troubling. But hey, troubling things happened sometimes. Every day, rational people are troubled by the discovery that they've had a premonitory dream or by the apparent clairvoyance of a card reader. Nancy and he were troubled when the Santa Barbara medium brought up the KGB restaurateur from Berkeley. Of course these sorts of events are troubling, but not so troubling as to upset your entire worldview, which has heretofore excluded the idea of extrasensory perception. Still, they are troubling.

Faced with Fat's inexplicable knowledge of his little boy's hernia, Phil counterattacked with the "know it by its fruits" argument. "Beware of false prophets who come to you in sheep's clothing but inwardly are ravenous wolves," Christ warns in Matthew 7:15. "You will know them by their fruits. Are grapes gathered from thorns, or figs from thistles? So, every sound tree bears good fruit, but the bad tree bears bad fruit."

Here, Phil told Fat, is the true criterion, the only way to distinguish between the man inspired by God and the mere lunatic. Of course, Christ was speaking of evil false prophets, of pied piper types like Hitler or Jim Jones, but the argument holds for the good guys, too, guys like you who think that hearing voices makes them prophets when in fact they are merely going off the rails: show us the fruits of your commerce with God, Phil asked Fat. Okay, you dreamed in Greek, you fired your agent, you've started trimming your nose hairs . . .

But I knew about the hernia!

Okay, but can you honestly say that knowing about Chris's hernia has made you a better person? For twenty years you've been speaking rapturously of empathy, of charity, of agape; you've been holding forth in long letters to your ex-wives, peppering your sermons with lines from Saint Paul. Well then, let's see what he says. Take his first Epistle to the Corinthians: "If I speak in the tongues of men and of angels, but have not love, I am a noisy gong or a clanging cymbal. And if I have prophetic powers, and understand all mysteries"—hear that, Fat?— "and all knowledge, and if I have all faith, so as to remove mountains, but have not love, I am nothing. If I give away all I have, and if I deliver my body to be burned, but have not love, I gain nothing."

Fat lowered his head in sadness as he listened to those words. Phil pursued his advantage. I know you're not evil, he told him, that you give to the poor, that you write checks to charitable organizations, that the suffering of children and cats can move you to tears. But that doesn't alter the fact that you remain incapable of empathy. Try as you do, and God knows you have tried, you have no more connection to others than you have to the real, sensorial world, the true world, from which a thick pane of glass still separates you. That's what mortal sin is and it isn't even your fault. You're more a victim than you are guilty. Sin is not a moral choice but a sickness of the mind that dooms it forever to have no commerce with anyone but itself, and thus to eternal repetition. You've got this sickness, Phil told Fat. Your mind is under house arrest; since the day you were born you've been confined to the labyrinth of your brain. What you're hearing now, all you've ever heard, and all you'll ever hear are the magnetic tapes of your own voice being played back to you in closed-circuit transmission. Don't kid yourself: that is exactly what you are hearing at this very moment. It's your own voice that's telling you this. You sometimes let yourself be fooled by it, because the voice wouldn't have been able to stand itself all these years without learning how to fake other voices, to echo them, to ventriloquize so that you think you're speaking with other people. The truth is that you're alone in there, just as Palmer Eldritch is alone in the world that he has emptied of its substance and whose inhabitants all bear his stigmata. You're alone the way Nixon was alone in the Oval Office with his hidden tape recorders whose reels started spinning every time he opened his mouth. Nixon at least was lucky in a way: he was forced to hand over his tapes, others listened to them, and then he got turned out of his bunker. No one is going to do you that favor. You're going to be able to go on listening to yourself, disagreeing with yourself, and telling yourself you're right until the day you die, and no one is going to stop you.

And that's what you mean when you say you agree with me?

That's exactly what I mean. And besides, you're right. At least, I can't prove you're wrong. No one can do that. Your whole system rests on the kind of reasoning that philosophers call a "sophism"—an argument that, though not necessarily correct, is logically unassailable. In your case, it goes as follows: "Maybe I'm not a prophet, but then by the same token neither was Isaiah. Maybe I confuse the gurglings of my unconscious with the voice of God, but the same could be said of Saint Paul. Tell me what difference there is between the light that blinded him on the road to Damascus and what I saw in the spring of 1974 in my apartment in Fullerton, Orange County, California. In the name of what and on what grounds can you distinguish one from the other? I can't guarantee you that you're wrong not to believe me, but I *can* guarantee you that you wouldn't have believed Paul. You would have shrugged your shoulders and maybe talked about epileptic fits or blows of the cane, just the way so many pious Jews and civilized Greeks did." Okay, Fat, I can't counter those explanations. Nor can I counter the objections of the ecology freaks who, when I tell them that it's ridiculous to grant trees and animals the same legal rights as people, point out that not so long ago it was considered just as ludicrous to grant those rights to women or to Blacks. I have no answer, either, for those who, if I concede that modern technology would have seemed like magic to our ancestors, oblige me to admit that what now seems inexplicable to us—troubling, as you put it so well—and what I try to ignore or sweep under the carpet will one day be just another branch of science: those who deny the existence of extrasensory perception today would have condemned Galileo. Personally, I doubt it, but it's a good argument, and now I'll keep quiet.

You can keep quiet, but I know what you're thinking. You're thinking I should read a few pages of my Exegesis. They speak for themselves and eloquently attest to their author's insanity. Compare the complication, the contradictions, the implausibility of his theories with the solidity, the clarity of Paul's Epistles. There is something self-evident about the truth, something that, apart from everything else, lets you know that it is true. The same goes for falsehood, and anyone who can't sense this has lost all faculties of judgment. That's what you're thinking, isn't it?

Of course that's what I'm thinking, and I know that you're going to say: that in thinking this, I prove nothing and merely demonstrate my laziness. The fact is I have your Exegesis right here in front of my nose, the ink still wet, whereas between me and the New Testament lie two thousand years of blind custom and habit. If I could somehow read it with fresh eyes, I'd see that nothing is so twisted and so contrary to common sense as Christian doctrine. The Greek gods have something human about them, something completely familiar, a little like those movies that people flock to because they are about the lives of people just like them but make those lives seem more glamorous. Christianity, on the other hand, goes against everything we believe we know about the way the world works. As I myself used to tell Anne back when we were attending church at Inverness, this crucified God, this ritualistic cannibalism that is supposed to transform the human species resembles nothing so much as science fiction. Christianity is every bit as unbelievable as science fiction, and if you're thinking that that's why it just may well be true, you wouldn't be the first person to think so.

All the same, you do find it strange, don't you, that my revelations are so much like my science fiction novels? Or maybe you think I've simply started to believe the stories I used to make up.

In fact that *is* what I think, but I'd put it another way. I'd say that you never made up any of it. I'd say this revelation of yours began invading the world, without your knowing it, through your novels. The more I think about it, the more it all strikes me as . . . how can I put this? Plausible? Logical? Cogent? Let's just say it doesn't surprise me that God would choose science fiction as His vehicle and put you in the driver's seat. That's always His way. He uses base materials—the stone that the masons have rejected. When He decides to choose His people, He doesn't take the Greeks or the Persians. No, He goes out and finds some obscure tribe wandering in the desert, nomads no one has ever heard of. And when He decides to send His son to His people, it's exactly the same. Everyone expects the triumphal arrival of a royal scion, and instead it all happens on the sly, among the down and out, in the annex of some motel in Bethlehem. One of the few things that we know about God's ways is that He manifests Himself where we least expect Him. That's what He Himself says so clearly in *Ubik*. Runciter doesn't use encyclicals to get his message across, he uses TV ads and graffiti on bathroom walls. One thing you can be sure of is that if God decides to speak to people today, He won't start with the pope or any other of His official representatives. And if for reasons of His own, He decides to speak to an American writer, it won't be Norman Mailer or Susan Sontag but some hack toiling away in the dark, grinding out cheap novels that no one takes seriously.

Well, if that's the case, joked Fat, you'll have to admit that I have conducted my career brilliantly to this point. On the other hand, all of that sounds a lot like the rantings of a loser, wouldn't you say?

Yes. But God might want to use the rantings of a loser to serve His designs. That would be just like Him—what with His inscrutable ways, and all that. You see, the problem with faith is that it never gives you any reason to call it quits. If you believe in the resurrection of Christ, then you have no grounds to deny the miracles—His virgin birth, for example. And if you believe in the Holy Virgin, then it's silly not to let her show up at Lourdes or Fatima or any of those other villages from which millions of pilgrims return transfigured. If you believe in these visions, in miracle cures and holy medallions, then why not in reincarnation too, or in the Great Pyramid's occult influence on world historical events, or in your Exegesis? Your trick, Fat, is to call yourself the bath water and then point out that, if it gets thrown out, the baby goes with it. But hang on a minute. What would happen if I agreed to sacrifice the baby?

You mean . . .

That's right. What if God doesn't exist?

Well, in that case, my Exegesis would be nothing but a load of crap.

But then the Gospels would be too. Isn't that what you'd say next?

Exactly, and that's basically what Saint Paul says: If Christ wasn't resurrected, everything that I've said to you is nonsense. So there's no difference between Isaiah and some paranoid schizophrenic, between Saint Paul and a lunatic who thinks he's Saint Paul—me, for example. All of us in the loony bin together. Does that make you happy?

You know very well that it doesn't. If you're right, then we both lose.

And then?

I don't know. I guess you've got me.

CHAPTER 20

END OF THE LINE

Under Phil's nervous gaze, Fat spent whole evenings immersed in his Exegesis. Like a man lost in some unknown territory who pores over whatever maps he finds in the glove compartment of his car—Michigan, Tanzania, the scenic byways of the Auvergne—he worked tirelessly trying to reconcile what had happened to him first to this, then to that form of spiritual experience or religious doctrine. His reference works, as he liked to announce grandly, ran the gamut from the *Encyclopedia Britannica* to the publications of the Church of Scientology, whose sales were fattening the pockets of fellow science fiction writer L. Ron Hubbard. He received catalogs from occult bookstores—the kind of place where Meister Eckhart rubbed elbows on a shelf with Madame Blavatsky. Thus armed and referenced, he spun out theory upon theory, each of which seeming as luminously plausible as the one before and the one after. Yet the novel that he told everyone he was going to write—the one that would be to the Exegesis what Christ's parables were to His secret teachings and whose advance he had long ago spent—was going nowhere. Meanwhile, his only income was from translations of his older works, he had to pay Nancy's alimony, and he and Tessa and Christopher were living hand to mouth. Tessa wanted to get a job, but Phil was dead set against it. He objected to her enrolling in the university to take a course in German, a language that he was using more and more often in their conversations without caring whether or not she understood what he was saying. He didn't like her to leave the house, whether to go shopping or to take Christopher for a walk, or even to accompany him when he went out. He insisted on his own autonomy without conceding her any at all. Her thoughts and opinions mattered very little to him, yet he couldn't stand her hiding them from him. He would ask her point-blank what was going on in her head and get angry if he suspected she was holding anything back, even though he himself had never offered the slightest explanation of what was going on in his all those months when Thomas had set up house inside his cranium and he had more or less stopped talking to Tessa, preferring to pass his days in front of the TV, exchanging asides and chuckles with his invisible companion. Not surprisingly, Tessa became angry and reproachful. Oblivious to his own role in their mutual unhappiness, he preferred to see it as part of a greater and more mysterious process whose significance defied rational explanation. The light had triumphed and reality had reclaimed its rightful place in the world, but everything seemed to be going downhill instead of getting better. His creative faculties were failing, his marriage was on the rocks, and now his car was ready to give up the ghost. It seemed the cycle of repetition in which he was trapped would go on forever.

Then he met a twenty-two-year-old named Doris, and, once again, he thought he had finally broken free. A chubby, determined young woman, Doris had just joined the Episcopal Church. She wanted to become a nun, she confided to him during the first of many long conversations they had in her studio apartment, whose walls were covered with religious posters. He thoroughly approved of that idea, even as he tried to figure out how to get her into bed with him. How wonderful life would be if they moved in together! They talked about theology, attended mass together, and participated in parish activities. Testing the waters with her, he complained that Tessa didn't understand him, that he was suffocating in the petty bourgeois cocoon that she had spun about him. This got him nowhere with Doris, who saw the problem differently: he was simply tired of being married, she told him, and was behaving like a child. Figuring it was time to bring out the heavy artillery, he began telling her about his own religious experiences.

It was a long story, and she listened patiently, though a little too dispassionately, he thought. He hadn't really known what to expect but was nevertheless hoping for something more enthusiastic than her comment that according to a *Time* magazine survey 40 percent of Americans claimed to have had a mystical experience at some point in their lives. Doris's reticence stemmed from her scrupulous orthodoxy. She would have liked to accept his arguments and not dimiss the possibility that he had been charged with a prophetic mission, but her priest had warned her against what people were beginning to call "New Age" ideas. She wanted doctrinal assurances. Phil swore to her that his Exegesis had nothing whatsoever to do with Pike's brand of syncretic religion, that he didn't see himself as creating a new sect, that, on the contrary, everything he was telling her had firm grounding in the original meaning of Christian observance. His was the God of Abraham, Isaac, and Jacob. Nevertheless, he insisted, the story of salvation wasn't finished: there had been the age of the Father, of which the Old Testament spoke, then the age of the Son, depicted in the New. And now the age of the Holy Spirit was at hand. Did he mean, asked an anxious Doris, that he thought of his books as the third part of the Bible? Or that he considered himself a new Messiah? He laughed modestly. No, of course not, more like John the Baptist—a forerunner, a man on the cusp between ages. The greatest in the Old Covenant, the smallest in the New. The last of the prophets, the one who emerges at a time when everyone is lamenting that God no longer speaks to His people. The voice crying in the wilderness. If she read the Bible carefully, he told her, she would see that John the Baptist was a bearded man, too, burning with the fire of the Holy Spirit. Would she have believed him?

Less receptive to Fat's rhetoric than Phil was, Doris dutifully asked herself that question but didn't bother to answer it. Phil's amorous feelings began to chill slightly. They heated up again in the spring of

1975, when she was diagnosed with lymphoma. Phil leapt into action, announcing that he wanted to live with her, take care of her, and never leave her side. What about Tessa? she objected. Her religious beliefs did not allow her to take the vows of marriage lightly. She forbade him to leave his wife and child, but they saw each other every day. In the evening, when he returned home, all he wanted to talk about was Doris's illness, Doris's piety, Doris's sublime resignation. Doris's doubts about his divine mission, on the other hand, he managed to forget, or, if he acknowledged them, it was to hold them up gratefully as a salutary lesson in humility. No human tresses had ever turned him on more than the wig that Doris wore in the months following her chemotherapy.

Finally, Tessa had enough and left, taking Christopher with her. Phil, busy talking with Tim Powers when his young brother-in-law came to get her things later that day, acted as though he didn't care. Powers was worried about how he really felt, but Phil assured him that he was fine and refused to let him stay to keep him company.

That evening, he swallowed forty-nine tablets of digitalin, thirty capsules of Librium, and sixty of Apresoline, washing them down with half a bottle of wine; then he opened his veins and lay down in the garage, having first closed the door and started up the car.

There was a hitch: the car kept stalling out. Irritated, and seeing no reason to put up with all this discomfort—the exhaust fumes were escaping anyway—Phil dragged himself back into the house and into bed. A little later, his door was broken down by an emergency medical team. Earlier, disoriented, he had called the pharmacy to refill his prescription of Librium; suspicious, the pharmacist had called the emergency medical services. Later, Dick decided something ought to be written about pharmacists and the part they play in life's grace.

His stomach was pumped and he was put on life support. At dawn, he regained consciousness. Lying on his back, he watching the EEG monitor at the head of his bed. The calm glowing line moving tirelessly across the black screen—that was who he was. Vague thoughts stirring about in his dull brain produced tiny, irregular spikes in the horizontal sweep of the glowing line. Losing himself in this spectacle, he tried to inflect the movement of the line by controlling the neural impulses emanating from his brain, the way one guides a toy electric car across the floor by remote control. At one point the spikes moved farther apart and the line became perfectly straight. It seemed to him that he had been staring for a long time at this straight line, whose peaceful, solid trace across the screen meant that he had died. Then, as though regretfully, the line took up its sinusoidal movement once more.

Three days later, an armed policeman pushed Phil's wheelchair down the long corridor connecting the intensive care unit to the hospital's psychiatric wing. Several hours went by without anyone's paying any attention to him. He could walk without assistance, but for one reason or another the policeman had left him sitting in the wheelchair. So there Phil stayed, parked along a corridor, watching the parade: white-coated doctors and nurses—never the same ones—walked by at irregular intervals, interspersed among a more regular flow of people in bathrobes—always the same ones—who seemed to him reasonably wild-eyed. They were probably completing some ritual circuit. Lacking the energy to get up out of his wheelchair and see for himself exactly what they were up to, he contented himself with observing the particular rhythm of each of the patients as they walked past. The mentally ill, he noted, moved about at a constant pace—each person had only one speed. But some of them dragged themselves along while others were always running. Several times he saw a fat, disheveled woman pass by who in a curiously sophisticated voice told anyone who cared to listen that her husband had tried to poison her by pumping toxic gas under the door of her bedroom. Phil noted with amazement that he was hearing a continuous narrative, even though it came in small snatches that lasted only a few seconds each and were separated by fairly long stretches of time. He shook his head, trying to shoo this puzzlement away as one would an insect.

To fend off the suffering that he had not yet begun to feel but that he sensed all around him, he tried to think about his Exegesis. Normally, he derived a certain self-satisfaction from devoting himself to the construction of a cosmogony, something few individuals were capable of doing—it was more the kind of thing civilizations, for example, did. But he wasn't interested now. Nor was God. *Eli, Eli, lama sabachthani*, he murmured, without awakening any responsive echo from within his mortal soul.

He thought about Donna. Sad as it was, he was relieved to think about her, the way an insomniac is relieved when he finally finds a comfortable position in bed or realizes he has stumbled onto a train of thought that is pulling him into the drift of sleep. He wondered whether she had become a heroin addict, or whether she was dead, or married, whether she was living in Oregon or Idaho. Maybe she had been in a car crash and was now paralyzed. For no apparent reason, this idea struck him as plausible.

He also thought about Kleo, trying to imagine what their life would have been like had he stayed with her. What books would he have written, what would their children have looked like? He had had a wife who loved him and he left her. A man does not receive such a gift twice in his life. What would she say if she saw him now, sitting in a wheelchair in a hospital, separated from his wife and his son, with a car he couldn't rely on even to kill himself and a totally fried brain? Probably she would weep.

He wept.

He watched television. An ad for *The Tonight Show* showed Sammy Davis Jr.—Johnny Carson's guest that evening—and Phil wondered what it would be like to have a glass eye. But first came the eleven o'clock news, offering brief, fuzzy images of Nixon on the grounds of his estate in San Clemente. The former president had nearly died from an attack of phlebitis, and now he, too, was being pushed around in a wheelchair. The camera was so far away that Nixon's face was just a smudge, his body a shriveled silhouette under a plaid throw. Again, Phil wept, both for himself and for his old enemy. The war was over and they had reached the same point in their lives. They were both defeated.

The next day, he submitted to various routine examinations. He tried to appear as normal as possible, but he could tell he was making a bad impression. And no one there even knew this wasn't the first time he had tried to kill himself: it was a good thing, he thought, that he had made his earlier suicide attempt in Canada.

He was told he would be kept under observation for three weeks—though it was made clear that it might also be three months. He thought about asking to be read his rights, then changed his mind. When you're nuts, you learn to keep your mouth shut.

Not much happened in the mental ward. Unlike in fiction, the patients didn't cow the staff, and the staff didn't torture the patients. Basically, the patients read, watched television, sat around, dozed, played cards. They talked a little, but in the way that people talk when they're waiting for a bus at a Greyhound terminal. Three times a day they ate meals served in plastic dishes on plastic trays, and three times a day they took their medication. Everyone got Thorazine, plus something else that the nurses refused to identify; they just stood by watching to make sure the pills were swallowed. Sometimes they made mistakes and brought the same tray of medications around twice. Even if you told them that you'd already taken your pills, the nurses insisted that you take them again. None of the patients Phil talked to, not even the most paranoid, believed that the nurses were double dosing on purpose, to make them more manageable. The nurses were stupid, the more cantankerous ones said; they were overworked, suggested the more generous ones. Even he no longer felt the desire to spin theories. He felt himself dying. His physical, mental, and spiritual life were draining from him like pus from an abscess. Soon he would be nothing more than an empty sac.

One day he found himself in a small room, waiting for an intern who was going to perform some sort of evaluation. Another patient was waiting there too, a Mexican girl, a Jehovah's Witness who proceeded to embark on a long description of God's Kingdom, where all the animals would lie together, the lion with the lamb. Phil was not even tempted to tell her that he knew a thing or two about the Kingdom of God and it had nothing to do with her picture-postcard vision of paradise.

Survivors of concentration camps who hear someone who has never been in one holding forth on the subject can't bring themselves to set the record straight either. They shake their heads and keep quiet.

He must have seen God too soon or too late. Either way, the meeting had not been a success from the point of view of his survival. Encountering the living God, if it was really Him he had met, had not given him the strength he needed to carry on the struggles of daily life, to hold on to his wife and child, to face with courage the trials that every man must face.

And was it really Him? Phil was no longer asking the question in the strictly academic terms in which he had posed it in the Exegesis, where all he had to do was prevent his adversary from proving the contrary. And what good had that done? He knew he had encountered something but now he discovered the encounter had done him absolutely no good. But what in life had ever done him any good?

Stacks of old newspapers lay on Formica tables. He read them methodically and distractedly. One day, he came across a short article, one of those human interest stories that are so devastating that there is no reason to develop them much beyond the bare facts. It was about a three-year-old boy whose parents had taken him to the hospital for a routine operation. He was supposed to be released the following day. The anesthesiologist had made a mistake, however, and, even after weeks of desperate efforts to correct the damage, the little boy remained deaf, dumb, blind, and paralyzed. Irreversibly.

As Phil read, he felt a sob rise in his throat, filling it but unable to come out. He spent the entire afternoon frozen in shock, staring blankly into space. Never had anything hurt so much. He could think of nothing else except the moment of the little boy's awakening, when he regained consciousness in the dark. At first he would be anxious, frightened the way one is frightened when one knows the fear is going to end. Wherever he was, his parents couldn't be far away. They would turn on the light and talk to him. But no one, nothing came to him. Not a sound. He tried to move but he wasn't able to. He tried to cry out but he couldn't hear his own screams. Maybe he felt it when someone touched him, when someone opened his mouth to feed him. Maybe they fed him intravenously. The article didn't say.

His parents and the hospital staff stood around him, dissolved in horror, but the boy didn't know this. They had no way to communicate with him. The electroencephalogram indicated that he was conscious, that there was something behind the waxy, contracted face, behind the pupils that no longer saw, and none of them could know that this someone, this little boy entombed within his own body, was silently howling with terror. No one could explain to him what had happened, and who would have had the heart to do so anyway? When and how would he understand what had happened to him? And that it would not end, that it would always be this way?

That night, as Phil lay awake in bed, unable to sleep, a sad and unshakable certainty invaded him.

He had indeed met something, had sensed its presence all its life, but it was neither God nor the devil. It was Jane. He had never had any other partner, any other adversary than this other half, this dead part of himself. Everything in his life had happened in a closed circuit. His life and all the weird stories that he had thought up were but a long dialogue between Phil and Jane. All the uncertainty from which he suffered, all the uncertainty that had been the stuff of his books came down to the question of which of the two of them was the dummy and which the ventriloquist. Was the real world the one in which he believed he lived and, like a medium, conjured up Jane in all her divine or diabolical disguises, or was it this tomb, this black hole, this eternal darkness in which Jane lived and imagined her surviving brother? He was merely the lead actor in a dead person's dream.

Or else it was not Jane who was dead, but he.

Lying at the bottom of a grave in a Colorado cemetery for the last forty-eight years, while Jane, in the world of the living, was thinking of him. Once again, it was either one or the other, but it hardly mattered now. The time for theories was finished.

His whole life he'd been searching for reality, and now he had found it. It was this tomb. His own.

He was in it.

He had always been there.

He was the little boy in the newspaper article.

And this time there was no doubt, no hidden truth behind this Ultimate Reality. He knew he had reached the end of the line.

He also knew that he would have to forget this knowledge. Light from the sun is better than artificial light, but artificial light is better than darkness. To say otherwise is pure bluster.

He would forget. He would believe that on this night he had merely come up with another theory, a particularly depressing one perhaps, yet understandable, given the circumstances. He would go back to his illusion, to the life he thought he had been leading; he would tinker with his Exegesis, which was the best way he knew of to hide his head in the sand. He would keep saying that he would give his life to know the truth, that nothing was more desirable than the truth, and each time he said it he would mean it. And happily for him, he would forget that it wasn't true.

It was like the story of the three wishes he had loved so much and told so many times to Jane during their childhood.

The first wish: I want to know the truth; I want to make my way up the river of forgetfulness; I want to be shown what's down there at the bottom of the sack.

Granted.

The second wish: I want to forget what I have seen and never think about it again; I want to forget the story of the little boy, forget about this whole business of the three wishes, forget that I have a third wish coming to me. I want to forget everything.

Granted.

You're still entitled to a third wish but you will never know that; you've forgotten it forever. That's a promise.

And now, sleep.

CHAPTER 21

CRITICAL MASS

Doris visited him faithfully in the psychiatric hospital. Each time she came he begged her to move in with him when he got out; he would keep her spirits up while she was in remission and, if her cancer came back, would take care of her the way she was taking care of him now—in the charity of Christ. He would love her and love himself, and God would love them both. Now that Tessa had left, no one could accuse them of adultery. This was the argument that won her over.

They found a three-room apartment in Santa Ana, in a new building at the edge of a Mexican barrio. The building, an apparent attempt on the part of the architect to strike a harmonious balance between modernism and local color, resembled a model prison. A magnetic card opened the underground parking garage; a closed-circuit television system monitored the entryway and the corridors; concealed loudspeakers piped in soft music. For a man who had spent his whole life living in single-family houses and who hated crowded spaces, it was a curious choice of residence, but Phil never complained about it and lived there until his death.

The apartment had the advantage of being close to Tim Powers's place and the Episcopal church where Doris ran an outreach program. Part of her job consisted of culling the true poverty cases from the raft of drug addicts who would show up every day with some new scam to extort money for their next fix. No matter how often Phil told her that drug addicts were no less deserving of sympathy than her poverty cases were, and in fact were every bit as poor, she considered them imposters and hated them. As she prepared dinner for him, she filled him in on the goings-on at the church. It amounted to the usual office gossip—rivalries, frustrations, petty resentments. The shining hero in all her stories was the priest who had converted her, Larry; she was in love with him, she said. When she told him how much she wanted to sleep with him, Larry, who was married and a grandfather, had given the rather Pike-like reply that he never mixed business and pleasure. Even after this rebuff, Larry remained Doris's constant point of reference. She invoked his authority every time Phil—in an effort to change the subject from parish gossip—tried to engage her in one of those theological discussions that he had assumed would be a side benefit of living with a devout Christian. "Larry says that's bullshit," was her response when he tried to tell her about the Gnostic foundations of her faith. And when he quoted Scripture, she would say, "I'll ask Larry if that's one of the corrupt parts of the Bible." When Larry and Doris found a verse in the Bible they didn't like, they pronounced it apocryphal. They had no stomach for speculation, controversy, or flirtation with heresy. As soon as her roommate went off in one of those directions, Doris knitted her brow and began grating her carrots with a fury that discouraged Phil from pursuing the matter further. Living with a dying woman turned out to be less uplifting than he had imagined.

Their friends found the whole arrangement unhealthy. So did Phil's new psychotherapist, who had treated him at the hospital and whom Phil had agreed to see once a week. As he is presented in *Valis*, "Maurice" is a huge man with a black beard who wears army fatigues. He says he's been involved in arms trafficking and once served in the Israeli army. He has a gruff, imperious manner and is fond of punctuating his pronouncements with an icy "And I mean it." It's an unnecessary stipulation; no one would ever accuse Maurice of kidding around.

Maurice's therapeutic project in Phil's case was to bully him into enjoying life so that he would stop trying to save other people. To Maurice, enjoying life meant balling some broad that's got big tits, not one who's dying. Unfortunately, Phil didn't share this idea—or any other of Maurice's ideas—about enjoying life. He understood only meaning, and he prudently abstained from sharing his thoughts on the subject with his therapist. When Maurice lit into Phil about Doris, he would stare at the floor and wait for the storm to pass.

All Phil wanted, Maurice insisted, was to believe he was a good person. If Doris didn't have cancer, he asked, would he want to sleep with her? Of course not. He was latching on to death so he could tell himself he was doing a good deed. He could go on thinking he was a saint while slinking off into his corner to kill himself. It was pathetically obvious. If Phil wanted to die, Maurice told him, he should just go and get it over with. Because he was going to die anyway.

He knew, Phil murmured penitently.

Actually, he thought that Maurice was an idiot, though that didn't mean that the man wasn't right. Phil even came around to seeing some truth in the psychosomatic theory of illness that Maurice favored, in the idea that organic disorders fulfill the unconscious wishes of the id. Although Phil couldn't honestly accuse Doris of having desired her cancer, he felt that she cultivated a repellently intimate relationship with it, one that grew even more intimate after her doctors announced that she was in remission. Phil was reminded of how he had felt when his cat Pinky had run away. He waited for weeks for him to come back and dreamed about him at night; he couldn't accept that Pinky was really gone forever. Each time he thought he heard a scratching at the door he jumped: maybe it was Pinky. In Doris's case, however, the question wasn't *whether* her disease would return but rather *when*. The doctors had warned her that it would, and the prospect made all joy a futile endeavor. If you laughed at a joke in her presence, you felt you were somehow insulting her. Common sense, thought Phil with his usual psychological penetration, should have made Doris draw every ounce of pleasure she could from life during her remission instead of waiting for it to end. He preached hedonism, forgetting that few people were less qualified than he to offer such advice and that an exuberant Doris would have put him off even more than the gloomy and pious Doris he now knew.

They spent the next three months together, keeping a watchful eye out for the return of her lymphoma. Phil, in his customary way, made living with him impossible. Either he was working on his Exegesis and couldn't be interrupted for any reason whatsoever or else he had stopped working and demanded that Doris be available to discuss with him whatever it was he had written. He objected to her going out with other men and hated the fact that she had a job; he preferred for her to be financially dependent on him and for himself to be praised for his generosity.

At the end of the summer, the apartment next door became available and Doris decided to move into it. She assured Phil that their relationship wouldn't change. They would help each other out as much as before and she would cook for him and come visit. Only now, they would each have a little more space and privacy, and didn't he think that was a good thing?

Phil did not think so. All he knew was that, once again, a woman had left him. He was so chagrined that he drove down the freeway in the wrong direction and wound up back in a psychiatric hospital, where he promptly fell in love with a young drug addict whom he hoped to save. After his release, he was afraid to get behind the wheel of a car again, and asked a friend, K. W. Jeter, to drive him to his weekly sessions with Maurice. As Phil insisted on being dropped off early and picked up late, Jeter assumed that Phil wanted to spare him from having to wait. He later discovered that Phil would return each week with his pockets stuffed with slips of paper with women's phone numbers on them. The mental health clinic had become the hub of his social life. Some people had their nightclubs, others their favorite beach; Phil's pickup place was the clinic.

His attempts to find another woman to live with met with no success. Schizophrenics, drug addicts, cancer patients—all these women, of whom he asked only that they let him love their defects, seemed to have put out the word among themselves that his rescue efforts were to be avoided at all costs. Living alone was entirely new to him and something he dreaded, yet either because his instinct for life and his death drive had by now been equally blunted or because he had finally become a little wiser, he got used to it. He settled into a routine to which he would adhere strictly throughout his final years, during which very little happened to him. He who had moved so many times in the course of his life was thrown into a panic when his prisonlike apartment building was put up for sale. He managed to buy his apartment and even became the president of the homeowners' association— an honor that he held out proudly to prove to people how much he had changed. Money was coming in. His old books continued to sell overseas and Warner Bros. had bought the film rights to *Do Androids Dream of Electric Sheep?* But he didn't know what to do with this godsend: it had come too late. He had grown accustomed to his bachelor existence, to his little apartment with its blinds always closed and its pervasive odor of cat piss. He labored every night on his Exegesis until the early hours of the morning, got up late, dressed himself in whatever was at hand—jeans, a rumpled floral-print shirt—and went out to buy frozen dinners, sweets, and cat food from the local convenience store. He spent his afternoons reading his reference books, listening to music, writing letters, making phone calls, and receiving visitors. Despite their separation, he had reconciled with Tessa and she brought Christopher to see him several times a week. Paul Williams's article had made him a popular subject for hip journalists, and they would often drop by, hoping for a bizarre interview, which most of the time they got. Above all, he continued to see a great deal of Doris. Not long after she moved out, her cancer returned and she became very sick. The wall between their two bathrooms was thin, and for hours on end Phil could hear her groaning, moaning, and trying to vomit. He proposed that she move back in with him so that he could help her, but Doris refused. When she was taken to the hospital, he spent whole days at her bedside, holding her hand. Her head sunk deep into her pillows, she looked like a bald old man. The chemotherapy had made her half deaf and blind. But when he asked her how she felt, she murmured, "I can feel that God is healing me." He shook his head sadly. God was a heartless bastard. Phil was vaguely irritated when, to everyone's surprise, Doris's condition steadily improved.

Every Thursday evening, Powers invited over to his apartment a small group of friends, fellow science fiction writers just starting out. While he was married, Phil had almost never gone to these gatherings, but now that he was a bachelor and lived in the neighborhood, he went all the time. There weren't any women at the sessions. Once this would have put him off but now it felt like a relief. He could be himself without second-guessing his intentions among these ingenuous young men, who seemed to be playing at being members of a Victorian men's club, comparing brands of whiskey and tobacco. But they talked, too, about books, films, and new albums. Phil's arrival brought a rich new topic one could call "Exegesis Update." Every Thursday evening Phil showed up with a good bottle of wine and a new theory as to the meaning of his experience, about which they had all been pledged to secrecy. One day he announced he had reconciled Pythagorism and Zoroasterism—whose falling out had previously escaped his companions' notice; the following week he was preaching the teachings of the Gnostic Basilides. Under Phil's influence, the little band of fans was transformed—whether they liked it or not—into a circle of theologians.

Besides him, two personalities, Powers and the aforementioned K. W. Jeter, dominated the group. They made a great comic duo—the Good Kid and the Punk. Blond, chubby, with smiling blue eyes, someone who was always willing to help out, Powers invested his stories with a hearty, impulsive imagination. His good fellowship, combined with a nearly legendary credulity that he must have liked to exaggerate, marked him for the role of sidekick, the Dr. Watson who, unfailingly amazed by Holmes's intellectual prowess, is ever the object of Holmes's gentle teasing. No one was quite so good as Powers at opening his eyes wide in a dumbfounded stare, rubbing his chin, and saying, "This time, Phil, I know you're pulling my leg. . . ."

As for Jeter, Phil at first mistrusted him. When he arrived in Fullerton and found Jeter hanging around Willis McNelly's class, Phil pegged him as an agent provocateur. With the passing years, Dick stopped giving him the cold shoulder and actually found it interesting to have for a friend someone as aggressively sinister as K.W. With his lanky frame, high cheekbones, and reptilian eyes, he looked like a hired gun out of a Western. Like Powers, he was a writer, but the novels he wrote were horror novels, filled with stomach-wrenching scenes of torture and mutilation. People who liked him spoke of his acerbic humor; everyone else found him odious.

Jeter's main fear in life was being taken for a ride. He listened to people as if they were all used-car salesmen. Where spiritual matters were concerned, his obsession with not being hoodwinked translated into a testy agnosticism. Powers was a Roman Catholic, and a stickler on matters of dogma, and Jeter and Phil loved nothing better than to shock him. Unlike Doris, whose response to irreligious or heretical remarks was to feign indifference and pick up her pace—the way she had been taught to do if she ever came upon a flasher—Powers got riled up and argued back, confident he could win Phil over by assuring him that, had they lived in the days of the Inquisition, he would have both set the match to Phil's pyre and prayed to God for Phil's salvation.

Powers was one of those Catholics who, unable to explain evil, deny its very existence. According to them, evil is simply good that has taken a wrong turn and gone astray, a teacher's ruler with which God, pedagogue that He is, instructs and edifies His charges. The role of Ivan Karamazov, who asks how a good God permits the suffering of children, fell naturally to Jeter. None of the members of Phil's little circle had kids, apart from him, and he never talked about them— except to make hay of his having diagnosed Christopher's hernia. What they had were cats, and so they adjusted the argument to fit their affective priorities. "What about my dead cat?" Jeter would ask whenever anyone mentioned God.

Some years earlier, Jeter's cat had been hit by a car. When Jeter ran to pick it up from the pavement, the poor creature was still alive, breathing bloody foam out its mouth. Jeter had seen in its eyes a look

of dreadful and unforgettable incomprehension. In *Valis*, Jeter's counterpart, Kevin, says:

> "On judgment day when I'm brought up before the great judge I'm
> going to say 'Hold on a second,' and then I'm going to whip out my dead
> cat. 'How do you explain *this*?' I'm going to ask." By then, Kevin would
> say, the cat would be stiff as a frying pan; he would hold out the cat by
> its handle, its tail, and wait for a satisfactory answer.
>
> Fat said, "No answer would satisfy you."
>
> "No answer you could give," Kevin sneered. "Okay, so God saved your
> son's life; why didn't he have my cat run out into the street five seconds
> later? *Three* seconds later? . . . I just think it's fucked. God is either
> powerless, stupid, or he doesn't give a shit. Or all three. He's evil, dumb,
> and weak. I think I'll start my own exegesis."
>
> "But God doesn't talk to you," I said.
>
> "You know who talks to Horse?" Kevin said. "Who really talks to
> Horse in the middle of the night? People from the planet Stupid. Horse,
> what's the wisdom of God called again? Saint what?"
>
> "Hagia Sophia," Horse said cautiously.
>
> Kevin said, "How do you say Hagia Stupid? St. Stupid?"
>
> "Hagia Moron," Horse said. "Moron is a Greek word like Hagia. I
> came across it when I was looking up the spelling of oxymoron."

Phil always defended himself by giving in to his adversary, and he
was grateful to Jeter for playing that part so faithfully. It was true that
Jeter lacked finesse—you couldn't count on him to play by the rules in
an argument. But with his rocklike brutality, he served as both foil and
springboard. On the one hand, he wouldn't let Phil forget that his conversations with God could be explained as a case of paranoid delirium.
On the other hand, if there was no alternative to insanity other than
the universal "bullshit" that summed up Jeter's philosophy of life, then
maybe it was better to be crazy. And, deep down, Jeter wasn't such a
bad guy. "We all deal with this bullshit the best we can. Who knows?
Maybe it will turn out that you've hit on a good thing."

Some days Phil could be very happy. He had everything he needed to live—a peaceful life, all the snuff he wanted, music, cats, and a group of loyal friends who, for all their teasing, admired him. And he had his Exegesis, which was slowly revealing to him the Savior's plans for him and for the world. Yes, it was all still obscure and contradictory and it still bounced him around from theory to theory, but he thought that one day the spirit slumbering within him would rouse itself from its torpor and, deciding that the joke had gone on long enough, would bring the monstrous manuscript to closure. Phil would be scribbling yet another of his speculations when suddenly whoever or whatever was hiding within the depths of his soul would grab the pen from him and write, "That's it. He was right." Then it would be revealed to the whole world, with dazzling clarity, that indeed that was it. If God had chosen him for His scribe, that was how it would have to happen. But who can say what God really wants? In imagining that we've guessed God's will, don't we incur His wrath? Phil feared that his fate would be to slog around in this heap of papers until he finally died. He was fairly certain that the secret of secrets lay somewhere among the debris, but that didn't guarantee he would know it if he found it. Perhaps someone on high had reserved for him this cruel vocation, this long torture of Tantalus: every moment of the day a voice told him that he was hot on the trail and kept leading him onward into the darkness. He would die certain of only one thing, if that: that he had been had. He could always tell himself that the second he crossed over to the Other Side the truth would be revealed and, as Saint Paul had promised, he would at last come face-to-face with reality. But who knew?

After almost four years of labor, the Exegesis seemed further away from being a book than when he had started. He joked about that with Powers and the others, but in fact he was deeply discouraged. He had filled thousands of sheets of paper that probably no one would ever read; he had constructed theory upon theory and compiled countless references—and day by day this enormous work seemed less and less likely to achieve its goal of providing a public accounting of what had happened to him in the spring of 1974. He got advances by setting down plot outlines of novels that everyone thought extremely promising—even he. But neither the sequel to *The Man in the High Castle* nor a project called *To Scare the Dead*, about a California businessman whose mind is invaded by a first-century Essene, saw the light of day. Once, when he had been a prolific writer, he would become deeply irritated when asked when he would get around to writing something serious. Now it was worse: people asked him if he was still writing. His famous imagination was reputed to have dried up, but he himself knew that the truth behind his writer's block lay elsewhere. He had never had imagination; he had merely written reports. For reasons of safety, he had long been kept in ignorance, allowed to believe that he had been making up his stories in the way that Ragle Gumm is allowed to believe that he is sending in answers to a contest in the local newspaper. A story needs a point, a meaning, yet in his case meaning in all its force and all its vast multiplicity had been dumped onto his head all at once. For years he had patiently cataloged and sorted, but he knew that the more he moved forward the less progress he made. As the pile of unreadable sheets of paper grew, so did the enigma.

He sometimes felt that he should have died in the spring of 1974. Not dying was apparently part of the program. Instead of experiencing final illumination and then dying, he had experienced illumination and survived. For one reason or another, the Programmer had revealed to him what is normally revealed only as one crosses over to the Other Side, and then He had left him here in this vale of tears. That was why it seemed that nothing more could happen to him, that life was going on without him. In a certain way, Philip K. Dick had died at the age of forty-six. In March 1974, the words *The End* had been printed at the bottom of the last page of his life's story. He had been granted a reprieve so that he could read it over again and fully grasp what he had only glimpsed the first time through. When he had managed to do that, he would be allowed to die for good.

The Programmer must have found something interesting about this experiment, Phil figured, but as far as he was concerned, he was no more than a rat in a maze. "I have become a machine which thinks and does nothing else. It scares me. How did this come about? I posed myself a problem and I cannot forget the problem but I cannot answer the problem, so I am stuck in flypaper. I can't get loose; it's like a self-imposed karma at work. Every day my world gets smaller. I work more, I live less."

Nothing more would happen to him. He would write no more books, meet no more women. Instead, he would be condemned to reread his old works, go back over his life, and fill the margins of his books with useless notes, never managing to put a satisfying coda to it all.

Yet something did happen to him in the end. Someone came into his life.

CHAPTER 22

THE ONE HE HAD BEEN WAITING FOR

In the Valley of the Moon, north of San Francisco, is the pretty town of Sonoma. And in this pretty town lived a pretty woman named Joan Simpson. She had black hair, a lithe but muscular body honed by martial arts, and a nonchalant way of sitting in a half-lotus position, one bronzed foot planted against her inner thigh. Her whole physical being expressed both a radiant sensuality and a degree of advancement on the path to serenity far greater than most people achieve. Joan worked in a psychiatric hospital and read Jung, R. D. Laing, and Sri Aurobindo. A slightly wandering eye only added to her charm.

Though not much interested in science fiction, Joan had come across one of Dick's novels—we don't know which—and then went about acquiring all the others. As many of his titles were out of print or otherwise hard to find, this meant getting in touch with specialty booksellers, with whom she enjoyed talking about her new favorite author, speaking of him as if she knew with absolute certainty that in a century or two the world would recognize him for what he was—a towering prophet and imposing thinker, one of the great minds of his day. It is quite possible that she told people what I myself, an adolescent in glasses and grubby desert boots, was going around saying at the time: that Dick was the modern Dostoevsky, a man who understood everything. Coming as it did from the mouth of an attractive, educated young woman who seemed to be neither a nut nor, like so many of his fans, a lumpen science fiction buff, her enthusiasm was striking. One of the booksellers knew Dick and wrote to him about his admirer. A series of letters and phone calls followed. Whether it was Phil or Joan who first brought up the ending of *The Man in the High Castle*, Joan, like Juliana Frink, put the *I Ching* in the trunk of her car and set off for Southern California to meet the author and to tell him that somehow, in some inexplicable way, everything he had written was true.

She was not at all surprised to find Phil living in a small apartment; after all, the Man in the High Castle himself lived in an ordinary suburban ranch house. And with his beard, his shining eyes, and the oddly distinguished air he had about him in spite of his careless getup and the cloud of snuff that rose from his clothing every time he moved, he did in fact resemble Hawthorne Abendsen. He was the right age now. When he asked her what she wanted to drink, she replied, "An old-fashioned, of course," and they both burst out laughing.

From the start they talked as if they'd known each other forever. Even the most commonplace words or phrases can resonate deeply and inexplicably, but it is rare for two people meeting for the first time to respond identically to the very same words, to hear the very same echoes. A believer in reincarnation would say that when perfect strangers understand each other perfectly at their first encounter, it is because they loved each other in a former lifetime. One need not believe in reincarnation to have experienced this phenomenon; romantic interest can account for it too, although Phil and Joan Simpson's remarkable rapport probably had more to do with memories from a past life than with physical attractions in this one. They were not lovers, technically speaking, for his all-consuming Exegesis had rendered Phil impotent. But they spent three weeks together, hardly ever leaving the apartment, enchanted by the certainty that, unbeknownst to them, what was happening had long been in preparation. Making up their dialogue as they went along, they discovered a script that had been written just for them. They forgot that Phil was the author of this play they seemed to be in, or perhaps they both believed that it had been dictated to him.

Phil and Joan sat facing each other in the darkened apartment, the blinds perpetually closed, and talked for days and nights on end, touching each other's faces with their fingertips, like blind people. "I knew that you would recognize me," Joan said, and from the tone of her voice and the faint glint of light reflecting off her teeth, he could tell that she was smiling. He told her that deep inside he knew that she would come. He had always known, he said, but in the past few weeks, his dreams had announced her imminent arrival.

He told her everything. Quietly and without hurry, he related the story of his awakening in the grand terms of a spiritual epic, and together, taking up his novels one by one in chronological order, they identified the stages of his journey. Joan was often a step ahead of him. Having read the novels, and without even knowing him, she had guessed it all: how he had been sent into the world, his memories occluded; the missing lamp cord that had been his first warning that something was amiss in the world, that had led him to suspect the universal simulacrum; his anxious attempts, in his novels of the 1960s, to explore the contours of this simulacrum; his indictment, in *The Three Stigmata of Palmer Eldritch*, of the demiurge responsible for it, who holds us all captive through drugs and false-memory implants; and, finally, in *Ubik*, the first appearance of the saving power, a force as quiet and humble as the enemy is brutal and oppressive. The Paraclete, Phil said, was nothing more than a little puff of cheap mist sold in handy spray cans to suburban housewives; that was the most important thing she needed to understand. He told her the reactions his works had garnered when they first came out, before he knew what they meant: he had made friends and enemies, the sons of light and the sons of darkness. He recounted the defeats his foes had dealt him—aimless wanderings, death wishes, the downward spiral that had been his life for ten years—until 1974, when he came back to the surface, his memories and vision restored. He should have been on the path to happiness, but everything was still going wrong. Thomas had left him. He had once again lost his family. He may have been on the winning side, and could even count himself among the architects of the victory, but he was a casualty of the war. All his premonitions had turned out to be true, light had triumphed over darkness, and yet he felt he had been duped. He was safe now, and free to live as he pleased, but what kind of life was this? Alone, unloved, holed up in a pathetic apartment in Santa Ana, he lived entirely within his mind, like a rat in a cage, spending his days listening to his own private Watergate tapes playing over and over in his brain, constructing a cosmogony that, irony of ironies, was undoubtedly false. The Programmer, as he had imagined Him, couldn't possibly treat him the way the Soviet Union had treated the veterans of the International Brigades who had taken refuge there after the Spanish Civil War—by delivering them up to Hitler. The ultimate Other, if it really was with Him that Phil was dealing, surely wouldn't have left him in this solipsistic hell. It just couldn't be. His life couldn't end like this. And then, in the depths of his despair and loneliness, he suddenly knew that it wouldn't, that this grim nightmare could only be that penultimate scene in which, just before the movie's happy ending, you're made to fear the worst. At night he would dream of a woman approaching him in the dark; he would sense her presence next to him on the mattress, the weight of her body, the warmth of her firm flesh. He knew the softness of her breasts; he had held them in his hands many times before. One night, awakening in the darkness, he had reached out his hand and found himself stroking a warm ball of fur that had nestled in his pillow. It was his cat, Pinky. He smiled: the Programmer was playing a practical joke on him, and it would soon be over. His reward would come. She would have traveled all day to see him, she would show up at his door wearing a T-shirt with no bra underneath, and when she sat she would place her foot against her inner thigh in the half-lotus position. Yes, just like that.

My God, how I've waited for you.

I know. I know all this. Now I'm here.

Joan's arrival reenergized him. The man who never left his apartment except for trips to the convenience store, to Powers's house, and to his

therapy sessions with Maurice, stunned the members of the Santa Ana
SF circle one day when he asked offhandedly whether one of them
might be willing to look after his cats for a few months while he was
out of town. He had decided to spend the summer in Sonoma with a
friend, he told them, a woman they didn't know. And then come September, he would be in France for a week, the guest of honor at a science fiction convention in Metz.

No one could believe it, and yet it was true—he did spend that
summer in Sonoma with Joan and he did go to France, also with her
and with her encouragement and loving care. That was what he always
wanted most from a woman—loving care—and for several months,
Joan gave it to him. She also gave him a large pectoral cross that he
wore around his neck on a heavy chain day and night.

He'd been asked to prepare a speech for the convention in France, and
the timing could not have been better. Juliana had come and confirmed
what he knew. Now he could tell the world the truth. How wondrous
were the ways of Providence, that He should let the French, who had
always been among his most fervent fans, be the first to hear his tidings.

Once he had settled on a title for his talk—"If You Find This World
Bad, You Should See Some of the Others"—he wrote as if in a trance.
Just as a puff or two from a spray can of Ubik turns back the forces of
entropy, so Joan's care revivified his thinking. From the shambles of his
Exegesis sprang up a model of the universe that, at last, was coherent
and precise. He simply had to pick up the thread from *The Man in the
High Castle*, follow it to the actual appearance of Joan at his door, and
everything made sense: his inklings of parallel universes, Christ's
teachings, the work of the Programmer during the stretch between his
experience in the spring of 1974 and Nixon's downfall in August of
that year. Naturally, his theological disquisition would double as a declaration of love and would end with Joan's arrival, which, in a way,
proved the existence of God. Perhaps at that moment in his talk a
spotlight could search out Joan in the audience and follow her as she
came down the aisle to join him onstage, and she would kiss the cross
that she had given him, then raise her face to kiss him on the lips . . .
No, better not. He had planned this sort of stage business once before,
with Donna, and it hadn't brought him any luck.

———

All summer long he practiced his speech, reading it into a tape recorder. Joan listened to it several times and helped him with his delivery. As to its content, she does not appear to have expressed any reservations. When they left for France, Fat felt that he was now fully in charge, lord of the castle once and for all. He spent the whole long night on the plane mumbling passages of the text, his eyes half closed, Joan's hand in his. Sometimes, anticipating the audience's reaction to this line or that, he chuckled softly to himself. He had given quite a few talks before roomfuls of fans at science fiction conventions, and he had sat through even more. Generally they consisted of a handful of entertainingly strung-together anecdotes, plus an inside joke or two, a tip of the hat to older writers for their work, and a nod of encouragement to those on the rise. Now, when he thought about what he was going to say, about the bomb snugly tucked away in his carry-on luggage, he felt as though he were the prophet Isaiah invited to say a few words at a Tupperware party.

He was nearly certain he was heading toward triumph. And if his listeners understood him and—this went without saying—believed him, his triumph would be no mere literary success. They would recognize his speech as the revelation it was. It would change their lives. Crowds would gather to hear him speak, each one larger than the one before, for naturally the speech he was coming to give would be but the first of many others like it. Like Ragle Gumm, he would make the cover of *Time* magazine as Man of the Year, yet even that designation people would come to regard as insignificant and somehow quaint, the way one regards the responses of distant ancestors to events whose true importance they could not yet fathom. He would be the Christopher Columbus of parallel universes. A new era, people would one day discover, had commenced on September 24, 1977.

In imagining his French audience as an army of potential disciples, ripe for conversion, he was greatly mistaken. It is true his arrival was keenly anticipated, but by veterans of May 1968 who admired him as a cranky iconoclast, as the Punk he took such pride in no longer being. They wanted Dick the Paranoiac, the Junkie, the Radical, the Unco-optable. Having bought the line that their idol's long creative silence had been due to "personal problems," the conventioneers expected to see, stepping off the plane from Los Angeles, a giggling, stumbling, drug-ruined wreck, and they felt a disappointment akin to what rock music critics feel when their favorite bad-boy rock idol shows up at his press conference sipping mineral water and extolling the virtues of family life and positive thinking. Phil looked in good shape—even in great shape. He laughed, ogled the girls, ate heartily, and reveled in all the attention. One of the other guests at his table at a dinner on the first evening asked him with a wink about the pills he had lined up next to his plate. They were for stomach problems, Phil told him, and the way he said it, as though it were self-evident, made it impossible not to believe that stomach problems were indeed what the pills were for.

To the listeners who gathered in the meeting hall of the Sofitel Hotel the following day to hear him speak, he seemed far less relaxed, from the moment he stepped onto the stage. The large cross that rested on his hairy chest, which his unbuttoned shirt exposed to general view, was surprising and somehow troubling—it had to mean something but just what no one could quite figure out. It couldn't be a profession of Christian faith—that much was certain. Indeed, the very idea was laughable. It had to be a parody of some sort, then. Perhaps Dick was camping, playing the vampire for them, but then where were the fake fangs and the garlic cloves?

Phil, for his part, was sweating nervously. Joan, furious at him for having openly flirted with a young journalist in her presence the night before, was pouting in her room. He felt alone, in dire need of her comfort and care, and no longer convinced of what he was about to say. The room had filled up by now, the last stragglers noisily making their way to their seats amid the clacking of folding chairs and the popping of flashbulbs. Phil tapped on the microphone to see if it was on, and it shrieked back at him like a Geiger counter on speed. The sound technicians asked him to say something into the microphone, so that they could adjust the sound level. Peering down at the front row, occupied by a phalanx of skinny, bearded young men in their duffel coats and watch caps, and feeling their eyes fixed on him from behind their wire-rimmed glasses, he recited in a quavering voice a verse from Saint Paul in which the bringer of the Word is assured that he need not worry, that the Holy Spirit will look after everything. Luckily, no one understood what he had said, but Phil realized he no longer believed in his apostolic mission. He felt the lucid panic of a man who, drunk, accepts an absurd dare and then, having sobered up, understands he has no way out and will be spending the rest of his days trying to live down his embarrassment. Phil began to fear that if he waited a moment longer he might simply run off the stage and into the street, so out of the blue he started reading his text without waiting for the signal to begin. Those who heard him that day recall that his voice sounded dead and metallic, so different from that of the expansive, good-humored dinner guest of the night before. It occurred to not a few people listening to him that, like a character in one of his novels, he had been replaced by a badly programmed robot that might short-circuit at any moment and explode right there on the stage, scorching everyone around him.

The speech began with some fairly banal observations about the emergence of new ideas, how they always seem obvious in hindsight, and the distinction between invention and discovery. He himself, Phil declared, was of the firm conviction that no one had ever invented anything. All we ever do, he said, is discover truths that have always been there, waiting to see the light of day and find their "inventor." The audience found the speaker tense and his translator's interruptions tedious, but they saw nothing particularly strange in his remarks; he seemed somehow to be talking about his novels. At his mention of the Kingdom of Heaven, however, those who had already been bothered by the cross he was wearing suddenly pricked up their ears, but the threat quickly passed. A learned critic leaned over to his neighbor and quoted with a wry smile Borges's famous description of theology as a branch of fantastic literature.

By now, in fact, Phil had launched into a fairly woolly theological theme, about a cosmic chess game in which the Programmer sits across the game board from His opponent, the "dark counterplayer," each of their moves working vast changes in the configuration of reality. He continued in this vein for a full half hour and might have been reading the phone book for all the interest he seemed to stir among the audience. The more attentive listeners, however, were beginning to shift in their seats, a vague uneasiness having descended on them. They seemed like passengers on an ill-fated train who, hearing suspicious noises and feeling foreboding little jolts and bumps that seem to bother no one else around them, try to convince themselves that they're wrong, that their nerves are merely playing tricks on them, that the noises and bumps and jolts are all normal. Suddenly, however, a terrible shaking begins, as though born of their anxiety, and, in an apocalyptic din, the train really and truly goes off the rails: the catastrophe is upon them.

Phil cleared his throat, fumbled with his papers, and then began to speak in a suddenly louder voice:

> What we need at this point is to locate, to bring forth as evidence, someone who has managed somehow—it doesn't matter how, really—to retain memories of a different present. . . . According to my theoretical view, it would almost certainly have to be memories of a worse world than this. For it is not reasonable that God the Programmer and Reprogrammer would substitute a worse world in terms of freedom or beauty or love or order or healthiness—by any standard that we know. When a mechanic works on your malfunctioning car he does not damage it further; when a writer creates a second draft of a novel he does not debase it further but strives to improve it. I suppose it could be argued in a strictly theoretical way that God might be evil or insane and would in fact substitute a worse world for a better one, but frankly I cannot take that idea seriously. . . . So let us ask, Does any one of us remember in any dim fashion a worse Earth circa 1977 than this? . . .
>   I [do] . . .

In *The Man in the High* Castle there is a novelist, Hawthorne Abendsen, who has written an alternate-world novel. . . . At the conclusion of

The Man in the High Castle, a woman appears at Abendsen's door to tell him what he does not know, that his novel is true. . . . The irony of this ending—Abendsen finding out that what he had supposed to be pure fiction spun out of his imagination was in fact true—the irony is this: that my own supposed imaginative work is not fiction—or rather is fiction only now. . . .

I am sure, as you hear me say this, you do not really believe me, or even believe that I believe it myself. But nevertheless it is true. . . . You are free to believe me or free to disbelieve, but please take my word on it that I am not joking; this is very serious, a matter of importance. I am sure that at the very least you will agree that for me even to claim this is in itself amazing. Often people claim to remember past lives; I claim to remember a different, very different, *present* life. I know of no one who has ever made that claim before, but I rather suspect that my experience is not unique; what perhaps is unique is the fact that I am willing to talk about it.

Which he did, to the bewilderment and then the consternation of the audience. He described what had happened to him three years earlier. He spoke of secret Christians and the role they had played in Nixon's demise. He explained that he himself was a reprogrammed variable in one of those insidious reality shifts that form the framework of the universe and that he had had direct contact with the Programmer. Normally, Phil went on, He remains hidden—*Deus absconditus,* as the theologians say. Although at work in every molecule of the world, He is seen by no one except those whom He grasps hold of, the way one grasps a chess piece from a gameboard to make a move. He, Phil Dick, had been this chess piece and now he could say from personal experience that Saint Paul was right: it is a terrible thing to fall into the hands of a living God—the Old Testament God who said: "For I am fashioning a new heaven and a new earth, and the memory of the former things will not enter the mind nor come up into the heart." Phil concluded:

When I read this I think to myself: I believe I know a great secret. When the work of restoration is completed, we will not even remember the tyrannies, the cruel barbarisms of the Earth we inhabited. . . . I believe that process is taking place now, has *always* been taking place now. And, mercifully, we are already being permitted to forget that which formerly was. And perhaps in my novels and stories I have done wrong to urge you to remember.

And now, apparently, he had erred again.

He stepped from the dais and surveyed the extent of damage. The translator, overwhelmed, had stopped translating, but those in the audience who understood English were explaining to their neighbors what Dick had said. Apparently, not only had he gone crazy but he had become a religious fanatic as well. The general feeling of admiration gave way to a stunned embarrassment. People were staring at him. No one quite knew what to say.

Throughout the rest of his stay in France, a stay he cut short, his hosts made enormous efforts to dispel the malaise, to maintain the joyous conviviality of an event at which everyone was supposed to be on the same wavelength. A consensus, albeit a halfhearted one, emerged among the conference attendees: the train wreck they had witnessed had been an enormous Phildickian hoax. Like Orson Welles, who had put one over on an entire nation with his radio adaptation of "The War of the Worlds," that rascal Dick had been having them on, trying out the subject of a future novel on his French audience. And to make the charade all the more convincing, he had pretended that he actually believed the nonsense he was spouting. Seeing this official version of events win the day, the subject in question decided the diplomatic course was to affirm it. Soon he was greeting people in the corridors and elevators of the hotel with cascades of Falstaffian laughter and exaggerated winks, as if to say, I really had you going there, didn't I?

Were I writing a novel and not a biography, I would say at this point that this failure proved an utter catastrophe for Dick—that every time he thought about the embarrassed silence with which his speech was received he was utterly mortified and that on his return to California he crawled into his bed and died. It would be a satisfying ending, dramatically speaking, but that is not what happened. Dick had an incredible ability to adapt; when one scenario he was applying to reality went awry, he simply adopted another. Fat lay low for a while, like a gambler who has gone for the big stakes and lost, while Phil took on the irritating restraint of the person who thinks, but doesn't say, I told you so. As for Dick himself, flying back over the Atlantic, he emanated the contented glow of a happy tourist, flattered by the royal treatment he had received though sorry, of course, about the misunderstanding that had marred his speech—but sorry in the way a foreign tourist dining out among the locals might be sorry for having, out of linguistic ignorance, ordered the one thing on the menu he didn't want to eat. It had been, in other words, one of those comic misadventures that often make for better memories than those times when everything goes exactly according to plan. (Nevertheless, he must have been vexed. In discussing the trip with Joan some days later, he told her that what he found strange about it all was that everyone was wondering whether or not he believed what he was saying—a question of secondary importance, as far as he was concerned—whereas no one had asked the important question, namely, whether or not what he was saying was true.)

Of all the women he had had in his life, Joan was the only one who managed to leave him without major drama. They didn't even break up. The distance between Sonoma and Santa Ana was great enough for them to justify the loosening of a connection that nevertheless remained warm. They looked back on their relationship with wistful nostalgia, the way we might look back on one of those wonderful but all-too-brief encounters we sometimes have while away on a trip, but for which the trip is the necessary condition.

The speech in France should have been the Advent of Horselover Fat, and Joan the high priestess of his cult. But it didn't work out, so Dick went back to his Exegesis, where once again he faced the old problem: how to tell a story whose meaning he hadn't figured out. He dreamed, theorized, drove himself to despair. And then, altogether unexpectedly, he found a solution.

He had been asked to write a preface to a collection of his stories. Not knowing what to write, he started talking about his childhood. Without any real idea where he was headed, he related anecdotes, presented and critiqued his ideas, all as if he were chatting with his friends. Letting himself go like this gave him a feeling of freedom. Suddenly he thought how great it was to write in this manner—to talk about what had happened to him in a chatty, intimate way, with no need to prove anything.

I don't have much to say about *Valis*, the resulting novel, which has served as the main source for the preceding two chapters. Written over the course of two weeks of intense but relaxed work, the book is about a circle of friends in Santa Ana, California, much like the group that its author was frequenting at the time. David the Roman Catholic, Kevin the big-hearted cynic, and Phil the science fiction writer are all very much concerned about their friend Horselover Fat. He smoked too much dope during the 1960s, suffered crushing disappointments, and ever since March 1974 has been claiming that he's seen God. Phil, an impartial though sympathetic witness, tells Fat's story and relates their conversations, while refraining from any attempt to make Fat's theories more coherent than they are. Here, for example, is the way he talks about his Exegesis:

> Knowing this, by direct route from the divine, made Fat a latter-day prophet. But, since he had gone crazy, he also entered absurdities into his *tractate*.
>
> *#50. The primordial source of all our religions lies with the ancestors of the Dogon tribe, who got their cosmology and cosmogony directly from the three-eyed invaders who visited long ago. The three-eyed invaders are mute and deaf and telepathic, could not breathe our atmosphere, had the elongated misshapen skull of Ikhnaton and emanated from a planet in the star-system Sirius. Although they had no hands, but had, instead, pincer claws such as a crab has, they were great builders. They covertly influence our history toward a fruitful end.*
>
> By now Fat had totally lost touch with reality.

CHAPTER 23

PENULTIMATE TRUTHS

I'm coming to the end of this story—unless, of course, it already ended, somewhere in the last hundred pages. What else happened to Dick? His mother died and he called Kleo, whom he hadn't seen in twenty years, and cried as he told her the news. Movie rights to *Do Androids Dream of Electric Sheep?* brought him lots of money. He gave a large part of it to charitable organizations, bought a house for Tessa and Christopher, and offered the apartment next to his—the one Doris had lived in for a time—as a wedding present to Tim Powers, who wouldn't accept it. He continued to go to Powers's house every Thursday, and every Friday he went to his therapist. He made an effort to lose weight, and he dressed better. A photo taken in the offices of Warner Bros. shows him standing next to the director Ridley Scott, looking rather convincingly like a successful writer—heftily built but not overweight, sporting a neatly trimmed beard and an elegant suede jacket. Joan Simpson may have been his last love but he still had a few friendships with women and perhaps a sexual tryst or two. A young actress for whom he tried in vain to open the doors of the studios remembers five qualities in Dick: his kindness, his warmth, his loyalty, his devotion to his art, and his melancholy. With the blinds drawn in his darkened apartment, he listened to Dowland's lute songs, bearing such titles as "Sorrow, Stay" and "Weep You No More, Sad Fountains," but his favorite of all remained "Flow, My Tears." From afar he watched his son grow up and for a while even considered getting remarried to Tessa. On bad days, he called her and asked her to come over and hold him.

God spoke to him no more. He had almost no more visions, and he dreamed less, too. Depending on how he felt, he saw this abandonment either as a new test of faith on the road to his salvation, as a sign of the Adversary's final victory, or as a return to lucidity after a long bout of delirium. One night, however, he smoked a roach that he found in his ashtray after a guest had left, and God broke His silence. To make sure he was dealing with the Almighty Himself, not some imposter, Phil tried to put Him to a test. The one he came up with on the spur of the moment seemed perfect: at long last he had found *the* question that would force Him—or whoever was passing himself off as Him—to show His cards and come clean. But alas, the next day he could remember neither this ultimate question nor the answer he received.

With nothing else to cling to, he continued to work on the Exegesis. He wrote two more books—or, to be exact, Horselover Fat wrote one book and Phil Dick another.

Fat's book, *The Divine Invasion*, treats that most intractable of subjects: the Incarnation. Everyone who has written a life of Jesus has racked his brains over this problem. What exactly did the carpenter's apprentice from Nazareth know about his divine nature? Did he become aware of it gradually, in a long, slow awakening? As he hung from the cross, could he possibly have thought that, by taking himself to be the Son of God, he had fallen prey to an illusion? And if not, and he knew all along that he would be resurrected, then how can one take the Passion seriously?

The Divine Invasion has as its protagonist a little boy named Emmanuel. Smuggled to Earth as an unborn child inside the womb of an ailing colonist who dies before giving birth to him, Emmanuel brings unhappy tidings to our planet. The universe, he announces, is both a prison and a simulacrum; the Creator has lost control of His Creation; and all of us are asleep, dreaming the dreams that the all-powerful Empire puts into our brains. The least deeply asleep among us, alerted by vague doubts and intuitions, by little glitches and inconsistencies in their daily lives, can sense the truth that the Empire tries to suppress. They dare not believe it, yet somehow they must—they must wake up. Whoever hears the words of Emmanuel and believes in him shall enter the Garden and make the world real again.

Various tutelary figures appear on the scene to help the child discover his origin and his mission: the prophet Elijah, in the guise of an old beggar, John the Baptist, Zoroaster, Athena, Yahweh Himself, and a sententious little girl whose name is the one used by Cabalists to refer to the spirit of God, His feminine element—Shekkinah.

This gathering of cosmic luminaries is reminiscent of those big-budget "prestige" films in which Hollywood studios used to give "guest appearances" to every last star they had under contract. Bedecked in an array of Essenian, Gnostic, and Hebraic references, the upper crust of the Exegesis mingle around an ample buffet of traditional Dickian specialties, like implanted memories and cryonic suspension, while a medley of John Dowland airs, as sung by Linda Ronstadt to the accompaniment of her vibrolute orchestra, plays in the background.

The usual, in other words.

The Transmigration of Timothy Archer is the exact opposite. Vicious and unpredictable, it is the work of the Rat at his confounding best.

In 1979, Joan Didion's *White Album*, a collection of essays on the 1960s, was published and instantly hailed as a classic of literary journalism. One of the essays, "James Pike, American," offered a devastating portrait of Phil's old friend, painting him as a religious opportunist, a philistine, an unintelligent intellectual, and a narcissist. Phil read the essay and found it very painful; given his tendency to adopt the point of view of anyone who attacked him, he probably saw that Didion was right about Pike in many ways, and that what she said about Pike applied to him as well.

Dick had subtitled his Exegesis "Apologia Pro Mia Vita." Now he thought he might write an apologia for Pike, who had been both a role model for him and the embodiment of what he feared becoming—in other words, a perfect alter ego.

The question was, who should tell the story? He briefly considered narrating it in his own voice, but he realized that he would soon find himself at the same impasse where he had left Phil and Fat caught up in their interminable duel. Every novelist has dreamed of escaping himself, of writing the thoughts of someone else, of telling a story in someone else's words. Dick, quite improbably, realized this dream, just as the end was drawing near. For the first time in his life he chose a woman as his protagonist—and not the dark-haired, empathetic woman of his dreams or the castrating bitch of his nightmares but a complex and believable character who bears no resemblance to the author who created her.

Angel, the narrator of this very mainstream novel, had been married to Jeff, the son of Timothy Archer, the celebrated Episcopal bishop of the diocese of California. Jeff Archer committed suicide in 1971, and the bishop and his mistress, Kirsten, claimed to be in contact with him, from the Other Side. Then Kirsten committed suicide, and shortly afterward the bishop himself died a strange death in the Judean desert. The book opens on December 8, 1980, the day John Lennon is shot. Three weeks before, Ronald Reagan had been elected president. It is a time, the *I Ching* indicates, "when inferior people are pushing forward and are about to crowd out the few remaining strong and superior men" (*Po*, "Splitting apart").

Angel manages a record store on Telegraph Avenue in Berkeley, and like so many others in the Bay Area, she dates the events of her life by the release of Beatles albums. Her marriage was falling apart around the time *Rubber Soul* came out. When Jeff moved into the hotel room where his body was later found, he brought Paul McCartney's first solo album with him; the room did not have a record player. Nine years later, Angel still wants to weep whenever she hears "Teddy Boy."

Despite the fact that her Sufi instructor—an Alan Watts clone who gives seminars on his houseboat in Sausalito—has been teaching the exact opposite lesson, she thinks that the only reason we're on earth is to make the discovery that what we most love will be taken from us. The day Lennon dies, she happens upon an article by the essayist Jane Marion, the darling of the New York literary establishment; it's about Angel's former father-in-law. Reading the essay, Angel bursts into tears and then decides to write her own version of events as she witnessed them.

Angel Archer loved and admired the bishop, whom she calls Tim, but she was not blind to his faults. Nor was Dick to his own; by taking the viewpoint of this grieving young woman who is trying to understand what went wrong, he lets the apologetic aspects of his project fall by the wayside. He had intended to eulogize his old friend Jim and, in doing so, to justify himself, but his portrait of Tim Archer, even less flattering than Didion's of Pike, presents a dry pedant of a man, someone who, deaf to his interlocutors, overwhelms them with learned quotations and lards his monologues with terms like *kerygma, parousia,* and *hypostasis.* Tim Archer had a moral lesson for everyone and spoke grandly of charity and love, but he elbowed his way through life without a thought to the consequences of his actions. No mundane concerns would ever stand between him and his zeal for truth. When he took the wrapping off a new shirt, he let the cellophane and pins and cardboard stays fall to the floor and then, since he was always in a rush, would stroll out of the room without picking them up. When he no longer got along with his wife, he declared their marriage annulled. When a commitment no longer served his interests, he ceased to honor it. After all, rather than persevering in an error, wasn't it better to simply turn the page? This rule of conduct, which Didion perceptively identified as a signal trait of the 1960s, guided his entire life—a succession of hastily turned pages, a book he skimmed. Christ Himself was but one of those pages, one experience among others. To remain loyal to Him in the face of doubt and temptation would have been unworthy of this spiritual Don Juan. And like certain Don Juans for whom each successive love affair is the one great and true love, the bishop believed that in his latest vision of the world he had found the final answer. But all it took was a new book or a seductive new theory and all his former certainties were called into question. As a five-year-old child, he had read the dictionary and telephone directory cover to cover—a feat his admirers held up as a sign of his zeal for knowledge; now, as an adult, he continued to seek objective answers to his every question in one book or another. He knew that somewhere there had to be an impartial, documented, dependable account of the Real Truth, just as there is one, for example, of agricultural policy in the Low Countries. Surely he had discovered that books contradict one another in the answers they offer to this type of question—and necessarily so, given that they reflect human opinions—but that discovery led him neither to relativism nor to throw in his lot with one camp; all it did was cause him to continually change his mind.

Characteristically, Dick's case study of intellectual and emotional faithlessness—a self-portrait in fact—was the occasion for yet another of his famous about-faces. In depicting the erring ways of Pike and those around him, he sided with Angel Archer. At least she had her feet on the ground and, without blaming the sinner, spoke out against his sin—an absurd quest for meaning that ultimatley had lured him into the Judean desert behind the the wheel of a Ford Cortina and left him stranded there with a gas station road map and those two bottles of Coke. There's nothing more pathetic than the mistrust of immediate reality by people who never stop splitting hairs over Ultimate Reality. They always think they're getting to the bottom of things, whose surfaces they turn away from as unworthy of their attention; they end up never knowing the flesh of the world, the softness and resistance it offers to the touch. They manage to bypass their own lives.

Yes, Phil thought with a sigh, I have bypassed my life.

Unsurprisingly, Dick went too far in his championship of reality. Not satisfied with giving his woeful-countenanced Knight of Meaning a worthy opponent in the figure of a lucidly unhappy yet loving young woman, he had to throw in a schizophrenic as well, whose inability to engage in abstract thinking makes him Dick's new model for humanity. As a teenager, Phil had been given the "proverb test" by a psychiatrist, the one that asks the subject to explain what sayings like "When the cat's away, the mice will play" mean. A person of reasonable mental capacities might talk about employees taking advantage of their boss's absence; someone less equipped to translate the proverb into more general, abstract terms will merely paraphrase it, never getting beyond its surface meaning. He or she will say something like, "If you have mice in your house, your cat will hunt them. And if your cat takes off, the mice will be happy because they'll be left alone, and that's why they'll play." In his newfound enthusiasm for the concrete, Dick came to vaunt this incapacity for abstract thinking as a welcome antidote to the excesses of which he knew he himself was guilty.

Hence the following conversation, as reported by Angel, between Bishop Archer and Bill, his mistress's schizophrenic son, who cannot make the abstract leap that would allow him to understand the analogical argument by which the bishop seeks to demonstrate that vague psychic phenomena can prove that his son has returned from among the dead:

"You look under your parked car and you find a pool of water. Now, you don't *know* that—the water—came from your motor; that is something you have to assume. You have evidence. As an attorney, I understand what constitutes evidence." . . .

"Is the car parked in your own parking slot?" Bill said. "Or is it in a public parking lot, like at the supermarket?"

Slightly taken aback, Tim paused. "I don't follow you."

"If it's your own garage or parking slot," Bill said, "where only you park, then it's probably from your car. Anyhow, it wouldn't be the motor; it'd be from the radiator or the water pump or one of the hoses. . . . Also, your transmission, if you have an automatic transmission, uses the same kind of fluid. Do you have power steering?"

"On what?" Tim said.

"On your car."

"I don't know. I'm speaking about a hypothetical car.". . .

"Okay. . . . The first thing to figure out is what kind of fluid it is. So you reach under the car—you may have to back it out first—and dip your finger in the fluid. Now, is it pink? Or brown? Is it oil? Is it water? Let's say it's water. Well, it could be normal; it could be overflow from the relief system of your radiator; after you turn off an engine, the water gets hotter sometimes and blows out through the relief pipe. . . . What kind of car are you driving?"

"I think it's a Buick," Tim said.

"It's a Chrysler," I said quietly.

"Oh," Tim said.

In life, what you need to know, Dick now insisted, is how to repair your car. Not some hypothetical car, not cars in general—because nothing exists *in general;* only particular things exist, and those that we happen to encounter along our path should suffice us. Those who want something else, something more, are looking for trouble: they start off noticing impossible repetitions and making ludicrous connections between unrelated events, and before they know it they're believing that everything that happens is the result of a secret master plan that it is their job to get to the bottom of; in short, they become paranoid. *Be careful, kids,* Dick seems to be saying in this novel, *it's all too easy to get caught up in this sort of thing. And I should know.*

And so, in this snakes-and-ladders game of a book we find ourselves back at space 16—irony and withdrawal, The Soul's Winter. Don Quixote has settled down, and before he dies, he undergoes one last conversion—to Sancho's vision of the world. And Cervantes, it seems, embraces Sancho's vision as well, for he ends his novel with Quixote's conversion, fully aware that the last chapter of a story traditionally carries its moral and meaning.

Timothy Archer being Dick's last novel, one might think that Phil—not Fat—came away with the final word. People who see the world in the same way as Jeter, Dick's apostle of bullshit, tend to read it as a final "testament," evidence of Dick's "return to reality," a disenchanted yet calm acceptance of the world in all its absurd, complex, and marvelous idiocy. There is no meaning, there is no Other Side, and maybe it's better that way. In any case, that's simply the way it is.

Or maybe not. Dick may have decided it was okay for him to live among windmills, but he would go on being a Rat. He just couldn't conquer the temptation to end his last book with the transmigration of the dead bishop's soul into the mind of Bill, his schizophrenic contradictor, as Bill and the narrator look on, stoned on some really good weed. Tired, Dick saw his death approaching and dreaded the moment when the roulette wheel would stop spinning and the little ball would land on a number—even or odd, it had to be one or the other. He knew that this moment would come, but he also knew that, for as long as he could, he would resist coming to a final conclusion and would go on contradicting himself to the bitter end, offering only penultimate truths.

In September 1981, he had one last vision. The new Savior had been born and was living in Sri Lanka among the poor; he went by the name of Tagore. Believing he had been chosen to prepare the world for this second incarnation of Christ, Dick summarized Tagore's teachings in a letter that he photocopied and sent to all his friends and acquaintances, as well as to the editor of an obscure fanzine. It was a clumsy interweaving of his usual religious obsessions with the philosophy of a fringe environmentalist movement—Deep Ecology—that was making its presence known on college campuses throughout California. The ecosphere is sacred, Tagore taught, and when the ecosphere is harmed, God is harmed. Tagore, the new Christ, had taken mankind's sins against the ecosphere upon himself.

The tone of this letter and others that Dick sent around this time shows how deadly serious he was about his new vision. That didn't prevent him, however, from attributing it to Horselover Fat or from writing a parodic article for another fanzine in which he expresses the following convictions—as firmly held, no doubt, as those he evinced in the Tagore letter—in regard to his recent output: "It is glib enough," he wrote,

> but apparently Dick is trying to work off the bad karma he allegedly acquired during his year or years with street-people, criminals, violent agitators and just by and large the scum of Northern California (this all took place, apparently, after the collapse of one of his many marriages).

This reviewer suggests that a better way to make amends would be to take some much-deserved R&R: stop writing, Phil, watch TV, maybe smoke a joint—one more bite of the dog won't kill you—and generally take it easy until both the Bad Old Days and the *reaction* to the Bad Old Days subside in your fevered mind.

Having written this, he gave a contented sigh and went back to his Exegesis.

CHAPTER 24

INDETERMINACY

By luck or by providence, he was spared the poisoned gift of a deathbed testament. He did not have an opportunity to choose his last words or to let the world know whether he was taking leave of it as Phil Dick or Horselover Fat.

On February 17, 1982, he gave an interview to a journalist who came to see him. He talked at great length about his latest enthusiasm: he had recently seen Benjamin Creme, a New Age guru of sorts, on television, and now considered him one of the great spiritual lights of our troubled time. Intrigued by the similarity between Tagore's teaching and Creme's message of hope for humanity in the Age of Aquarius, he had sent Creme a few of his books, along with a user's guide he extracted from the Exegesis; he expected great things to come of their meeting. All this he explained to the journalist, then, after asking him to turn off the tape recorder, confessed his doubts about the whole thing. That evening, he phoned the journalist to tell him that the off-the-record comments were perhaps a better reflection of his real thoughts than those the journalist had on tape. It was hard to tell whether he was agonized or amused. That was his last conversation.

The next day, worried that they hadn't seen him, his neighbors knocked on his door, then forced their way into his apartment. They found him lying unconscious on the floor. The doctors diagnosed a stroke and thought at first that he would recover, but he had two more in the days that followed. He could neither speak nor eat; only his eyes revealed that he was conscious. He received the sacraments of the Church, though there was no way of telling whether he wanted them or not. Then he fell into a coma. For three days he lingered, connected to life by a battery of tubes and pumps. The monitor beside his bed indicated an extremely diminished level of electrical activity in his brain, as those in the room with him kept their eyes fixed on the screen, watching the crests on the wavy line grow smaller and smaller. To what sorts of thoughts might these ripples correspond? In what sort of limbo was what remained of Phil now drifting? Did an answer lie somewhere in its deepest depths, and if so, was someone there to hear it?

I don't know whether someone reminded him of his third wish. Nor do I know whether, during his last moments or after, he came face-to-face with whatever it was he had once glimpsed in a mirror darkly and had chased after during most of his stay on earth. I don't know whether God exists, but I do know that the question is not the province of a biographer.

Doris spent three nights at his bedside, praying.

From what he had told her of his spiritual experiences, she had concluded that he had lost his way, that in his searching for the Living God all he had found was himself and the misery of his own flesh. But he had searched for Him, had desired Him with all his heart and soul, and Doris wanted to believe that, with so strong a desire, a person might lose his way but not his soul. If God did not pity Phil, how could we call Him merciful? How could there be a Communion of Saints?

She prayed for his salvation, certain that her prayers would be answered, certain that, indeed, all of us will be saved. That was why Christ had come among us. And precisely because she was certain of this, she vowed that she would offer this prayer every day for the rest of her life. (At the time of writing, she is still alive, still praying for his soul's salvation.)

Then the EEG went flat. It remained so for the next five days—a straight line splitting the screen in two. On March 2, the wires and tubes were disconnected and the monitor was turned off.

Edgar Dick, very old now, came to retrieve his son's body and took it to Fort Morgan, Colorado, where Phil's gravesite had been waiting for him for fifty-three years. Only the date of his death needed to be engraved on the stone. When Phil was laid next to Jane, the old man, who until then had shown no emotion, saw the tiny coffin again and burst into sobs.

ABOUT THE AUTHOR

One of France's most critically acclaimed writers, EMMANUEL CARRÈRE is the author of several screenplays and three novels, including *The Mustache* and *Class Trip*, which won the prestigious Prix Femina. His work of nonfiction, *The Adversary*, was a *New York Times* Notable Book of 2001 and has been published in eighteen countries. He lives in Paris.